Quilted Legends
Of the West

That Patchwork Place®

**Judy Zehner &
Kim Mosher**

CREDITS

Technical Editor .... Sally Schneider
Managing Editor .... Greg Sharp
Copy Editor .... Tina Cook
Proofreader .... Leslie Phillips
Design Director .... Judy Petry
Text and Cover Designer .... David Chrisman
Production Assistant .... Shean Bemis
Illustrator .... Laurel Strand
Illustration Assistant .... Lisa McKenney
Photographer . ... Brent Kane
Photography Assistant .... Richard Lipshay

QUILTED LEGENDS OF THE WEST

That Patchwork Place, Inc., PO Box 118
Bothell, WA 98041-0118 USA

Printed in the United States
00 99 98 97 96 95   6 5 4 3 2 1

Library of Congress Cataloging–in–Publication Data

Zehner, Judy,
    Quilted legends of the West / Judy Zehner & Kim Mosher.
      p. cm.
    ISBN 1-56477-125-3
    1. Patchwork—West (U.S.)—Patterns. 2. Patchwork quilts—West (U.S.)—Themes, motifs. 3. Wildlife art—West (U.S.) 4. Indian art—West (U.S.) I. Mosher, Kim. II. Title.
    TT835.Z45 1995
    746.46—dc20   95–38730
                     CIP

ACKNOWLEDGMENTS

Judy: My daughter and collaborator, Kimberley Zehner Mosher, has always been my dearest friend. While she claims to be my student, she has been both a teacher and a guide in my quilting endeavors and in my life. This project could not have been accomplished without her.

Kim: My thanks to my mother, Judith L. Zehner, my friend and mentor. She had a dream and allowed me to be a part! Thanks also to my husband and lifelong companion, Lucky Mosher, for his love and support, and to our daughters, Lacey and Lindsey, who are God's blessings to us.

Our thanks to:

The family, friends, and former students who tested the quilt patterns: Maxine Gillaspy, Jimmy C. Jones, Cynthia Maddox, Beth Soderquist, Rose Alter, Paula Cooper Black, Rosemary Pearson, Paulette Bray, Kathleen Faucett, Patricia Zabel, and Cheryl Bush.

Sharon Haynes, for her quilting expertise; Beth Soderquist and Anne Muhme, for their computer assistance; Freda Holleman, for her knowledge of Native American lore; and the Delectable Mountains Quilter's Guild, for their encouragement.

David J. Zehner, husband and dad, who made all this possible.

MISSION STATEMENT

Contents

Introduction

"What is man without the beasts? If all the beasts were gone, men would die from great loneliness of spirit, for whatever happens to the beasts also happens to the man. All things are connected. Whatever befalls the earth befalls the children of the earth."

Chief Seattle

As a young woman, I became interested in my heritage and in genealogy. I found that my great-great grandfather on my mother's side, John Lewis Martin, was a full-blooded Cherokee, as was my great-great grandmother on my father's side. Although some people may dispute the phenomenon of racial memories, I believe they are real. Throughout my life, my art has reflected nature, wildlife, and ethnic designs. I was not raised in a tribal culture, and I do not claim to be a mystic. I merely share this information to explain why I rejoice in the development of wildlife designs in my quilting.

When I learned of my heritage, I commented to my great-aunt, Bernice Martin Summers (whom we called Aunt Squaw), how wonderful it must be to be an Indian. She looked at me in my ignorance and said, "Honey, it wasn't wonderful when I was a child; we were ashamed to be Indian." Maturity brought her pride in her heritage, and it is her legacy to her family.

I offer the work of my heart and my hands to you. These designs embody beauty, strength, symbolism, and spirituality. They also remind me how fragile life is and why we must tread lightly upon the earth. I encourage you to create works of comfort and art that are meaningful to you and in which you take pride. As you choose colors, fabrics, quilting designs, and embellishments, listen to your heart and let your story tell itself.

Judy

In 1987 my mother, Judy Zehner, opened a quilt shop called "Traditions" in the small town of Hayden, Colorado. This wonderful endeavor prompted her to teach me to quilt. Not only did I learn a traditional skill, but I also found a way to express myself, to create something with my hands and my heart that I could be proud of and that I could share with friends and family.

These animal designs are not only an expression of God's beautiful creation, but also an attempt to retain pieces of the past.

As interest in the Native American heritage of this country continues to grow, many people seek to create environments within their homes that reflect this interest. In our quilts and wall hangings, we try to emulate the Native American ability to combine artistry with utility.

Our designs are based on simple piecing methods, and they are strong and graceful rather than cute. We adapted the quilting designs from traditional quilting motifs and Native American symbols. The quilts are intended for the intermediate quilter, but can be made by a beginner with basic skills.

Kim

Gallery

The Messenger by Kimberley L. Mosher, 1994, Steamboat Springs, Colorado, 54" x 56". Directions begin on page 25. The eagle, our nation's symbol, is brilliant in Kim's choice of colors. Quilted by Judith L. Zehner.

Wings in the Wind by Maxine M. Gillaspy, 1994, Craig, Colorado, 84" x 97". Maxine is Judy's mother and Kim's grandmother. She added wide borders and used the Prehistoric Wind Symbol block in each corner to make her quilt larger. Maxine made wonderful usc of a fabric printed with Native American designs. Quilted by Sharon Haynes.

White Bear by Kimberley L. Mosher, 1994, Steamboat Springs, Colorado, 47" x 38". Directions begin on page 31. Mountain goats are amazing acrobats, with a supreme sense of balance and a complete lack of fear of high places. Judy used the mountain goat as a background for petroglyphic quilting designs. Quilted by Judith L. Zehner.

Goat at Sperry Chalet by Pat Zabel, 1994, Steamboat Springs, Colorado, 40" x 48". Three generations of Pat's family have worked at Glacier National Park during the summer. A favorite spot is Sperry Chalet, reached after a hard 6.7 mile hike. It boasts a spectacular mountain vista and a resident population of shaggy mountain goats. Pat's quilt was made to commemorate good times there.

Setting Sun by Kimberley L. Mosher, 1994, Steamboat Springs, Colorado, 43" x 34". Directions begin on page 37. Straight-line and stipple quilting create reflections and refractions, echoing sound and light in the Rockies. Quilted by Judith L. Zehner.

Lightning Strikes by Cheryl Bush, 1994, Craig, Colorado, 38" x 47". Cheryl made enough Tesque Lightning Symbol blocks to go all around her quilt, adding size as well as interest to the design.

Bear Dreamer by Kimberley L. Mosher, 1994, Steamboat Springs, Colorado, 52" x 37". Directions begin on page 43. The bear was honored and revered for his healing powers as well as for his special relationship to humans. Quilted by Judith L. Zehner.

Black's Bear by Paula Cooper Black, 1994, Steamboat Springs, Colorado, 35" x 50". Paula's bear is completely hand quilted. She made it for her mountain cabin.

Spirit of the Mountains by Judith L. Zehner, 1994,
Routt County, Colorado, 56" x 51". Directions
begin on page 49. America's native lion has a shy
and secretive nature.

Cougars by Paulette Bray, 1994, Craig, Colorado,
51" x 57". Paulette's daughter attends a college
whose mascot is a cougar. This hangs in her room.

Red Dog by Judith L. Zehner, 1994, Routt County, Colorado, 38" x 44". Directions begin on page 56. The border fabric, which features little creatures, adds to the sense of fun.

Butterscotch by Rosalie R. Alter, 1994, Craig, Colorado, 32" x 37". Rose's color choices made her title for this quilt a natural. Quilted by Judith L. Zehner.

We Were Here by Judith L. Zehner, 1994, Routt County, Colorado, 48" x 49". Directions begin on page 62. Symbolic quilting adds poignancy to the real story of the near extinction of the American bison.

Big Buff by Elizabeth Soderquist, 1994, Steamboat Springs, Colorado, 52" x 64". Beth added a border using the Pinwheel Symbol blocks to enlarge the quilt and enhance the design. It hangs in her office.

Spirit Companions by Kimberley L. Mosher, 1994, Steamboat Springs, Colorado, 44" x 41". Directions begin on page 68. The pronghorn antelope lives in the wild only in North America. Quilted by Judith L. Zehner.

Hurrah for the Prairies by Maxine Gillaspy, 1994, Craig, Colorado, 36" x 39½". Maxine likes adding little creative touches to her quilts, such as the piecing in the border. Quilted by Judith L. Zehner.

Life Giver by Kimberley L. Mosher, 1994, Steamboat Springs, Colorado, 48" x 52". Directions begin on page 75. Spirited deer are abundant in our country's woodlands. Quilted by Judith L. Zehner.

Christmas Night by Kathy Faucett, 1994, Hayden, Colorado, 38" x 50½". Kathy loved using metallic fabric to add holiday elegance to her wall hanging.

In the Presence of the Arrow by Kimberley L. Mosher, 1994, Steamboat Springs, Colorado, 51" x 49". Directions begin on page 82. The beautiful foliage fabric inspired Kim's color choices for the elk. Arrow quilting follows the design elements. Quilted by Judith L. Zehner.

Wapiti by Rosemary Pearson, 1994, Steamboat Springs, Colorado, 44" x 54". The addition of a border to just one side of the quilt accentuates this elk design. Rosemary added trapunto and quilted with metallic thread.

Sunrise by Kimberley L. Mosher, 1994, Steamboat Springs, Colorado, 89" x 101". Different values add depth to the scene in this multiple-figure design.

Quilted by Sharon Haynes. See "Creating a Pair or Herd" on page 90 for information on how to combine several animals in your quilt design.

Peaceable Kingdom by Kimberley L. Mosher and Judith L. Zehner, 1994, Routt County, Colorado, 188" x 120". Color choices and design placement were exciting challenges for Judy and Kim when they combined all ten animal designs. Quilted by Sharon Haynes.

Native American Symbolism

Color

Use color to put special significance into the "legend" that your quilt tells. The significance of color in Native American lore varies from tribe to tribe. According to Cherokee legend, red was the color of sacred fire. It was connected with the sun and with blood, and therefore with life. Black was the color of death, associated with the west, the region of the souls of the dead.

To the Arapaho, red meant man or blood or earth. It was associated with the east, the direction of the rising sun, and was the color of success.

To the Crow, black was the color of victory, while to the Sioux, black symbolized night.

The Sioux used colors to represent the cardinal directions. East, the abode of the sun and the morning star, was yellow. North was the source of knowledge regarding health, and its color was red. West was the home of the Thunder Beings, and its color was black. South, the source of knowledge and power, was symbolized by white.

The Hopi perceived six geographic directions, including up and down. Each was represented by a color: northwest, yellow; southwest, red; southeast, blue; northeast, white; up, purple; and down, speckled.

In Ute rituals, red symbolized earth and longevity, white stood for winter and purity, blue meant sky and water, and yellow represented sunlight and the dawning of a new day.

Motifs

Using Native American motifs as quilting designs can be a great way to tell a story with your quilt. It has been fascinating to observe the similarity of symbols among different cultures and to discover how many traditional quilting designs were adapted from Native American origins. Although the symbols we used to enhance our designs are not exactly the same as the original form, we use them to honor cultures that we respect and admire.

Use a photocopy machine to enlarge the designs on these pages for use as quilting designs.

We used many design motifs found in North American petroglyphs and pictographs. A petroglyph is a carving on stone, while a pictograph is a painting on stone. Though techniques and styles vary greatly across the country, the human hand, the bear track, and the Thunderbird are found in almost every location where rock art appears in North America.

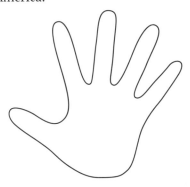

Human Hand

Hand prints may mean something as simple as "I was here," or where they exist in large numbers, they may represent identification with a tribal unit or ceremony.

Bear Track

Bears have always been objects of wonder. As a living symbol of strength and courage, the bear played a major part in tribal ritual mythology.

Shields, arrows, and clouds are common motifs associated with hunting magic and rainmaking.

Thunderbird

The Thunderbird is a supernatural being, considered a clan ancestor and guardian spirit. It brought success in war and long life. Some Plains tribes believed that thunderstorms were the result of struggles between the Thunderbird and a huge rattlesnake.

In some areas there are thousands of well-executed engravings of mountain sheep. They are depicted in various forms but are always recognizable. These engravings may have been made for hunting rituals.

You can find Kokopelli, the hump-backed flute player, carved or painted on rocks and painted on pottery. Among the Hopi, he was the symbol of the Flute Clan. He is widely known as a symbol of fertility or as a trickster.

Kokopelli

Mountain Sheep

Deer, elk, bison, and pronghorn antelope symbols are common from the Great Basin to the Great Plains. They were honored as life-givers.

Pronghorn Antelope

Bison

Deer

Elk

Fabric and Supplies

Fabric Selection Tips

You can often identify the work of a friend merely by the color and style of fabrics used in a project. You may find that you tend to repeat color combinations you find pleasing and that you have to force yourself to use a different color scheme. Our thoughts on color and fabric selection are only suggestions, and we encourage you to use your creativity and color sense (or non-sense)!

We learned some important lessons while piecing our first "legends" quilts. We found that a busy allover print, rather than a directional pattern, is best for backgrounds. Because the backgrounds in these quilts are composed of many pieces, a neutral background is better than directional or scenic prints. Directional prints appear haphazard after they have been cut up and reassembled, which is distracting.

Good contrast between the animal design and the background is essential. To make the animal appear more realistic, you can use several fabrics with either subtle or dramatic changes of shading or patterning. If we want only a slight contrast, we use both the front and back of one fabric. Natural colors work well for the animals and background, but we also love the excitement of vivid, unexpected, brilliant colors.

We looked for rich colors and designs and chose not to use obvious floral prints; however, your fabric choices are your personal trademark, and the story you tell is your own.

We used only 100% cotton fabric. For ease in cutting and piecing, we choose not to prewash it. We prefer to wash the finished product and let all the parts shrink together for an old-fashioned look. We have not had a catastrophe yet, but it might happen, so prewash if you prefer. Use a light coat of spray starch after washing for a crisp finish.

Give some thought to your quilting method when considering background and backing. Remember that your quilting will show more readily on fabric that appears solid than it will on a busy print. Since we machine-quilted our quilts, we wanted our quilting to blend with the backing, and chose our fabric accordingly. If you do beautiful hand quilting, let it show by using a subtle print or a solid-colored fabric for the background.

Basic Sewing Tools

Basic quilting tools are the only ones required to make these quilts. The tools we use most are:

  Sewing machine
  Rotary cutter and mat
  6" x 24" ruler
  6" x 12" ruler
  6" x 6" ruler
  Small, glass-head pins
  Sharp #2 pencil
  Assorted marking pencils
  Iron and ironing board
  Seam ripper
  Scissors
  Design board (optional)

We use a piece of Styrofoam™ insulation board as a design board. Use anything you can pin into that is light and portable. Prop it close to your sewing machine, so that as you assemble the units you can pin them up and stand back to get a better perspective of your work. You will be able to quickly see if your color choices were appropriate and if there is enough contrast in your design.

Quiltmaking Techniques

You need only basic cutting and sewing skills to make these patterns, but they are certainly not "first project" material. There are many excellent beginning quiltmaking books in the marketplace, and we suggest that you learn your skills from them.

Seam Allowances

Use the method you prefer to sew an exact ¼"-wide seam allowance. Some options are a ¼"-wide presser foot, a seam guide, alternate needle position, or a taped guideline on the bed of your sewing machine.

¼" grid line

Use ¼" graph paper to mark an accurate seam guide.

Put masking tape or moleskin in front of needle along edge of graph paper to guide fabric.

Rotary Cutting

Cut all pieces with a rotary cutter and an acrylic ruler. Use a rotary mat that has a grid of 1" squares. Place the fabric on the mat with the fold toward you. Fold the fabric again, keeping the folded edge parallel to the selvage edge. You now have four layers of fabric, with the double fold facing you. Place the folded edge of the fabric on a horizontal grid line on the mat. Align the ruler with a vertical line on the mat and trim the raw edges by making a vertical cut. You are now ready to cut straight strips.

Selvages

Fold

Selvages

Fold

Trim this edge away.

To cut strips that are wider than your ruler, place two or more rulers next to each other to measure the required strip width.

TIP: Hold your rotary cutter at a right angle (90°) to the mat. Slanting the cutter either inward or outward creates a slight discrepancy in the size of your strips.

Timesaving Piecing

We used several timesaving sewing techniques to make the quilts in this book, including the 45 Flip, the Piggyback Flip, and the 45 Joint. Rather than repeat the directions for these in each quilt, you will be referred to the directions that follow. These are easy ways to add 45° angle triangle corners to squares and rectangles. It is particularly useful because it is much easier to cut and handle a small square than it is a small triangle.

The 45 Flip: Place fabrics right sides together, keeping the smaller square on top and the raw edges even. Using a sharp pencil and a small ruler, draw a diagonal line from corner to corner across the small square. Stitch on the drawn line. Trim excess fabric, leaving a ¼"-wide seam allowance. Press from the front, pressing the seam allowance toward the outside edge. (See "Pressing" on page 23.) Use the 45 Flip with any square on any larger square or rectangle.

Trim away

TIP: Before you cut, stitch another line ½" from the first, toward the corner. Cut between the two lines; then press the 45 Flip as shown above. The remaining piece is a half-square triangle, which you can save for your scrap basket or use to construct an interesting back for your quilt.

Cut

Piggyback Flip: Start with a 45 Flip as described above. Place a smaller square on the corner of the completed 45 Flip; then repeat the technique for the 45 Flip.

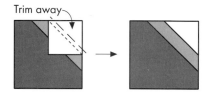

Trim away

Use 45 Flips and Piggyback Flips on one, two, three, or all four corners of any square or rectangle. You can use the same fabric color for each flip or a combination of colors.

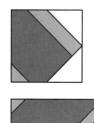

45 Joint: Rather than work with difficult trapezoids, use this technique to join rectangles at a 45° angle. Join binding strips this way as well.

With right sides together, make an **L** with your fabric rectangles. Using a sharp pencil and a small ruler, draw a diagonal line, starting where the rectangles meet at the top and ending where the rectangles meet at the bottom. (Refer to the illustration below; the intersections are marked

with a *.) Stitch on the line and trim away excess fabric, leaving a ¼"-wide seam allowance. Press from the right side. Make a reverse **L** to make a seam in the opposite direction. In the directions for each quilt we describe these units as right and left 45 Joints.

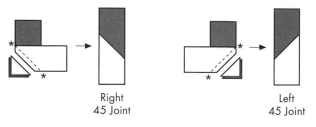

Right
45 Joint

Left
45 Joint

You can also make 45 Joints one after another in either direction.

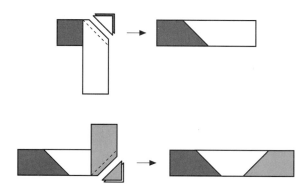

Practically Perfect Pinning

It takes patience and practice to match seams "practically perfectly." We found these methods to be useful.

- Use fine, glass-head pins. Large quilting pins distort fabric edges.
- Seams must match on the ¼" stitching line, so insert your pin at that spot. Be sure to insert your pins straight up and down rather than at an angle.

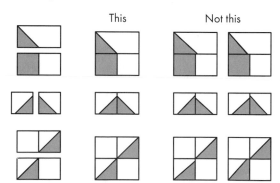

This   Not this

❖ Our rule of thumb is to try three times to match a seam. If it still doesn't suit you after the third try, leave it and go on. Either you will acquire more skill and come back to it later, or you will decide that it is "close enough," and continue to enjoy your project.

If you sew a consistent ¼"-wide seam and cut accurately, you will be amazed at how many seams you can match with little effort!

Pressing

Set up a small pressing pad beside your sewing machine, or position your ironing board beside your chair and lower it to a comfortable height. This allows you to sew and press without getting up, or at least without moving far.

❖ To reduce stretching and distortion, press lightly; do not iron.

❖ Press 45 Flips, Piggyback Flips, and 45 Joints from the right side, using the side of your iron to position the triangle. This helps prevent small tucks that can alter the size of your finished piece.

❖ Press toward the darker fabric if you can. Some pieces will naturally press better in one direction than in another.

❖ To facilitate matching, press seams that must match in opposite directions.

Adding Borders

We designed the animals as wall hangings, but you can make them bed size with the addition of borders. We always use squared borders, attaching the sides first, then the top and bottom.

❖ The symbol included in each design makes a wonderful pieced border when repeated around the edge of the quilt. See "Lightning

Strikes" on page 7. See other pieced border options below.

❖ Multiple fabrics make effective borders, as shown in "Black's Bear" on page 8.

❖ Add borders to just two sides as we did in "Red Dog" on page 10.

❖ Use a small framing border and finish with a wider border of background fabric. See "White Bear" on page 6.

It is important that borders fit properly and do not ripple, especially on a wall hanging. To make a quilt that hangs straight, square and trim the pieced top before adding each border. Repeat after all the borders have been added, and once more after it is quilted and before you bind it.

To square up a quilt, lay the pieced top on a 30" x 36" cutting mat. Line up a stitched seam with a grid line on the mat. Using the grid lines on the mat, trim the outer edges of the quilt to make them square.

To determine the length of the side borders, measure the right and left sides and through the center of the quilt top. All three measurements should be the same. If they are not, average the three measurements and cut your side borders to that length.

To determine the length of the top and bottom borders, measure the width of the quilt through the center and at the top and bottom edges, including the added side borders.

Match the center and both ends of the pieced top to the center and both ends of the border; then stretch or ease as necessary to make the quilt fit the border.

Square the quilt each time you add borders. You will be pleased with the result.

Quilt Plans

The animal patterns in this book are completely rotary cut and Template-Free®. Like cross-stitch, they are based on a graph of squares, each square equaling one inch. As you work with the patterns you will quickly learn how to identify which fabric to cut and what size to cut it just by its position on the graph. We found these patterns exciting and addicting; we couldn't wait to finish one before beginning another.

While none of these designs is difficult, we would rank them in order of challenge as they appear in the table of contents, with the least challenging being "The Messenger."

Following the Plans

✤ Each pattern is divided into lettered units (A, B, C, and so on). Each unit is subdivided into sections, and each section is made of pieces that are numbered, sized, and diagrammed. Use the 45 Flip, Piggyback Flip, 45 Joint, and Practically Perfect Pinning to easily assemble each unit.

✤ The directions for each animal begin with a strip-cutting chart. Cut each of the strips as described; then cut pieces from the strips as called for in the directions for each unit.

✤ Arrange all the unit pieces before beginning to sew. Pin the pieces to your design board as you sew them together. As your picture takes shape, it becomes easier to envision the finished project.

You can start with any unit, but it makes sense to begin with one that has fewer pieces, working toward more complex units when you have some experience. For example, do not start with the antler sections of the mule deer or elk!

Adjusting the Size

It is possible to make these quilts in a smaller size. Use the quilt plans, which show the placement of each piece, but cut your pieces smaller. For a quilt that is half as wide and half as long as the samples, reduce the size of the piece as follows:

Piece Size	Subtract ½"	Divide in Half	Add ½"
3½" x 4½"	3" x 4"	1½" x 2"	2" x 2½"

The number in the last column is the size to cut the new piece. Repeat this calculation with each piece that you cut; then follow the piecing diagrams for the quilt plan of your choice. The same method works for strip sizes. Subtract ½" from the width of the strip size, divide it in half, then add ½" to find the new strip size to cut. You will need fewer strips than called for in the strip-cutting charts if you adjust the size downward. We do not recommend adjusting upward in size.

The Messenger

Cheyenne legend portrays the eagle as a principal intermediary between the Above Beings and humans because he flies so high and is so powerful and sharp-eyed.

Quilt Size: 54" x 56"

Eagle Image Size: 38" x 42"

Symbol: Prehistoric Wind

Color Photo: Page 5

Materials: 44"-wide fabric

2¼ yds. for background and outer border
1⅛ yds. purple for body
⅜ yd. white #1 for head and tail
⅛ yd. black for west wind symbol
⅛ yd. fuchsia for north wind symbol
⅛ yd. gold for east wind symbol
⅛ yd. white #2 for south wind symbol
Scrap of gold for beak
3¼ yds. for backing
⅝ yd. for binding
58" x 60" piece of batting

Strip Cutting

Cut the following strips across the fabric width (crosswise grain). For additional cutting directions, see the chart with each design unit.

Fabric	No. of Strips	Strip Width
Background	1	1½"
	2	2½"
	1	3½"
	1	4½"
	1	5½"
	1	9½"
Purple	1	1½"
	1	2½"
	1	3½"
	1	4½"
	1	5½"
	1	7½"
	1	8½"
White #1	1	1½"
	1	8½"
Black	1	3½"
Fuchsia	1	3½"
Gold	1	3½"
White #2	1	3½"
Gold scrap	1	2½"

Unit Cutting and Assembly

Using the strips you just cut, cut the required number of pieces for each fabric listed in the unit cutting charts. In most cases you will simply crosscut the strips; occasionally you will need to trim pieces to the dimensions given in the chart.

Units A and C: Eagle

Note: These units are mirror images.

Unit A   Unit C

CUTTING

Cut 2 of each of the pieces listed for each fabric, cutting them from the strips called for in the chart at left.

Fabric	Strip Width	Piece #	Dimensions
Background	2½"	2	2½" x 4½"
	9½"	1	9½" x 9½"
Purple	4½"	3	4½" x 7½"
	7½"	1a	7½" x 7½"

ASSEMBLY

Refer to the piecing diagram below.

1. Assemble section 1a for Unit A, using the 45 Flip (page 21). Repeat for Unit C, reversing the placement of the pieces and the direction of the seam so that the sections are mirror images.
2. Arrange all the sections and join to complete Units A and C.

Unit A

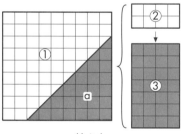

Unit C

Unit B: Eagle

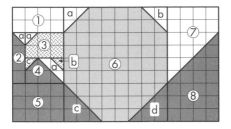

7. Join the finished sections to complete Unit B. See illustration at left.

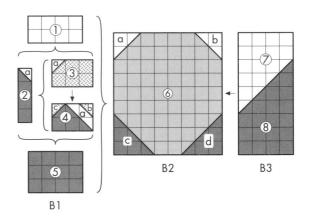

CUTTING

Use the strips listed in the chart on page 26.

Fabric	Strip Width	Piece #	Dimensions
Background	1½"	2a, 3a	1½" x 1½"
	2½"	1	2½" x 4½"
		4a, 6a, 6b	2½" x 2½"
	4½"	7	4½" x 6½"
White #1	8½"	6	8½" x 9½"
Beak	2½"	3	2½" x 3½"
		4b, 4c	1½" x 1½"*
Purple	1½"	2	1½" x 4½"
	2½"	4	2½" x 3½"
	3½"	6c, 6d	3½" x 3½"
	4½"	5	3½" x 4½"
		8	4½" x 7½"

*Cut from the larger strip and trim to the proper size.

ASSEMBLY

Refer to the piecing diagram above right. To make the construction easier, we divided Unit B into 3 parts.

1. Arrange the pieces for each section of Unit B.
2. Assemble 2a and 3a, using the 45 Flip.
3. Sew piece 4a and 4c to piece 4, using the 45 Flip; add piece 4b, using the Piggyback Flip.
4. Join the pieced units to complete Unit B1.
5. Add pieces 6a, 6b, 6c, and 6d to piece 6 (45 Flip) to complete Unit B2.
6. To complete Unit B, join pieces 7 and 8 using the left 45 Joint.

Units D and F: Eagle

Note: These units are mirror images.

Unit D   Unit F

CUTTING

Cut 2 of each of the pieces listed for each fabric, cutting them from the strips called for in the chart on page 26.

Fabric	Strip Width	Piece #	Dimensions
Background	5½"	1	3½" x 5½"
		2, 3	4½" x 5½"
		4	5½" x 5½"
Purple	3½"	1a	3½" x 3½"
	4½"	2a, 3a	4½" x 4½"
	5½"	4a	5½" x 5½"
	8½"	5	8½" x 16½"

ASSEMBLY

1. Assemble sections 1a, 2a, 3a, and 4a for Unit D, using the 45 Flip. Repeat for Unit F, reversing the placement of the pieces and the direction of the seams so that the sections are mirror images. Refer to the illustration below.

2. Arrange all the sections for each unit and join to complete.

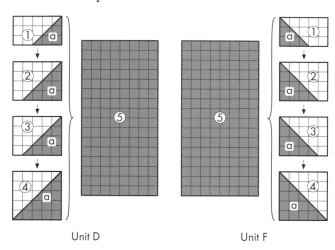

Unit D   Unit F

Unit E: Wind Symbol

Note: If you choose not to use the Symbol block, do not cut the pieces in the chart that follows. Replace them with a 16½" x 16½" square of purple fabric.

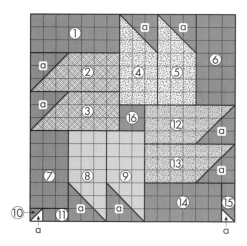

CUTTING

Use the strips listed in the chart on page 26.

Fabric	Strip Width	Piece #	Dimensions
Background	1½"	10a, 15a	1½" x 1½"
Purple	1½"	10	1½" x 1½"
		11	1½" x 2½"
	2½"	16	2½" x 2½"
	3½"	2a, 3a, 4a, 5a, 8a, 9a, 12a, 13a	3½" x 3½"
		14	3½" x 6½"
		15	1½" x 3½"
	7½"	1, 6	3½" x 7½"
		7	3½" x 6½"*
Black	3½"	2, 3	3½" x 7½"
Fuchsia	3½"	4, 5	3½" x 7½"
White #2	3½"	8, 9	3½" x 7½"
Gold	3½"	12, 13	3½" x 7½"

*Cut from the larger strip and trim to the proper size.

ASSEMBLY

1. Assemble 2a, 3a, 4a, 5a, 8a, 9a, 10a, 12a, 13a, and 15a, using the appropriate colors (as shown in the unit illustration at left) and the 45 Flip.

2. Arrange the pieces for each section of the wind symbol and sew together as shown.

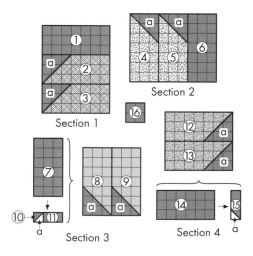

Section 1   Section 2   Section 3   Section 4

3. Sew section 4 to piece 16 with a partial seam, beginning at the upper edge and ending at the center of 16 as shown in step 4.

4. Add the remaining 3 sections in a counter-clockwise direction, beginning with section 2 and ending with section 3.

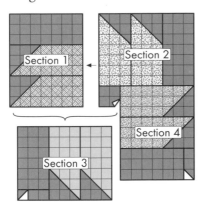

5. Complete the seam between sections 3 and 4.

Finish sewing this seam.

Units G and I: Eagle

Note: These units are mirror images.

Unit G   Unit I

CUTTING

Cut 2 of each of the pieces listed for each fabric, cutting them from the strips called for in the chart on page 26.

Fabric	Strip Width	Piece #	Dimensions
Background	3½"	1a	3½" x 3½"
		4	3½" x 4½"
	4½"	2	4½" x 10½"
	9½"	5	6½" x 7½"*
		6	6½" x 9½"
Purple	4½"	1	3½" x 4½"
	7½"	5a	6½" x 6½"*
		3	3½" x 6½"*

*Cut from the larger strip and trim to the proper size.

ASSEMBLY

Refer to the piecing diagram below.

1. Assemble 1a and 5a for Unit G, using the 45 Flip. Repeat for Unit I, reversing the placement of the pieces and the direction of the seams so that the units are mirror images.

2. Sew piece 3 to piece 4, using the left 45 Joint. Use the right 45 Joint to sew the pieces for Unit I.

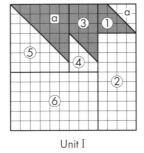

Left 45 Joint   Right 45 Joint

3. Arrange all the pieces for each unit and join to complete Units G and I.

Unit G   Unit I

Unit H: Eagle

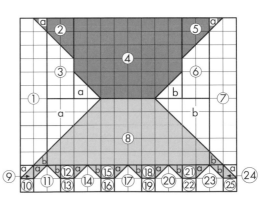

CUTTING

Use the strips listed in the chart on page 26.

Fabric	Strip Width	Piece #	Dimensions
Background	1½"	9a, 10, 13, 16, 19, 22, 24a, 25	1½" x 1½"
	2½"	1, 7	2½" x 11½"
		4a, 4b,	2½" x 2½"
		11, 14, 17, 20, 23	
	4½"	8a, 8b	4½" x 4½"
	5½"	3, 6	2½" x 5½"
Purple	1½"	1a, 7a	1½" x 1½"
	2½"	2, 5	2½" x 3½"
	8½"	4	6½" x 8½"
White #1	1½"	1b, 7b, 9, 11a, 11b, 12, 14a, 14b, 15, 17a, 17b, 18, 20a, 20b, 21, 23a, 23b, 24	1½" x 1½"
	8½"	8	5½" x 12½"*

*Cut from the larger strip and trim to the proper size.

ASSEMBLY

Refer to the piecing diagram above right. To make the construction easier, we divided Unit H into 2 parts.

1. Assemble sections 1a/b, 4a/b, 7a/b, and 8a/b, using the 45 Flip.
2. Sew piece 2 to piece 3, using the right 45 Joint. Repeat with pieces 5 and 6, using the left 45 Joint.

Right
45 Joint

Left
45 Joint

3. Arrange the completed sections and sew together as shown to complete Unit H1.

4. Referring to the numbered piecing diagram below, assemble each of the units, using the 45 Flip to add pieces a and b where required.

5. Arrange all the sections and join to complete Unit H2. Sew to the bottom edge of Unit H1, completed in step 3 above.

Quilt Top Assembly

1. Arrange the completed units as shown in the quilt plan on page 25.
2. Sew the units together in rows. Press the seams in opposite directions from row to row. Sew the rows together to complete the design area of the quilt top.
3. For side borders, cut 2 strips, each 6½" x 42". Measure the quilt top for side borders as shown in "Adding Borders" on page 23. Trim the borders to fit; then sew them to opposite sides of the quilt top.
4. From the background fabric, cut 3 strips, each 9½" x 42". Cut 1 strip in half crosswise and sew 1 short piece to each of the remaining strips. Measure the quilt and trim border strips to fit. Sew the strips to the top and bottom edges of the quilt top.

Finishing

1. Layer the quilt with backing and batting; baste.
2. Quilt as desired and bind the edges. The background is quilted with diagonal lines. See page 25 for other quilting suggestions.

White Bear

The Mountain Goat has been mistaken for many different creatures. When Indians brought goat skins to explorer Captain Cook in 1778, he thought they were white bear. Explorer Alexander MacKenzie saw the animals and decided they were white buffalo, and Lewis and Clark thought they were mountain sheep. The mountain goat is not a goat at all, but an antelope.

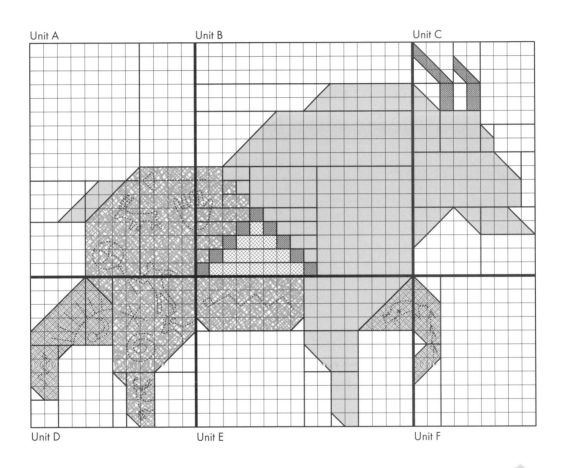

Unit A Unit B Unit C

Unit D Unit E Unit F

Quilt Size: 47" x 38"

Mountain Goat Image Size: 28" x 37"

Symbol: Acoma Mountain

Color Photo: Page 6

Materials: 44"-wide fabric

1½ yds. for background and outer border
½ yd. off-white #1 for body
½ yd. off-white #2 for body
¼ yd. off-white #3 for body
1½" x 20" strip of blue for symbol 2
1½" x 14" strip of teal for symbol 1
4" x 9" piece of brown for horn
¼ yd. black print for inner border
1½ yds. for backing
½ yd. for binding
42" x 51" piece of batting

Strip Cutting

Cut the following strips across the fabric width (crosswise grain). For additional cutting directions, see the chart with each design unit.

Fabric	No. of Strips	Strip Width
Background	1	1½"
	1	2½"
	1	3½"
	1	4½"
	1	8½"
Off-white #1	1	1½"
	1	4½"
	1	7½"
Off-white #2	1	4½"
	1	6½"
Off-white #3	1	4½"
Blue	1	1½"
Teal	1	1½"

Unit Cutting and Assembly

Using the strips you just cut, cut the required number of pieces for each fabric listed in the unit cutting charts. In most cases you will simply crosscut the strips; occasionally you will need to trim pieces to the dimensions given in the chart.

Unit A: Mountain Goat

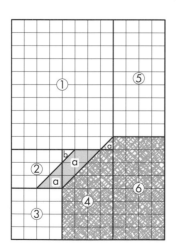

CUTTING

Use the strips listed in the chart at left.

Fabric	Strip Width	Piece #	Dimensions
Background	1½"	4b	1½" x 1½"
	3½"	2	3½" x 4½"
	4½"	3	4½" x 4½"
		5	4½" x 9½"
	8½"	1	8½" x 10½"
Off-white #1	7½"	2a	2½" x 2½"*
		4a	3½" x 3½"*
Off-white # 2	4½"	4	4½" x 7½"
		6	4½" x 8½"
	6½"	1a	1½" x 1½"*

*Cut from the larger strip and trim to the proper size.

ASSEMBLY

Refer to the piecing diagram below.
1. Assemble 1a, 2a, and 4a, using the 45 Flip (page 21).
2. Sew piece 4b to 4a, using the Piggyback Flip (page 22).
3. Arrange all the sections and join them to complete Unit A.

Units B1 and B2: Mountain Goat

To make the construction easier, we divided Unit B into 3 parts.

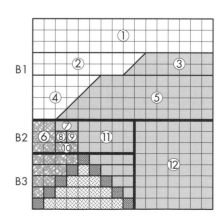

CUTTING

Use the strips listed in the chart on page 32.

Fabric	Strip Width	Piece #	Dimensions
Background	2½"	2	2½" x 10½"
	3½"	1	3½" x 16½"
	4½"	4	4½" x 6½"
Off-white #1	1½"	9	1½" x 1½"
		7	1½" x 2½"
	4½"	5	4½" x 14½"
	7½"	11	3½" x 5½"*
		3	2½" x 8½"*
		12	7½" x 8½"
Off-white #2	4½"	6	2½" x 3½"*
	6½"	8	1½" x 1½"*
		10	1½" x 2½"*

*Cut from the larger strip and trim to the proper size.

ASSEMBLY

Refer to the piecing diagram below.

1. Sew piece 2 to piece 3, using a right 45 Joint. Repeat with pieces 4 and 5.

2. Join piece 2/3 to piece 4/5; then sew piece 1 to the top edge to form Unit B1.

Right 45 Joint

Unit B1

3. Sew pieces 7, 8, 9, and 10 together; then add piece 6 to the left side of the unit and piece 11 to the right side to make Unit B2.

Unit B2

Unit B3: Acoma Mountain Symbol

Note: If you choose not to use the Symbol block, do not cut the pieces in the chart that follows. Replace them with a 5½" x 9½" rectangle of off-white #2.

CUTTING

Use the strips listed in the chart on page 32.

Fabric	Strip Width	Piece #	Dimensions
Off-white #1	1½"	8	1½" x 3½"
		13	1½" x 2½"
		18	1½" x 1½"
	4½"	3	1½" x 4½"
Off-white #2	4½"	1	1½" x 4½"
		4	1½" x 3½"*
	6½"	9	1½" x 2½"*
		14	1½" x 1½"*
Blue	1½"	6	1½" x 1½"
		11	1½" x 3½"
		16	1½" x 5½"
		20	1½" x 7½"
Teal	1½"	2, 5, 7, 10, 12, 15, 17, 19, 21	1½" x 1½"

*Cut from the larger strip and trim to the proper size.

ASSEMBLY

1. Arrange the pieces for Unit B3. Sew them together to form rows. Sew the rows together to complete Unit B3.

Unit B3

2. Arrange all parts for Unit B with piece 12.
3. Sew the sections together to complete Unit B.

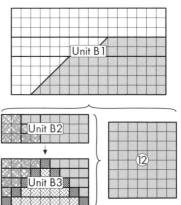

Unit C: Mountain Goat

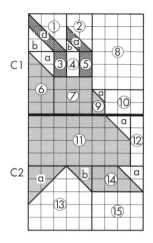

CUTTING

Use the strips listed in the chart on page 32.

Fabric	Strip Width	Piece #	Dimensions
Background	1½"	2b, 9a	1½" x 1½"
		4	1½" x 2½"
		12	1½" x 4½"
	2½"	1b, 6a,	2½" x 2½"
		11a, 14a	
	3½"	1	3½" x 3½"
		2, 10	2½" x 3½"
		15	3½" x 4½"
	4½"	8	4½" x 6½"
	8½"	13	5½" x 5½"*
Off-white #1	1½"	9	1½" x 2½"
	4½"	11	4½" x 8½"
		14	2½" x 4½"
	7½"	6	2½" x 5½"*
		7, 13a	3½" x 3½"*
		13b	2½" x 2½"*
Brown	3½"	1a	3½" x 3½"
	3½"	2a	2½" x 2½"*
	3½"	3, 5	1½" x 2½"*

*Cut from the larger strip and trim to the proper size.

ASSEMBLY

Refer to the piecing diagram above right. To make the construction easier, we divided Unit C into 2 parts.

1. Assemble 1a, 2a, 6a, and 9a, using the 45 Flip.

2. Sew piece 1b to 1a and piece 2b to 2a, using the Piggyback Flip.
3. Arrange all the sections with pieces 3, 4, 5, 7, 8, and 10, and join to complete Unit C1.

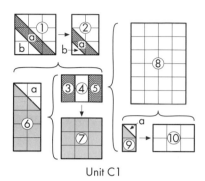

Unit C1

4. Assemble 11a, 13a/b, and 14a, using the 45 Flip.
5. Arrange the sections with pieces 12 and 15, and join to complete Unit C2.

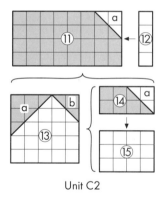

Unit C2

6. Sew Unit C1 to the top edge of Unit C2 to complete Unit C.

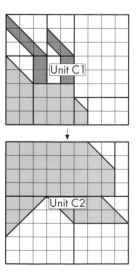

Unit D: Mountain Goat

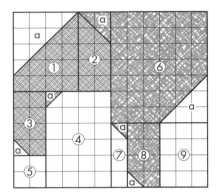

2. Arrange all the sections with pieces 5 and 9 and join to complete Unit D.

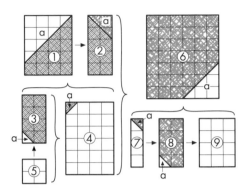

CUTTING

Use the strips listed in the chart on page 32.

Fabric	Strip Width	Piece #	Dimensions
Background	1½"	3a	1½" x 1½"
		7	1½" x 4½"
		8a	1½" x 1½"
	2½"	5	2½" x 2½"
	3½"	6a	3½" x 3½"
		9	3½" x 4½"
	4½"	1a	4½" x 4½"
		4	4½" x 6½"
Off-white #2	4½"	2a	2½" x 2½"*
		8	2½" x 4½"
	6½"	6	6½" x 7½"
		7a	1½" x 1½"*
Off-white #3	4½"	1	4½" x 5½"
		2	2½" x 5½"*
		3	2½" x 4½"
		4a	1½" x 1½"*

*Cut from the larger strip and trim to the proper size.

ASSEMBLY

Refer to the piecing diagram above right.
1. Assemble 1a, 2a, 3a, 4a, 6a, 7a, and 8a, using the 45 Flip.

Unit E: Mountain Goat

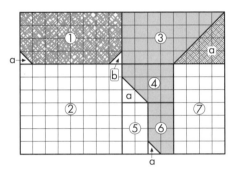

CUTTING

Use the strips listed in the chart on page 32.

Fabric	Strip Width	Piece #	Dimensions
Background	1½"	1a, 1b	1½" x 1½"
		6a	
	2½"	4a	2½" x 2½"
	4½"	5	2½" x 4½"
		7	4½" x 7½"
	8½"	2	7½" x 8½"
Off-white #1	4½"	3	4½" x 8½"
		4	3½" x 4½"
		6	2½" x 4½"
Off-white #2	4½"	1	4½" x 8½"
Off-white #3	4½"	3a	4½" x 4½"

ASSEMBLY

Refer to the piecing diagram below.
1. Assemble sections 1a/b, 3a, 4a, and 6a, using the 45 Flip.
2. Arrange all the sections with pieces 2, 5, and 7, and join to complete Unit E.

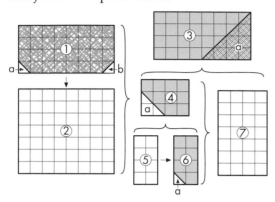

Unit F: Mountain Goat

CUTTING

Use the strips listed in the chart on page 32.

Fabric	Strip Width	Piece #	Dimensions
Background	1½"	1b, 2a	1½" x 1½"
	2½"	1a	2½" x 2½"
		3	2½" x 5½"
	8½"	4	7½" x 11½"*
Off-white #3	4½"	1	2½" x 5½"*
		2	2½" x 3½"*

*Cut from the larger strip and trim to the proper size.

ASSEMBLY

Refer to the piecing diagram above right.
1. Assemble 1a/b, using the 45 Flip.

2. Sew piece 2 to piece 3, using the left 45 Joint; then add piece 2a, using the 45 Flip.

3. Arrange completed sections with piece 4 and join to complete Unit F.

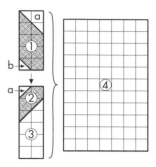

Quilt Top Assembly

1. Arrange the completed units as shown in the quilt plan on page 31. Sew the units together in rows, and press the seams in opposite directions from row to row. Sew the rows together.
2. For the inner border, cut 4 strips of black print, each 1½" x 42". Measure the quilt top for side borders as shown in "Adding Borders" on page 23. Trim 2 border strips to fit and sew them to opposite sides of the quilt top.
3. Measure the quilt top for top and bottom borders. Trim the remaining 2 border strips to fit and sew them to the top and bottom edges of the quilt top.
4. For the outer border, cut 4 strips of background fabric, each 4½" x 42". Measure the quilt top for side borders, trim the strips to fit, and sew them to opposite sides of the quilt top. Sew the pieces trimmed from the side border strips to the remaining 2 border strips. Measure the quilt top for top and bottom borders, trim the strips to fit, and sew them to the top and bottom edges of the quilt top.

Finishing

1. Layer the quilt with backing and batting; baste.
2. Quilt as desired and bind the edges. We stipple-quilted the front of the goat and quilted several designs adapted from petroglyphs on his hindquarters.

Setting Sun

Thousands of petroglyphs remain as silent records of the presence of the bighorn sheep from Alaska to the Desert Southwest. In these petroglyphs, you can almost see the setting sun and hear the mountains echo with the collision of two rams fighting to dominate the herd.

Quilt Size: 43" x 34"

Bighorn Sheep Image Size: 26" x 35"

Symbol: Tesque Lightning

Color Photo: Page 7

Materials: 44"-wide fabric

1¾ yds. for background and outer border
⅝ yd. rose print for body
¼ yd. rose solid for body
¼ yd. off-white for body
⅜ yd. maroon for horn and legs
Scrap of green solid for symbol
1⅜ yds. for backing
½ yd. for binding
38" x 47" piece of batting

Strip Cutting

Cut the following strips across the fabric width (crosswise grain). For additional cutting directions, see the Unit Cutting chart with each design unit.

Fabric	No. of Strips	Strip Width
Background	1	1½"
	1	2½"
	1	3½"
	2	6½"
	1	9½"
Rose print	1	2½"
	1	3½"
	1	7½"
Rose solid	1	4½"
Off-white	1	4½"
Maroon	1	2½"
	1	3½"
Green	1	2½"

Unit Cutting and Assembly

Using the strips you just cut, cut the required number of pieces for each fabric listed in the unit cutting charts. In most cases you will simply make crosscuts; occasionally you will need to trim pieces to the dimensions given in the chart.

Unit A: Bighorn Sheep

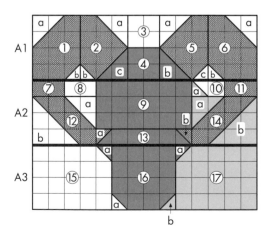

CUTTING

Use the strips listed in the chart at left.

Fabric	Strip Width	Piece #	Dimensions
Background	1½"	1b, 2b, 5c, 6b, 16a	1½" x 1½"
	2½"	1a, 2a, 3, 5a, 6a, 12a	2½" x 2½"
		8, 10	1½" x 2½"
	3½"	12b	3½" x 3½"
	6½"	15	4½" x 5½"*
Rose print	2½"	10a, 16b	1½" x 1½"*
		14a	2½" x 2½"
	3½"	14b	3½" x 3½"
	7½"	17	4½" x 5½"*
Rose solid	4½"	2c, 4, 5b	2½" x 2½"*
		9	3½" x 6½"*
		13	1½" x 6½"*
		15a, 17a	1½" x 1½"*
		16	4½" x 4½"
Maroon	2½"	7, 11	1½" x 2½"
		13a, 13b	1½" x 1½"
	3½"	1, 2, 5, 6, 12, 14	3½" x 4½"

*Cut from the larger strip and trim to the proper size.

ASSEMBLY

Refer to the piecing diagrams below and on the next page. To make the construction easier, we divided Unit A into 3 parts.

1. Assemble sections 1a/b, 2a/b, 5a/b, and 6a/b, using the 45 Flip (page 21).
2. Add piece 2c to 2a/b, and piece 5c to 5a/b in the same manner.
3. Join the pieced units with pieces 3 and 4 to complete Unit A1.

Unit A1

4. Construct 10a, 12a/b, 13 a/b, and 14 a/b, using the 45 Flip.

5. Join the pieced units with pieces 7, 8, 9, and 11 to complete Unit A2.

Unit A2

6. Assemble sections 15a, 16a/b, and 17a, using the 45 Flip.
7. Join the pieced units to complete Unit A3.

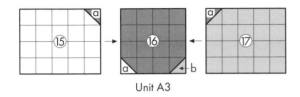

Unit A3

8. Sew Unit A1 to the top edge of Unit A2; then sew Unit A3 to the bottom edge to complete Unit A.

Unit B: Bighorn Sheep

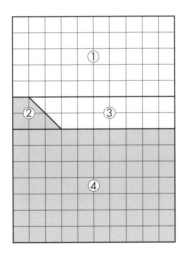

CUTTING

Use the strips listed in the chart on page 38.

Fabric	Strip Width	Piece #	Dimensions
Background	6½"	1	5½" x 10½"*
	9½"	3	2½" x 9½"
Rose print	3½"	2	2½" x 3½"
	7½"	4	7½" x 10½"

*Cut from the larger strip and trim to the proper size.

ASSEMBLY

Refer to the piecing diagram below.
1. Sew piece 2 to piece 3, using the left 45 Joint.

2. Sew piece 1 to the top edge of piece 2/3. Sew piece 4 to the bottom edge to complete Unit B.

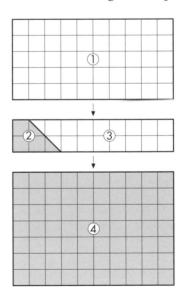

Unit C: Bighorn Sheep

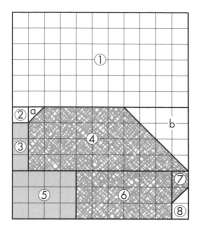

CUTTING

Use the strips listed in the chart on page 38.

Fabric	Strip Width	Piece #	Dimensions
Background	1½"	2, 4a	1½" x 1½"
		8	1½" x 2½"
	6½"	1	6½" x 11½"
		4b	4½" x 4½"*
Rose print	3½"	3	1½" x 3½"
		5	3½" x 4½"
Off-white	4½"	4	4½" x 10½"
		6	3½" x 6½"*
		7	1½" x 2½"*

*Cut from the larger strip and trim to the proper size.

ASSEMBLY

Refer to the piecing diagram above right.
1. Assemble 4a/b, using the 45 Flip.
2. Join piece 7 to piece 8, using the left 45 Joint.

3. Arrange the sections with pieces 1, 5, and 6 and join to complete Unit C.

Unit D: Bighorn Sheep

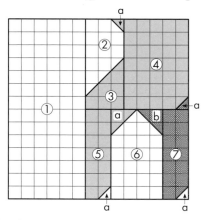

CUTTING

Use the strips listed in the chart on page 38.

Fabric	Strip Width	Piece #	Dimensions
Background	1½"	5a, 7a	1½" x 1½"
	6½"	1	6½" x 14½"
		2	3½" x 6½"
	9½"	6	4½" x 7½"*
Rose print	2½"	2a	1½" x 1½"*
		6a	2½" x 2½"
	3½"	3	3½" x 4½"
	7½"	4	5½" x 7½"
		5	2½" x 7½"
Maroon	2½"	4a	1½" x 1½"*
		6b	2½" x 2½"
		7	2½" x 7½"

*Cut from the larger strip and trim to the proper size.

ASSEMBLY

Refer to the piecing diagram below.

1. Sew piece 2 to piece 3, using the left 45 Joint.

2. Assemble sections 4a, 5a, 6a/b, and 7a, using the 45 Flip.
3. Arrange all the sections with piece 1 and join to complete Unit D.

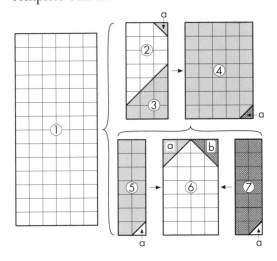

Unit E: Tesque Lightning Symbol

Note: If you choose not to use the Symbol block, eliminate pieces 1a and 2a from the chart above right, and do not sew sections 1a and 2a in step 1 of "Assembly."

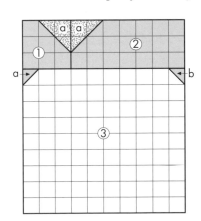

CUTTING

Use the strips listed in the chart on page 38.

Fabric	Strip Width	Piece #	Dimension
Background	9½"	3	9½" x 10½"
Rose print	2½"	3a	1½" x 1½"*
		3b	1½" x 1½"*
	3½"	1	3½" x 3½"
		2	3½" x 7½"
Green	2½"	1a	2½" x 2½"
		2a	2½" x 2½"

*Cut from the larger strip and trim to the proper size.

ASSEMBLY

1. Assemble sections 1a, 2a, and 3a/b, using the 45 Flip.
2. Arrange all the sections and join to complete Unit E.

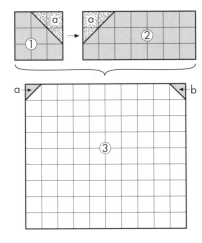

Unit F: Bighorn Sheep

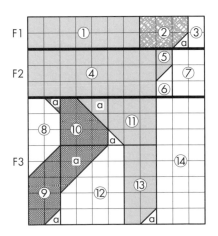

CUTTING

Use the strips listed in the chart on page 38.

Fabric	Strip Width	Piece #	Dimension
Background	1½"	2a, 9a, 11a, 13a	1½" x 1½"
	2½"	3, 6	1½" x 2½"
		7	2½" x 3½"
		8	2½" x 5½"
	3½"	14	3½" x 8½"
	6½"	12	4½" x 5½"*
Rose print	2½"	5	1½" x 2½"
		10a	2½" x 2½"
		13	2½" x 5½"
	3½"	4	3½" x 8½"
		11	3½" x 3½"
	7½"	1	2½" x 7½"
Off-white	4½"	2	2½" x 3½"*
Maroon	2½"	8a	1½" x 1½"*
		9	2½" x 5½"
	3½"	10, 12a	3½" x 3½"

*Cut from the larger strip and trim to the proper size.

ASSEMBLY

Refer to the piecing diagram below, and the unit diagram on page 41. To make the construction easier, we divided Unit F into 3 parts.

1. Assemble 2a, using the 45 Flip.
2. Sew to pieces 1 and 3 to complete Unit F1.

Unit F1

3. Sew piece 5 to piece 6, using the left 45 Joint.

4. Sew piece 4 to the left side of 5/6 and sew piece 7 to the right side to complete Unit F2.

Unit F2

5. Sew piece 8 to piece 9, using the left 45 Joint. Add piece 8a and 9a, using the 45 Flip.

6. Assemble 10a, 11a, 12a, and 13a, using the 45 Flip.
7. Arrange the assembled pieces with 8/9a and piece 14 to complete Unit F3.

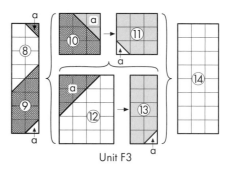

Unit F3

8. Arrange all the sections and join them to complete Unit F.

Quilt Top Assembly

1. Arrange all the units as shown in the quilt plan on page 37. Sew the units together in rows and press the seams in opposite directions from row to row. Sew the rows together.
2. For the side borders, cut 2 strips of background fabric, each 4½" x 42". Measure the quilt top for borders as shown in "Adding Borders" on page 23. Trim the strips to fit; then sew them to opposite sides of the quilt top.
3. For the top and bottom borders, cut 3 strips of background fabric, each 4½" x 42". Cut 1 strip in half crosswise and sew 1 short piece to each remaining strip. Measure, trim to fit, and sew the borders to the top and bottom edges of the quilt top.

Finishing

1. Layer the quilt with backing and batting; baste.
2. Quilt as desired and bind the edges. We used straight lines and stipple quilting to create the impression of sound and light in the Rockies.

Bear Dreamer

Indians believed that there must be a relationship between bear and man because they both walk on two legs and eat the same food. However, they deemed the bear the smarter of the two because man does not know how to live all winter without eating! Black bears can also be dark brown, cinnamon colored, or white.

Unit A   Unit B   Unit C

Unit D   Unit E   Unit F

Quilt Size: 52" x 37"

Bear Image Size: 40" x 25"

Symbol: Bear Paw

Color Photo: Page 8

Materials: 44"-wide fabric

1⅝ yds. for background and outer border
1⅛ yds. black print for bear
⅜ yd. black solid for bear
¼ yd. off-white for muzzle (or a 7" x 7" scrap)
¼ yd. green for Bear Paw symbol (optional)
¼ yd. red for Bear Paw symbol (optional)
1½ yds. for backing
½ yd. for binding
41" x 56" piece of batting

Strip Cutting

Cut the following strips across the fabric width (crosswise grain). For additional cutting directions, see the chart with each design unit.

Fabric	No. of Strips	Strip Width
Background	1	1½"
	2	2½"
	1	3½"
	1	4½"
	1	6½"
Black print	1	1½"
	1	2½"
	1	3½"
	1	5½"
	1	14½"
Black solid	1	1½"
	1	2½"
	1	3½"
	1	4½"
Off-white		6½" square
Green	1	1⅞"
Red	1	2½"

Unit Cutting and Assembly

Using the strips you just cut, cut the required number of pieces for each fabric listed in the unit cutting charts. In most cases you will simply make crosscuts; occasionally you will need to trim pieces to the dimensions given in the chart.

Bear Paw Block

Note: If you choose not to use the Symbol block, do not cut the pieces in the chart that follows. Replace them with a 10½" x 10½" square of black print fabric.

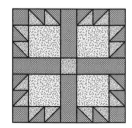

CUTTING

Use the strips listed in the chart at left.

Fabric	Strip Width	Cut	Unit Dimensions
Black print	1½"	4	1½" x 1½"
	3½"	4	1½" x 3½"
	14½"	2	5¾" x 5¾"*
		8	1⅞" x 1⅞"*
Green	1⅞"	8	1⅞" x 1⅞"
Red	2½"	4	2½" x 2½"
		1	1½" x 1½"

*Cut from the larger strip and trim to the proper size.

ASSEMBLY

1. Cut each green and black 1⅞" square once diagonally to yield 16 black and 16 green triangles. Sew each black triangle to a green triangle to make half-square triangle units.

Make 16

2. Sew pairs of half-square triangle units together as shown.

Make 4   Make 4

3. Assemble the half-square triangle units with squares and rectangles as shown. Join to construct 1 Bear Paw block.

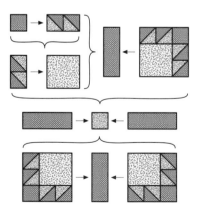

4. Cut both 5¾" x 5¾" black squares once diagonally to yield 4 triangles.

6. Sew triangles to 2 opposite sides of the block; press seams toward the triangles. Sew the remaining 2 triangles to the remaining sides; press seams toward the triangles. Reserve for Unit A assembly below.

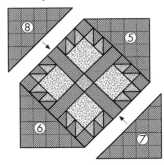

Unit A: Black Bear

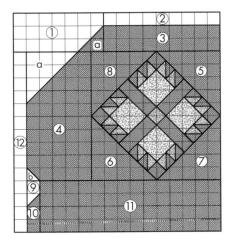

CUTTING

Use the strips listed in the chart on page 44.

Fabric	Strip Width	Piece #	Dimensions
Background	1½"	2	1½" x 9½"
		4b	1½" x 1½"
		9	1½" x 2½"
		12	1½" x 14½"
	3½"	1	3½" x 7½"
	4½"	4a	4½" x 4½"
Black print	2½"	1a	2½" x 2½"
		3	2½" x 9½"
	3½"	10	1½" x 3½"
	5½"	4	5½" x 10½"
	14½"	11	4½" x 14½"

ASSEMBLY

Refer to the piecing diagram below.

1. Assemble 1a and 4a/b, using the 45 Flip (on page 21).
2. Sew piece 9 to piece 10, using the left 45 Joint.

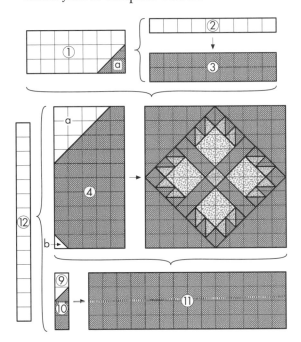

3. Arrange all the completed sections with pieces 2, 3, 11, and 12 and the reserved Bear Paw block. Join to complete Unit A.

Unit B: Black Bear

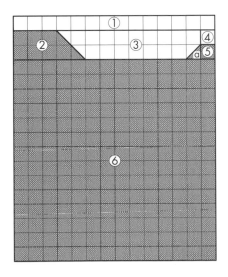

CUTTING

Use the strips listed in the chart on page 44.

Fabric	Strip Width	Piece #	Dimensions
Background	1½"	1	1½" x 14½"
		4	1½" x 1½"
	2½"	3	2½" x 10½"
Black print	1½"	3a, 5	1½" x 1½"
	5½"	2	2½" x 5½"
	14½"	6	14½" x 14½"

ASSEMBLY

Refer to the piecing diagram below.

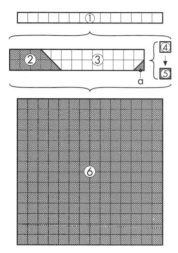

1. Sew piece 2 to piece 3, using the left 45 Joint.
2. Assemble piece 3a, using the 45 Flip.
3. Arrange all the sections with pieces 1, 4, 5, and 6. Join to complete Unit B. Refer to illustration at the botom of page 45.

Unit C:

Black Bear

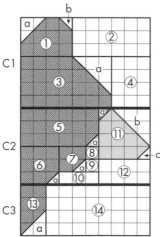

CUTTING

Use the strips listed in the chart on page 44.

Fabric	Strip Width	Piece #	Dimensions
Background	1½"	1b, 6a, 7a, 9, 11c	1½" x 1½"
	2½"	1a, 13a	2½" x 2½"
	3½"	3a, 11b	3½" x 3½"
		10	1½" x 3½"
	4½"	4	3½" x 4½"
		12	2½" x 4½"
		14	4½" x 8½"
	6½"	2	3½" x 6½"
Black print	1½"	11a	1½" x 1½"
	2½"	7	2½" x 2½"
	3½"	1	3½" x 4½"
		5	3½" x 6½"
		6	3½" x 3½"
	5½"	3	4½" x 7½"*
		13	2½" x 4½"*
Off-white		5a, 8	1½" x 1½"**
		11	4½" x 4½"**

*Cut from the larger strip and trim to the proper size.

**Cut from the 7" square.

ASSEMBLY

Refer to the piecing diagrams below and on the next page. To make the construction easier, we divided Unit C into 3 parts.

1. Assemble 1a/b and 3a, using the 45 Flip.
2. Arrange the pieced units with pieces 2 and 4 and join to complete Unit C1.

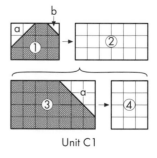

Unit C1

3. Sew piece 5a, 6a, and 7a, using the 45 Flip.
4. Sew piece 11a and 11c to piece 11, using the 45 Flip. Trim and press. Add piece 11b.

5. Arrange the pieces for Unit C2 and join them to complete the unit.

Unit C2

6. Assemble 13a, using the 45 Flip.

7. Sew piece 14 to the right side of 13a to complete Unit C3.

Unit C3

8. Arrange all parts and join them to complete Unit C.

Unit D: Black Bear

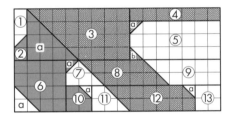

CUTTING

Use the strips listed in the chart on page 44.

Fabric	Strip Width	Piece #	Dimensions
Background	1½"	10a, 12a	1½" x 1½"
	2½"	6a, 13	2½" x 2½"
		7, 11	2½" x 3½"
	3½"	1	1½" x 3½"
		5	3½" x 7½"
	6½"	9	2½" x 6½"
Black print	1½"	4	1½" x 7½"
		5a, 5b	1½" x 1½"
	2½"	8, 12	2½" x 7½"
	5½"	3	4½" x 8½"*
Black solid	2½"	2	1½" x 2½"
		7a	1½" x 1½"*
		10	2½" x 2½"
	4½"	3a, 6	4½" x 4½"

*Cut from the larger strip and trim to the proper size.

ASSEMBLY

Refer to the piecing diagram below.

1. Assemble 3a, 5a/b, and 6a, using the 45 Flip.
2. Join piece 1 to piece 2, using the left 45 Joint. Repeat with pieces 7 and 8 and pieces 11 and 12.

3. Sew piece 7/8 to piece 9, using the left 45 Joint. Add piece 7a, using the 45 Flip.
4. Arrange all the pieces with pieces 4 and 13 and join to complete Unit D.

Unit E: Black Bear

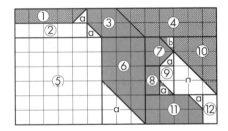

CUTTING

Use the strips listed in the chart on page 44.

Fabric	Strip Width	Piece #	Dimensions
Background	1½"	1a, 3a, 7a, 11a	1½" x 1½"
	1½"	2	1½" x 5½"
	1½"	9, 12	1½" x 2½"
	3½"	6a, 10a	3½" x 3½"
	6½"	5	6½" x 6½"
Black print	1½"	1	1½" x 5½"
		7b	1½" x 1½"
	2½"	4	2½" x 7½"
	3½"	10	3½" x 4½"

Continued next page

Fabric	Strip Width	Piece #	Dimensions
Black solid	2½"	3	2½" x 4½"
		8	1½" x 2½"
		9a	1½" x 1½"*
		7	2½" x 2½"
	4½"	6	3½" x 6½"*
		11	2½" x 4½"

*Cut from the larger strip and trim to the proper size.

ASSEMBLY

Refer to the piecing diagram below.

1. Assemble 1a, 6a, 7a/b, 9a, 10a, and 11a, using the 45 Flip.
2. Sew piece 3 to piece 4, using the left 45 Joint. Add piece 3a to piece 3/4, using the 45 Flip.
3. Arrange all the pieces and join to complete Unit E.

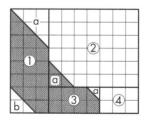

Unit F: Black Bear

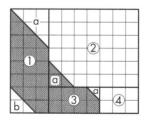

CUTTING

Use the strips listed in the chart on page 44.

Fabric	Strip Width	Piece #	Dimensions
Background	1½"	3a	1½" x 1½"
	2½"	4	2½" x 3½"
		1b	2½" x 2½"
	3½"	1a	3½" x 3½"

Continued next column

Fabric	Strip Width	Piece #	Dimensions
Background	6½"	2	6½" x 7½"
Black print	2½"	2a	2½" x 2½"
	3½"	1	3½" x 8½"
	5½"	3	2½" x 4½"*

*Cut from the larger strip and trim to the proper size.

ASSEMBLY

Refer to the piecing diagram below.

1. Assemble 1a/b, 2a, and 3a, using the 45 Flip.
2. Arrange the pieces with piece 4 and join to complete Unit F.

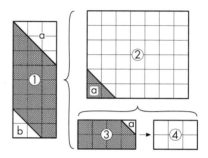

Quilt Top Assembly

1. Arrange all the units as shown in the quilt plan on page 43. Sew the units together in horizontal rows, pressing seams in opposite directions from row to row. Sew the rows together.
2. For side borders, cut 2 strips of background fabric, each 6½" x 42". Measure the quilt top for borders as shown in "Adding Borders" on page 23. Trim the strips to fit and sew them to opposite sides of the quilt top.
3. For the top and bottom borders, cut 3 strips of background fabric, each 6½" x 42". Cut 1 strip in half crosswise and sew 1 short piece to each of the remaining strips. Measure, trim to fit, and sew the pieced border strips to the top and bottom edges of the quilt top.

Finishing

1. Layer the quilt with backing and batting; baste.
2. Quilt as desired and bind the edges. We stipple quilted the entire quilt, treating each part of the bear's body separately. We used a more widely spaced stipple design in the background.

Spirit of the Mountains

According to Zuni mythology, the mountain lion guarded the north, while other sacred animals watched over the remaining five directions. Puma, panther, painter, cougar, and catamount are all names for the same secretive and nocturnal cat that some Native Americans called "Spirit of the Mountains."

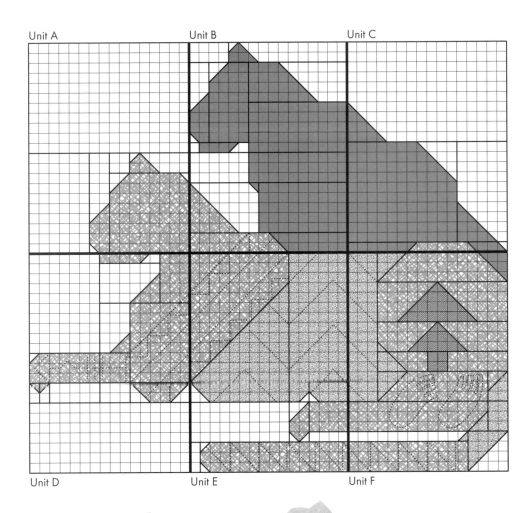

❖

Quilt Size: 56" x 51"

Cougar Image Size: 43" x 48"

Symbol: Hopi Tree

Color Photo: Page 9

❖

Materials: 44"-wide fabric

2¼ yds. for background and border
1¼ yds. light gold #1 for cougar body
⅝ yd. light gold #2 for cougar body (We used the wrong side of the light gold fabric above.)
½ yd. medium gold for cougar #2
¼ yd. green for Hopi tree symbol
3 yds. for backing
¾ yd. for binding
55" x 60" piece of batting

Strip Cutting

Cut the following strips across the fabric width (crosswise grain). For additional cutting directions, see the chart with each design unit.

Fabric	No. of Strips	Strip Width
Background	1	1½"
	2	2½"
	1	3½"
	1	4½"
	2	11½"
Light gold #1	1	1½"
	1	2½"
	3	3½"
	2	10½"
Light gold #2	1	2½"
	1	3½"
	1	10½"
Medium gold	1	2½"
	1	10½"
Green	1	4½"

Unit Cutting and Assembly

Using the strips you just cut, cut the required number of pieces for each fabric listed in the unit cutting charts. In most cases you will simply make crosscuts; occasionally you will need to trim pieces to the dimensions given in the chart.

Unit A: Cougar

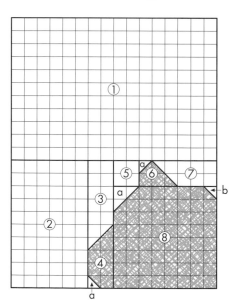

CUTTING

Use the strips listed in the chart at left.

Fabric	Strip Width	Piece #	Dimensions
Background	1½"	4a, 6a, 8b	1½" x 1½"
	2½"	3	2½" x 7½"
		5, 8a	2½" x 2½"
		7	2½" x 5½"
	11½"	1	11½" x 16½"
		2	6½" x 10½"*
Light gold #1	2½"	4	2½" x 5½"
	3½"	6	2½" x 3½"
	10½"	8	8½" x 8½"*

*Cut from the larger strip and trim to the proper size.

ASSEMBLY

Refer to the piecing diagram below.
1. Sew piece 3 to piece 4, using the left 45 Joint. Repeat with pieces 6 and 7.

2. Add piece 4a to 3/4.
3. Assemble 8a/b, using the 45 Flip (page 21).
4. Arrange and sew together pieces 2–8 as shown below. Add piece 1 to complete Unit A as shown at left.

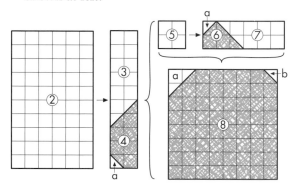

Unit B1: Cougar

To make the construction easier, we divided Unit B into 2 parts.

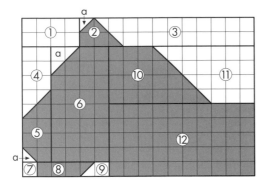

2. Add piece 2a to 2/3 and add piece 6a to 4/6, using the 45 Flip.
3. Assemble 5a, using the 45 Flip.
4. Assemble all pieces and join to complete Unit B1, shown at left.

CUTTING

Use the strips listed in the chart on page 50.

Fabric	Strip Width	Piece #	Dimensions
Background	1½"	2a, 6a, 7	1½" x 1½"
		9	1½" x 2½"
	2½"	1	2½" x 4½"
		3	2½" x 11½"
		4	2½" x 5½"
		5a	2½" x 2½"
	4½"	11	4½" x 7½"
Medium gold	2½"	2	2½" x 3½"
		5	2½" x 5½"
		8	1½" x 4½"*
	10½"	6	4½" x 8½"*
		10	4½" x 7½"*
		12	5½" x 10½"

*Cut from the larger strip and trim to the proper size.

ASSEMBLY

Refer to the piecing diagram above right.
1. Sew piece 4 to piece 6, using the left 45 Joint. Repeat with pieces 10 and 11 and pieces 8 and 9. Check color placement.

Unit B2: Cougar

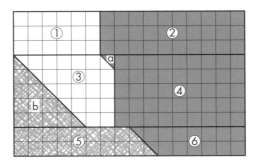

CUTTING

Use the strips listed in the chart on page 50.

Fabric	Strip Width	Piece #	Dimensions
Background	3½"	1	3½" x 6½"
	11½"	3	5½" x 7½"*
Light gold #1	10½"	3b	5½" x 5½"*
		5	2½" x 10½"
Medium gold	10½"	2	3½" x 10½"
		4	5½" x 9½"*
	2½"	3a	1½" x 1½"*
		6	2½" x 8½"

*Cut from the larger strip and trim to the proper size.

ASSEMBLY

Refer to the piecing diagram below.
1. Assemble 3a/b, using the 45 Flip.
2. Sew piece 5 to piece 6, using the left 45 Joint.

3. Arrange all the pieces; join to complete Unit B2.

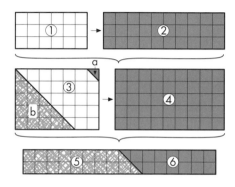

4. Sew Unit B2 to the bottom edge of Unit B1.

Unit C: Cougar

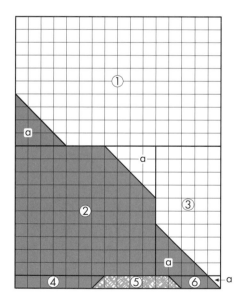

CUTTING

Use the strips listed in the chart on page 50.

Fabric	Strip Width	Piece #	Dimensions
Background	1½"	6a	1½" x 1½"
	4½"	2a	4½" x 4½"
	11½"	3	5½" x 10½"*
		1	10½" x 16½"*
Light gold #1	1½"	5	1½" x 7½"
Medium gold	2½"	4	1½" x 7½"*
		6	1½" x 4½"*
	10½"	1a, 3a	4½" x 4½"*
		2	10½" x 11½"

*Cut from the larger strip and trim to the proper size.

ASSEMBLY

Refer to the piecing diagram below.
1. Assemble 1a, 2a, and 3a, using the 45 Flip.
2. Sew piece 4 to piece 5, using the right 45 Joint.

Right
45 Joint

3. Sew piece 4/5 to piece 6, using the left 45 Joint. Add piece 6a to 4/5/6, using the 45 Flip.

Left
45 Joint

4. Assemble all the pieces and join them to complete Unit C.

Unit D: Cougar

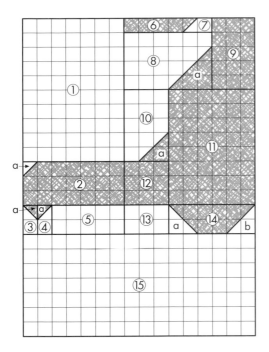

CUTTING

Use the strips listed in the chart on page 50.

Fabric	Strip Width	Piece #	Dimensions
Background	1½"	2a,	1½" x 1½"
		3, 4, 7	1½" x 2½"
	2½"	5	2½" x 5½"
		13	2½" x 3½"
		14a, 14b	2½" x 2½"
	3½"	10	3½" x 5½"
	4½"	8	4½" x 6½"
	11½"	1	7½" x 10½"*
		15	7½" x 16½"*
Light gold #1	1½"	3a, 4a	1½" x 1½"
		6	1½" x 5½"
	2½"	10a	2½" x 2½"
		14	2½" x 6½"
	3½"	2	3½" x 7½"
		8a, 12	3½" x 3½"
		9	3½" x 5½"
	10½"	11	6½" x 8½"*

*Cut from the larger strip and trim to the proper size.

ASSEMBLY

Refer to the piecing diagram below.

1. Assemble 2a, 3a, 4a, 8a, 10a, and 14a/b, using the 45 Flip.
2. Sew piece 6 to piece 7, using the right 45 Joint.

3. Arrange all the pieces and join to complete Unit D.

Unit E: Cougar

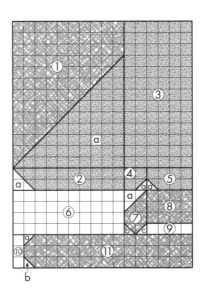

CUTTING

Use the strips listed in the chart on page 50.

Fabric	Strip Width	Piece #	Dimensions
Background	1½"	4a, 5a, 7b, 7c, 11a, 11b	1½" x 1½"
		10	1½" x 3½"
	2½"	2a, 7a	2½" x 2½"
	4½"	6	4½" x 10½"
		9	1½" x 4½"
Light gold #1	2½"	7	2½" x 4½"
	3½"	8	3½" x 4½"
		11	3½" x 15½"
	10½"	1	10½" x 13½"
Light gold #2	2½"	4	2½" x 2½"
		5	2½" x 4½"
	10½"	1a	10½" x 10½"
		2	2½" x 10½"
		3	6½" x 13½"*

*Cut from the larger strip and trim to the proper size.

ASSEMBLY

Refer to the piecing diagram below.
1. Assemble 1a, 2a, 4a, 5a, 7a/b/c, and 11a/b, using the 45 Flip (page 21).
2. Arrange all units and join to complete Unit E as shown on page 53.

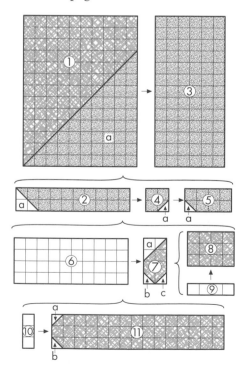

Unit F: Hopi Tree Symbol

To make the construction easier, we divided Unit F into 2 parts.

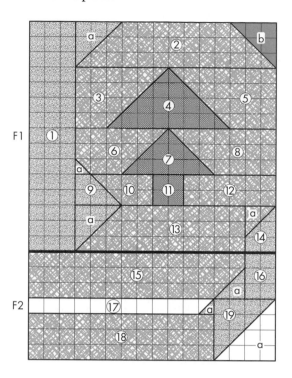

Note: If you prefer not to use the Symbol block, do not cut pieces 3–12. Replace them with a 9½" x 13½" rectangle of light gold #1 and a 3½" x 3½" square of light gold #2. Sew the light gold #2 square to the lower left corner of the light gold #1 rectangle, using the 45 Flip.

CUTTING

Use the strips listed in the chart on page 50.

Fabric	Strip Width	Piece #	Dimensions
Background	1½"	17	1½" x 2½"
	4½"	19a	4½" x 4½"
Light gold #1	1½"	17a	1½" x 1½"

Continued next page

Fabric	Strip Width	Piece #	Dimensions
Light gold #1	2½"	10	2½" x 4½"
		12	2½" x 6½"
		14a	2½" x 2½"
	3½"	15	3½" x 14½"
		2	3½" x 13½"
		18	3½" x 12½"
		6	3½" x 6½"
		8	3½" x 7½"
		13	3½" x 11½"
	10½"	3	4½" x 6½"*
		5	4½" x 7½"*
Light gold #2	1½"	6a	1½" x 1½"
	2½"	15a	2½" x 2½"
	3½"	1	3½" x 15½"
		16	2½" x 3½"
		2a, 13a,	3½" x 3½"
		9, 14	2½" x 3½"
	10½"	19	4½" x 4½"
Medium gold	10½"	2b	3½" x 3½"*
Green	4½"	4	4½" x 8½"
		7	3½" x 6½"*
		11	2½" x 2½"*

*Cut from the larger strip and trim to the proper size.

ASSEMBLY

Refer to the piecing diagram above right.
1. Assemble 2a/b, 13a, and 14a, using the 45 Flip.
2. Sew piece 3 to piece 4, and piece 6 to piece 7, using the right 45 Joint.

Right
45 Joint

3. Join piece 5 to piece 3/4, piece 8 to piece 6/7, and piece 9 to piece 10, using the left 45 Joint.

Left
45 Joint

4. Add piece 6a to 6/7/8, using the 45 Flip.

5. Arrange all the pieces and join to complete Unit F1 as shown at right and in the finished unit on page 54.

6. Assemble 15a, 17a, and 19a, using the 45 Flip.

7. Arrange all the pieces and join to complete Unit F2.

8. Sew Unit F2 to the bottom edge of Unit F1 to complete Unit F.

Quilt Top Assembly

1. Arrange the completed units as shown in the quilt plan on page 49.
2. Sew units together in rows. Press seams to opposite sides from row to row. Join rows.
3. For side borders, cut 3 strips of background fabric, each 4½" x 42". Cut 1 strip in half crosswise and sew 1 piece to each of the remaining strips. Measure the quilt top for borders as described in "Adding Borders" on page 23. Trim the strips to fit and sew them to opposite sides of the quilt top.
4. For top and bottom borders, cut 3 strips of background fabric, each 4½" x 42". Join the strips as described in step 3, measure, and trim to fit. Sew the strips to the top and bottom edges of the quilt top.

Finishing

1. Layer the quilt with backing and batting; baste.
2. Quilt as desired and bind the edges. We stipple quilted the darker cougar and quilted parallel diagonal lines and petroglyph symbols on the lighter cougar.

Red Dog

In the Blackfoot warrior hierarchy, kit foxes were more powerful than braves. In their dances, Blackfoot braves jumped from side to side, mimicking the wily fox. A rust red coat makes him one of nature's handsomest dogs, although the fox can also be black, or more rarely, silver.

Unit A
Unit B
Unit C
Unit D

Quilt Size: 38" x 44"

Fox Image Size: 21" x 27"

Symbol: Arapaho Frog

Color Photo: Page 10

Materials: 44"-wide fabric

1 yd. for background and top and right borders
½ yd. red #1 for body
¼ yd. red #2 for body
¼ yd. black for body
⅛ yd. green for symbol
1⅜ yds. striped fabric for bottom and left borders
1½ yds. for backing
½ yd. for binding
42" x 48" piece of batting

Strip Cutting

Cut the following strips across the fabric width (crosswise grain). For additional cutting directions, see the chart with each design unit.

Fabric	No. of Strips	Strip Width
Background	1	1½"
	1	2½"
	1	7½"
Red #1	2	2½"
	1	3½"
	1	4½"
Red #2	1	2½"
Black	1	2½"
	1	3½"
Green	2	2⅝" x 4⅛" rectangles

Unit Cutting and Assembly

Using the strips you just cut, cut the required number of pieces for each fabric listed in the unit cutting charts. In most cases you will simply make crosscuts; occasionally you will need to trim pieces to the dimensions given in the chart.

Unit A: Fox

CUTTING

Use the strips listed in the chart above.

Fabric	Strip Width	Piece #	Dimensions
Background	1½"	2a, 13a	1½" x 1½"
	2½"	2b, 4	2½" x 2½"
		3	2½" x 4½"
		6, 12	2½" x 3½"
	7½"	1	4½" x 5½"*
		7	4½" x 6½"*
		14	7½" x 8½"

Continued next column

Fabric	Strip Width	Piece #	Dimensions
Red #1	2½"	3a, 7b	2½" x 2½"
		5, 9, 13	2½" x 3½"
	3½"	6a, 6b, 7a	1½" x 1½"*
	4½"	2, 11	3½" x 4½"
		8	1½" x 4½"
Black	2½"	10	1½" x 2½"
	3½"	8a, 9a, 11a	1½" x 1½"*

*Cut from the larger strip and trim to the proper size.

ASSEMBLY

Refer to the piecing diagrams below. To make the construction easier, we divided Unit A into 2 parts.

1. Assemble 2a/b, 3a, and 6a/b, using the 45 Flip (page 21).
2. Arrange these pieces with pieces 1, 4, and 5 and join to complete Unit A1.

Unit A1

3. Assemble 7a/b, 8a, 9a, and 11a, using the 45 Flip.
4. Sew piece 12 to piece 13, using the right 45 Joint. Add piece 13a to piece 12/13.

5. Arrange these pieces with piece 10 and join to complete Unit A2.

Unit A2

6. Sew Unit A2 to the bottom edge of Unit A1; then add piece 14 to the right side to complete Unit A.

Unit B: Arapaho Frog Symbol

CUTTING

Use the strips listed in the chart on page 57.

Fabric	Strip Width	Piece #	Dimensions
Background	1½"	2, 11	1½" x 2½"
	2½"	1	2½" x 5½"
		4	2½" x 3½"
		9	2½" x 2½"
	7½"	6	3½" x 3½"*
Red #1	2½"	3	1½" x 2½"
		5a	2½" x 2½"
	3½"	1a	1½" x 1½"*
Black	2½"	4a	2½" x 2½"
		10	1½" x 2½"
	3½"	5	3½" x 6½"
		6a, 6b, 9a	1½" x 1½"*
		8	3½" x 4½"

*Cut from the larger strip and trim to the proper size.

ASSEMBLY

Note: If you choose not to use the Symbol block, replace the pieces in steps 1 and 2 with a 4½" x 6½" rectangle of black print fabric.

Refer to the piecing diagram above right.

1. To construct the Arapaho Frog symbol, place the 2 green 2⅝" x 4⅛" rectangles right sides together. Cut once diagonally to yield 4 triangles. Arrange the triangles as shown and sew them together to form a diamond.

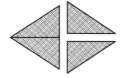

2. From black fabric, cut 2 rectangles, each 3¼" x 4½", and place them right sides together. Cut once diagonally to yield 4 triangles. Sew 1 triangle to each side of the green diamond. Trim the resulting rectangle to 4½" x 6½".

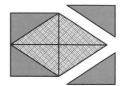

3. Assemble sections 1a, 4a, 5a, 6a/b, and 9a, using the 45 Flip.
4. Arrange these pieces with pieces 2, 3, 8, 10, 11, and the Arapaho Frog symbol, and join to complete Unit B.

Unit C: Fox

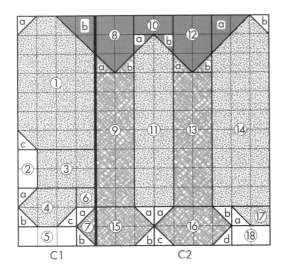

C1   C2

CUTTING

Use the strips listed in the chart on page 57.

Fabric	Strip Width	Piece #	Dimensions
Background	1½"	1a, 1c,	1½" x 1½"
		4a, 4b, 4c,	
		7a, 7b, 14b, 15a, 15b,	
		16a, 16b, 16c, 16d, 17a	
		2, 18	1½" x 2½"
		5	1½" x 3½"
Red #1	2½"	3, 4	2½" x 3½"
		11	2½" x 9½"
		17	1½" x 2½"
	3½"	6	1½" x 1½"*
		14	3½" x 10½"
	4½"	1	4½" x 7½"
Red #2	2½"	7	1½" x 2½"
		8a, 8b,	1½" x 1½"*
		12a, 12b	
		9, 13	2½" x 7½"
		15	2½" x 3½"
		16	2½" x 4½"
Black	2½"	1b, 14a	2½" x 2½"
		10	1½" x 2½"
	3½"	8, 12	2½" x 3½"
		11a, 11b	1½" x 1½"*

*Cut from the larger strip and trim to the proper size.

ASSEMBLY

Refer to the piecing diagrams below. To make the construction easier, we divided Unit C into 2 parts.

1. Assemble 1a/b/c, 4a/b/c, and 7a/b, using the 45 Flip.
2. Arrange these pieces with pieces 2, 3, 5, and 6, and join to complete Unit C1.

Unit C1

3. Assemble 8a/b, 11a/b, 12a/b, 14a/b, 15a/b, 16a/b/c/d, and 17a, using the 45 Flip.
4. Arrange these pieces with pieces 9, 10, 11, 13, and 18, and join to complete Unit C2.

Unit C2

5. Sew Unit C2 to the right edge of Unit C1 to complete Unit C.

Unit D: Fox

ASSEMBLY

Refer to the piecing diagram below.

1. Assemble sections 1a, 2a/b, 6a, 12a, and 16a, using the 45 Flip.
2. Join pieces 9, 10, and 11, using the left 45 Joint.

3. Arrange these sections with pieces 3, 4, 5, 7, 8, 13, 14, and 15, and join to complete Unit D.

CUTTING

Use the strips listed in the chart on page 57.

Fabric	Strip Width	Piece #	Dimensions
Background	1½"	2b, 6a, 12a	1½" x 1½"
		8	1½" x 2½"
		13	1½" x 3½"
	2½"	2a, 15	2½" x 2½"
	7½"	1	4½" x 6½"*
		9	3½" x 5½"*
		11	3½" x 4½"*
		16	5½" x 8½"*
Red #1	2½"	5	1½" x 2½"
		7, 14	2½" x 3½"
	3½"	1a, 3	1½" x 1½"*
		10	3½" x 10½"
		16a	3½" x 3½"
	4½"	12	3½" x 4½"
Black	2½"	2	2½" x 4½"
		6	2½" x 2½"
	3½"	4	1½" x 1½"*

Quilt Top Assembly

1. Arrange the units as shown in the quilt plan on page 56.
2. Sew Unit C to the bottom edge of Unit B. Add Unit D to the right side; then sew Unit A to the top of B/C/D.
3. For the top and right side borders, cut 2 strips of background fabric, each 9" x 42". Measure the quilt for 1 side border as shown in "Adding Borders" on page 23. Trim the strip to fit; then sew it to the right side of the quilt top. Measure the remaining strip, trim to fit, and sew it to the top edge of the quilt top.
4. For the left side and bottom borders, cut the striped fabric lengthwise into 2 strips, each 6" x 49". Follow a line of the stripe to make the cutting easier. Measure the quilt top for side and bottom borders, and add 7" to each measurement. Pin 1 border strip to the left side of the quilt, with the top edge even with the quilt top and extra fabric at the bottom edge. Sew it to the left side of the quilt, stopping the stitching ¼" from the bottom left corner. Pin the bottom border as you did above, with the right-side edges even and extra fabric on the left side. Stitch in place, stopping the stitching ¼" from the bottom left corner.

Quilt front

¼" from quilt corner

5. To miter the corner, fold the quilt top diagonally from the corner, right sides together, and arrange the border strips so that the long edges are aligned.

Wrong side of quilt top

6. Align the 45° angle of the ruler on the stitching line. Draw a line on the wrong side of each strip, from the intersection of the stitching lines to the outer edge.

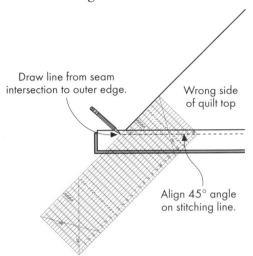

Draw line from seam intersection to outer edge.

Wrong side of quilt top

Align 45° angle on stitching line.

7. Pin carefully, matching the drawn lines on both border strips, and sew on the line. Backstitch at both ends. Trim seams to ¼" and press open.

Finishing

1. Layer the quilt with batting and backing; baste.
2. Quilt as desired and bind the edges. We stipple quilted the legs and black area of the fox and quilted a moon and Thunderbird design, which radiates from the top right corner. We quilted in-the-ditch around the fox.
3. You may use yarn or floss to chain-stitch four little legs to the corners of the Frog symbol if you desire. See the color photo on page 10.

We Were Here

In The American Bison, *Martin S. Garretson relates a Kiowa legend. The Great Spirit said to the people, "Here are the Buffalo. They shall be your food and your raiment, but in the day you shall see them perish from off the face of Earth, then know that the end of the Kiowa is near. . . ."*

The outline of a hand is one of the most powerful of symbols. It says to future generations, "We were here." We use this somber symbol to speak for the spirit of the buffalo.

Finished Quilt Size: 48" x 49"

Buffalo Image Size: 44" x 33"

Symbol: Pinwheel

Color Photo: Page 11

Materials: 44"-wide fabric

2 yds. for background and border
⅝ yd. medium tan for body
⅝ yd. light tan for body
½ yd. black for body and symbol
⅓ yd. gold for symbol
2¾ yds. for backing
⅝ yd. for binding
52" x 53" piece of batting

Strip Cutting

Cut the following strips across the fabric width (crosswise grain). For additional cutting directions, see the chart with each design unit.

Fabric	No. of Strips	Strip Width
Background	2	2½"
	2	3½"
	1	4½"
	1	7½"
	1	9½"
Medium tan	2	3½"
	1	10½"
Light tan	1	2½"
	1	5½"
	1	9½"
Black	1	2½"
	1	10½"
	1	10" square
Gold	1	10" square

UNIT CUTTING AND ASSEMBLY

Using the strips you just cut, cut the required number of pieces for each fabric listed in the unit cutting charts. In most cases, you will simply make crosscuts; occassionally you will need to trim pieces to the dimensions given in the chart.

Unit A: Buffalo

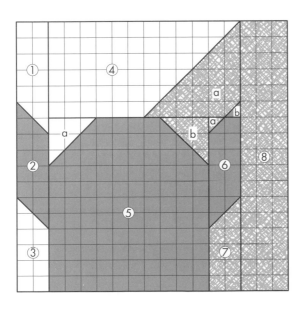

CUTTING

Use the strips listed in the chart at left.

Fabric	Strip Width	Piece #	Dimensions
Background	2½"	3	2½" x 6½"
	3½"	5a	3½" x 3½"
	7½"	1	2½" x 7½"
		4	6½" x 12½"*
Medium tan	3½"	5b	3½" x 3½"
		6a	1½" x 1½"*
		7	2½" x 6½"*
		8	3½" x 17½"
	10½"	4a	6½" x 6½"*
Black	2½"	2	2½" x 8½"
		4b	1½" x 1½"*
		6	2½" x 7½"
	10½"	5	10½" x 11½"

*Cut from the larger strips and trim to the proper size.

ASSEMBLY

Refer to the piecing diagram below.

1. Sew pieces 1, 2, and 3 together, using the right 45 Joint. Repeat with pieces 6 and 7, using the left 45 Joint. Add piece 6a to piece 6/7.

Right 45 Joint

Left 45 Joint

2. Assemble sections 4a and 5a/b, using the 45 Flip (page 21).
3. Arrange these sections with piece 8 and join to complete Unit A.

Unit B: Buffalo

Unit C: Buffalo

CUTTING

Use the strips listed in the chart on page 63.

Fabric	Strip Width	Piece #	Dimensions
Background	7½"	1a	7½" x 7½"
Medium tan	3½"	2	3½" x 8½"
	10½"	1	10½" x 14½"
		3a	6½" x 6½"*
Light tan	5½"	1b	3½" x 3½"*
	9½"	3	8½" x 11½"*

*Cut from the larger strip and trim to the proper size.

ASSEMBLY

Refer to the piecing diagram below.
1. Assemble sections 1a/b and 3a, using the 45 Flip.
2. Arrange these sections with piece 2 and join to complete Unit B.

CUTTING

Use the strips list in the chart on page 63.

Fabric	Strip Width	Piece #	Dimensions
Background	3½"	4a	3½" x 3½"
	4½"	1	4½" x 7½"
	9½"	3	9½" x 9½"
Light tan	2½"	2	2½" x 4½"
		3a	2½" x 2½"
	9½"	4	9½" x 13½"

ASSEMBLY

Refer to the piecing diagram below.
1. Assemble sections 3a and 4a, using the 45 Flip.
2. Arrange these sections with pieces 1 and 2, and join to complete Unit C.

Unit D: Buffalo

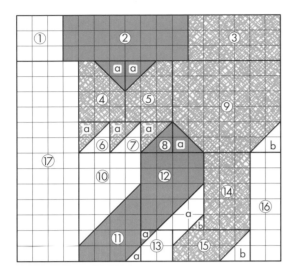

ASSEMBLY

Refer to the piecing diagram below.

1. Assemble sections 4a, 5a, 6a, 7a, 8a, 9a/b, 12a, 13a, and 15a/b for Unit D, using the 45 Flip.
2. Add piece 12b to section 12a, using the Piggy-back Flip (page 22).
3. Sew piece 10 to piece 11, using the left 45 Joint. Add piece 11a to section 10/11.

4. Arrange all the sections and join to complete Unit D.

CUTTING

Use the strips listed in the chart on page 63.

Fabric	Strip Width	Piece #	Dimensions
Background	2½"	6, 7, 9b, 13, 15b	2½" x 2½"
		11a, 15a	1½" x 1½"*
	3½"	1, 12a	3½" x 3½"
	4½"	10	4½" x 6½"
		17	4½" x 13½"
	7½"	16	2½" x 7½"
Medium tan	3½"	3	3½" x 6½"
		4, 5	3½" x 4½"
		6a, 7a, 8a	2½" x 2½"*
		12b	1½" x 1½"*
		14	3½" x 5½"
		15	2½" x 5½"*
	10½"	9	6½" x 7½"*
Black	2½"	4a, 5a, 8, 9a	2½" x 2½"
		13a	1½" x 1½"*
	10½"	2	3½" x 8½"*
		11, 12	4½" x 5½"*

*Cut from the larger strip and trim to the proper size.

Unit E: Buffalo

CUTTING

Use the strips listed in the chart on page 63.

Fabric	Strip Width	Piece #	Dimensions
Background	9½"	1, 2	7½" x 9½"
Light tan	2½"	1a, 2a	2½" x 2½"

ASSEMBLY

Refer to the piecing diagram below.
1. Assemble sections 1a and 2a, using the 45 Flip.
2. Sew section 2a to the right side of section 1a to complete Unit E.

Unit F: Buffalo

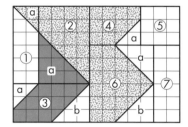

CUTTING

Use the strips listed in the chart on page 63.

Fabric	Strip Width	Piece #	Dimensions
Background	2½"	1	2½" x 6½"
		3a, 4a	2½" x 2½"
		7	2½" x 6½"
	3½"	3b, 5, 6a	3½" x 3½"
		6b	
Light tan	2½"	1a	2½" x 2½"
	5½"	2	4½" x 6½"*
		4	3½" x 4½"*
		6	5½" x 6½"
Black	10½"	2a	4½" x 4½"*
		3	3½" x 6½"*

*Cut from the larger strip and trim to the proper size.

ASSEMBLY

Refer to the piecing diagram below.
1. Assemble sections 1a, 2a, 3a/b, 4a, and 6a/b for Unit F, using the 45 Flip.
2. Arrange the sections with pieces 5 and 7 and join to complete Unit F.

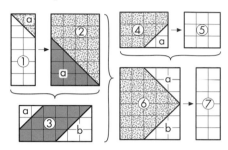

Unit G: Pinwheel Symbol

Note: If you choose not to use the Symbol block, eliminate steps 1–6 and replace the pieced unit with a rectangle of light tan fabric, 6½" x 24½". Sew a 3½" x 3½" square of medium tan to the upper left corner of this rectangle, using the 45 Flip. Finish piecing the unit beginning with step 7 of "Assembly" on page 67.

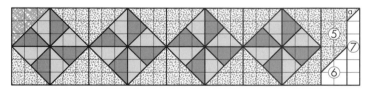

Unit G

CUTTING

Use the strips listed in the chart on page 63.

Fabric	Strip Width	Piece #	Dimensions
Background	2½"	6	2½" x 3½"
	7½"	7	1½" x 6½"*
Medium tan	10½"	1a	4" x 4"*
Light tan	2½"	7a	1½" x 1½"*
	5½"	5	2½" x 5½"
		2 squares	4" x 4"*
	9½"	2 squares	7" x 7"*
Gold		1 square	10" x 10"
Black		1 square	10" x 10"

Use the 10" gold square with these strips.

*Cut from the larger strip and trim to the proper size.

ASSEMBLY

Refer to the piecing diagram below.

1. To make half-square triangles for the pinwheel sections, place the black and gold 10" squares right sides together. Press to prevent them from slipping. Draw a grid of 3" x 3" squares on the back of the gold fabric. Draw diagonal lines in every other square in one direction as shown below. Draw diagonal lines in the opposite direction in the remaining squares.

2. Sew ¼" from each side of each diagonal line; then cut the grid apart on each drawn line. You will have 18 half-square triangle units. Press the seam toward the darker fabric in each one.

 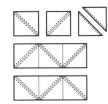

3. Sew half-square triangle units together as shown to make 4 Pinwheel blocks.

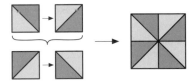

4. For corner triangles, cut the 4" squares of light tan and medium tan once diagonally to yield 4 triangles of light tan and 2 triangles of medium tan. (Set aside 1 of each color.)

5. For the side setting triangles, cut the 7" squares of light tan twice diagonally to yield 8 triangles. (You will have 2 extra triangles.)

6. Arrange the Pinwheel blocks and the corner and side setting triangles as shown. Join them in diagonal rows.

7. Sew piece 5 to piece 6, using the left 45 Joint.

8. Assemble section 7a, using the 45 Flip.

9. Arrange these sections with the pinwheel section and join to complete Unit G.

Quilt Top Assembly

1. Arrange all the units as shown in the quilt plan on page 62.

2. Sew Unit B to the bottom edge of Unit A.

3. Sew Unit C to the right side of Unit B; then add Unit G to the bottom edge.

4. Sew Unit F to the right side of Unit E; then add this section to the bottom edge of B/C/G.

5. Sew Unit A/B to the left side of B/C/E/F/G to complete the buffalo.

6. For side borders, cut 2 strips of background fabric, each 2½" x 42". Adding the quilt top for borders as shown in "Adding Borders" on page 23. Trim the strips to fit and sew them to opposite sides of the quilt top.

7. For top and bottom borders, cut 3 strips of background fabric, each 8½" x 42". Cut 1 strip in half crosswise; sew 1 short piece to each of the remaining strips. Measure the quilt top and trim the borders to fit; sew the strips to the top and bottom of the quilt top.

Finishing

1. Layer the quilt with batting and backing; baste.

2. Quilt as desired and bind the edges. We quilted several hand prints, both large and small, on the buffalo's hindquarters and quilted the remainder of the top with wavy lines.

Spirit Companions

Choovio, the antelope, was the animal representative of Kuskurza, the Hopi Third World. The fastest of American hoofed animals, he was difficult to hunt. Sometimes his curiosity was greater than his caution. The child wrapped in antelope skins was sure to be swift, dancing, and curious.

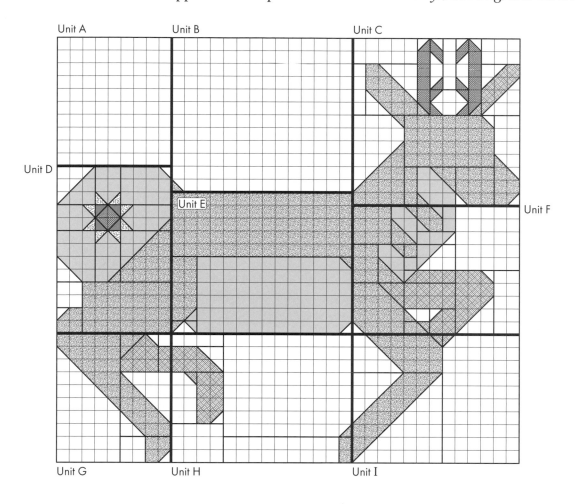

Quilt Size: 44" x 41"

Antelope Image Size: 36" x 33"

Symbol: Navaho Great Star

Color Photo: Page 12

Materials: 44"-wide fabric

1¾ yds. for background and outer border
¾ yd. turquoise #1 for body
⅜ yd. turquoise #2 for body
¼ yd. white for body and tail
⅛ yd. tan for horn and symbol
2½" x 2½" square of maroon for symbol
3 yds. for backing
½ yd. for binding
45" x 48" piece of batting

Strip Cutting

Cut the following strips across the fabric width (crosswise grain). For additional cutting directions, see the chart with each design unit.

Fabric	No. of Strips	Strip Width
Background	1	1½"
	2	2½"
	1	4½"
	1	7½"
	1	12½"
Turquoise #1	1	1½"
	1	2½"
	1	4½"
	1	7½"
Turquoise #2	1	2½"
	1	6½"
White	1	1½"
	1	6½"
Tan	1	1½"

Unit Cutting and Assembly

Using the strips you just cut, cut the required number of pieces for each fabric listed in the unit cutting charts. In most cases, you will simply make crosscuts; occasionally you will need to trim pieces to the dimensions given in the chart.

Units A and B: Antelope

Unit A

Unit B

ASSEMBLY

1. For Unit A, cut a 9½" x 10½" rectangle from background fabric.
2. For Unit B, cut a 12½" x 14½" rectangle from background fabric and a 1½" square of turquoise #1.
3. To assemble Unit B, sew the 1½" turquoise square to the lower left corner of the 12½" x 14½" background rectangle, using the 45 Flip (page 21).

Unit C: Antelope

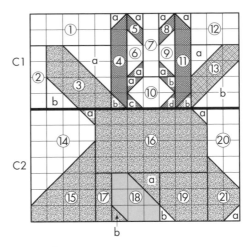

CUTTING

Use the strips listed in the chart at left.

Fabric	Strip Width	Piece #	Dimensions
Background	1½"	4a, 5a, 8a, 11a, 16a, 19a, 21a	1½" x 1½"
		6, 9	1½" x 3½"
	2½"	1, 20	2½" x 5½"
		10, 12	2½" x 3½"
		3b, 13a	2½" x 2½"
	4½"	2, 7	1½" x 4½"
		14	4½" x 6½"
	7½"	3a, 13b	3½" x 3½"*
Turquoise #1	1½"	4b, 14a, 18b	1½" x 1½"
		17	1½" x 3½"
	2½"	18a	2½" x 2½"
	4½"	3	4½" x 4½"
		15	4½" x 5½"
		19	3½" x 3½"*
		21	2½" x 4½"
		16	4½" x 7½"
Turquoise #2	2½"	11b	1½" x 1½"*
	6½"	13	3½" x 4½"*
White	6½"	18	3½" x 3½"*
Tan	1½"	4, 11	1½" x 6½"
		5, 8	1½" x 2½"
		6a, 9a, 10a, 10b, 10c, 10d	1½" x 1½"

*Cut from the larger strip and trim to the proper size.

ASSEMBLY

Refer to the piecing diagram below. To make the construction easier, we divided Unit C into 2 parts.

1. Assemble sections 3a/b, 4a/b, 10a/b/c/d, 11a/b, 13a/b, using the appropriate fabrics (as shown in the unit illustration below) and the 45 Flip.

2. Sew piece 5 to piece 6, using the right 45 Joint; then add 5a and 6a, using the 45 Flip.

Right
45 Joint

3. Sew piece 8 to piece 9, using the left 45 Joint; then add 8a and 9a, using the 45 Flip.

Left
45 Joint

4. Arrange these sections with pieces 1, 7, and 12, and join to complete Unit C1.

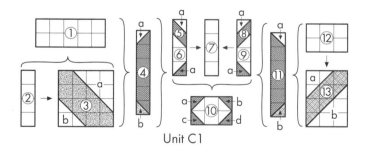

Unit C1

5. Assemble sections 16a, 18a/b, and 19a, using the appropriate fabrics and the 45 Flip.

6. Sew piece 14 to piece 15, using the left 45 Joint; then add 14a to the upper right corner, using the 45 Flip.

Left
45 Joint

7. Sew piece 20 to piece 21, using the right 45 Joint. Add 21a to the lower right corner, using the 45 Flip.

Right
45 Joint

8. Arrange all the sections and join to complete Unit C2.

Unit C2

9. Sew Unit C2 to the bottom edge of Unit C1 to complete Unit C.

Unit D: Small Navajo Star Symbol

Note: If you prefer not to include the small Navaho Star symbol, eliminate the turquoise #2 and tan pieces and replace the maroon square with a white square. See the illustration below right.

Alternate Symbol Block

CUTTING

Use the strips listed in the chart on page 69.

Fabric	Strip Width	Piece #	Dimensions
Background	1½"	3a, 11a	1½" x 1½"
	2½"	7a, 10	2½" x 2½"
	7½"	1a	3½" x 3½"*
Turquoise #1	1½"	6c, 8c	1½" x 1½"
	2½"	11	2½" x 2½"
	4½"	9	4½" x 4½"
		12	4½" x 7½"
Turquoise #2	2½"	5a, 5b,	1½" x 1½"*
		5c, 5d	
White	6½"	2, 4	2½" x 3½"*
		6, 8	2½" x 4½"*
		1, 9a	3½" x 3½"*
		3, 7	3½" x 4½"*
Tan	1½"	2a, 2b, 4a,	1½" x 1½"
		4b, 6a, 6b,	
		8a, 8b	
Maroon	2½"	5	2½" x 2½"

*Cut from the larger strip and trim to the proper size.

ASSEMBLY

Refer to the piecing diagram below.
1. Assemble sections 1a, 2a/b, 3a, 4a/b, 5a/b/c/d, 6a/b/c, 7a, 8a/b, 9a, and 11a, using the appropriate fabrics (as shown in the unit illustration on the facing page) and the 45 Flip.
2. Arrange the sections with pieces 10 and 12, and join to complete Unit D.

Unit E: Antelope

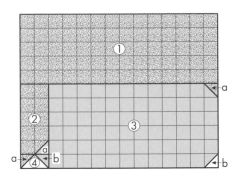

CUTTING

Use the strips listed in the chart on page 69.

Fabric	Strip Width	Piece #	Dimensions
Background	1½"	4	1½" x 2½"
		3b	1½" x 1½"
Turquoise #1	1½"	3a, 4a	1½" x 1½"
	2½"	2	2½" x 5½"
	7½"	1	5½" x 14½"*
White	1½"	2a, 4b	1½" x 1½"
	6½"	3	6½" x 12½"

*Cut from the larger strip and trim to the proper size.

ASSEMBLY

Refer to the piecing diagram below.
1. Assemble sections 2a, 3a/b, and 4a/b, using the 45 Flip.
2. Arrange the sections with piece 1 and join to complete Unit E.

Unit F: Antelope

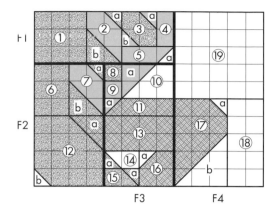

F3   F4

CUTTING

Use the strips listed in the chart on page 69.

Fabric	Strip Width	Piece #	Dimensions
Background	1½"	5a, 12b, 16a, 17a,	1½" x 1½"
	2½"	10	2½" x 3½"
		14	1½" x 2½"
		18	2½" x 5½"
	7½"	17b	3½" x 3½"*
		19	5½" x 5½"*
Turquoise #1	1½"	2a, 7a, 14a, 8	1½" x 1½"
		15	1½" x 2½"
	2½"	2b, 3, 7b	2½" x 2½"
		6	2½" x 3½"
	4½"	1	3½" x 3½"*
		12	4½" x 4½"
Turquoise #2	2½"	12a, 16	2½" x 2½"
		13	2½" x 4½"
		15a	1½" x 1½"*
	6½"	11	1½" x 4½"*
		17	3½" x 5½"*
White	1½"	3a, 3b, 9, 11a	1½" x 1½"
		4	1½" x 2½"*
		5	1½" x 3½"*
	6½"	2, 7	2½" x 3½"*
		10a	2½" x 2½"*

*Cut from the larger strip and trim to the proper size.

ASSEMBLY

Refer to the piecing diagram below. To make the construction easier, we divided Unit F into 4 parts.

1. Assemble sections 2a/b, 3a/b and 5a, using the 45 Flip.
2. Arrange the sections with pieces 1 and 4, and join them to complete Unit F1.

Unit F1

3. Assemble sections 7a/b and 12a/b, using the 45 Flip.
4. Arrange the sections with piece 6 and join them to complete Unit F2.

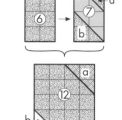

Unit F2

5. Assemble sections 10a, 11a, 14a, 15a, and 16a, using the 45 Flip.
6. Arrange these sections with pieces 8, 9, and 13, and join them to complete Unit F3.

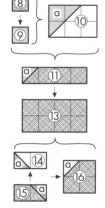

Unit F3

7. Assemble section 17a/b, using the 45 Flip.
8. Arrange 17a/b with pieces 18 and 19 and join them to complete Unit F4.

Unit F4

9. Sew Units F2 and F3 together; then add Unit F1 to the top edge. Sew Unit F4 to the right side of Unit F1/2/3 to complete Unit F.

Unit G: Antelope

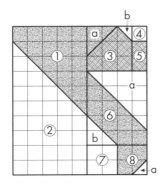

CUTTING

Use the strips listed in the chart on page 69.

Fabric	Strip Width	Piece #	Dimensions
Background	1½"	3b, 4, 8a	1½" x 1½"
	2½"	6b, 7	2½" x 2½"
	4½"	6a	4½" x 4½"
	7½"	2	5½" x 9½"*
Turquoise #1	2½"	3a, 8	2½" x 2½"
	4½"	6	4½" x 5½"
	7½"	1	5½" x 6½"*
Turquoise #2	2½"	5	1½" x 2½"
	6½"	3	3½" x 3½"*

*Cut from the larger strip and trim to the proper size.

ASSEMBLY

Refer to the piecing diagram above right.
1. Assemble sections 3a/b, 6a/b, and 8a, using the 45 Flip.

2. Sew piece 1 to piece 2, using the right 45 Joint.

3. Arrange all the sections with pieces 4, 5, and 7, and join to complete Unit G.

Unit H: Antelope

CUTTING

Use the strips listed in the chart on page 69.

Fabric	Strip Width	Piece #	Dimensions
Background	1½"	4a	1½" x 1½"
	2½"	2a	2½" x 2½"
		7	2½" x 9½"
	4½"	1	1½" x 4½"
		3	2½" x 4½"
		5	3½" x 4½"
	12½"	6	8½" x 10½"*
Turquoise #1	1½"	6a	1½" x 1½"
		8	1½" x 2½"
Turquoise #2	2½"	2, 4	2½" x 4½"
		3a	1½" x 1½"*

*Cut from the larger strip and trim to the proper size.

ASSEMBLY

Refer to the piecing diagram below.

1. Assemble sections 2a, 3a, 4a, and 6a, using the 45 Flip.
2. Arrange all the sections with pieces 1, 5, 7, and 8, and join to complete Unit H.

Unit I: Antelope

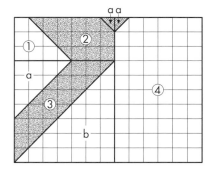

CUTTING

Use the strips listed in the chart on page 69.

Fabric	Strip Width	Piece #	Dimensions
Background	4½"	1	3½" x 4½"
		3a	4½" x 4½"
	7½"	3b	7½" x 7½"
		4	6½" x 10½"*
Turquoise #1	4½"	2	3½" x 6½"*
	7½"	3	7½" x 7½"
Turquoise #2	2½"	2a, 4a	1½" x 1½"*

*Cut from the larger strip and trim to the proper size.

ASSEMBLY

Refer to the piecing diagram below.

1. Sew piece 1 to piece 2, using the left 45 Joint; then add piece 2a to the upper right corner of section 1/2.

2. Assemble sections 3a/b and 4a, using the 45 Flip.
3. Arrange all the sections and join them to complete Unit I.

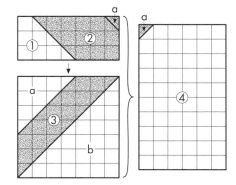

Quilt Top Assembly

1. Arrange all the units as shown in the quilt plan on page 68. Sew the units together in vertical rows, pressing seams in opposite directions from row to row. Sew the rows together.
2. For side borders, cut 2 strips of background fabric, each 4½" x 42". Measure the quilt top for borders as shown in "Adding Borders" on page 23. Trim the strips to fit and sew them to opposite sides of the quilt top.
3. For the top and bottom borders, cut 3 strips of background fabric, each 4½" x 42". Cut 1 strip in half crosswise and sew 1 short piece to each remaining strip. Measure the quilt top, trim strips to fit, and sew them to the top and bottom edges of the quilt top.

Finishing

1. Layer the quilt with backing and batting; baste.
2. Quilt as desired and bind the edges. We outlined five antelope heads in the background and stipple quilted inside some of the outlines.

Life Giver

The American Indian has stalked the deer with bows and arrows. He has eaten its flesh, warmed himself in its hide, and made tools and weapons from its antlers. Native Americans were grateful to the deer for its gift of life. Of all the members of the four-footed antlered tribe, the deer was considered to be the purest.

Quilt Size: 48" x 52"

Deer Image Size: 31" x 42"

Symbol: Arapaho Deer Tracks

Color Photo: Page 13

Materials: 44"-wide fabric

2⅜ yds. for background and outer border
⅞ yd. blue #1 for body and border
⅜ yd. blue #2 for ear and legs
⅜ yd. blue #3 for body
¼ yd. blue #4 for tail
⅝ yd. black for horn, symbol, and border
3⅛ yds. for backing
⅝ yd. for binding
52" x 56" piece of batting

Strip Cutting

Cut the following strips across the width of the fabric (crosswise grain). For additional cutting directions, see the chart with each design unit.

Fabric	No. of Strips	Strip Width
Background	2	1½"
	5	2½"
	2	3½"
	1	6½"
	1	15½"
Blue #1	1	2½"
	3	4½"
	1	6½"
Blue #2	1	2½"
	1	4½"
Blue #3	1	2½"
	1	5½"
Blue #4	1	3½"
Black	1	1½"
	4	2½"
	1	3½"

Unit Cutting and Assembly

Using the strips you just cut, cut the required number of pieces for each fabric listed in the unit cutting charts. In most cases you will simply make crosscuts; occasionally you will need to trim pieces to the dimensions given in the chart.

Unit A: Deer

Because of the complexity of the piecing, you may prefer to piece this unit last.

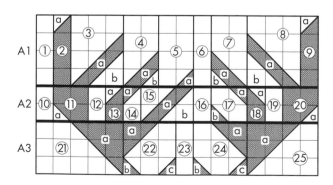

CUTTING

Use the strips listed in the chart at left.

Fabric	Strip Width	Piece #	Dimensions
Background	1½"	1, 6	1½" x 4½"
		2a, 4b,	1½" x 1½"
		7b, 9a, 11a,	
		13a, 18a, 20a	
	2½"	3b, 8b,	2½" x 2½"
		15a, 15b, 17,	
		4, 5, 7	2½" x 4½"
		10, 12,	1½" x 2½"
		14, 16, 19	
	3½"	3, 8, 25	3½" x 4½"
		21	3½" x 5½"
		22, 24	3½" x 3½"
		23	1½" x 3½"
Black	1½"	2, 9	1½" x 4½"
		5a, 14a,	1½" x 1½"
		17a, 17b, 22b,	
		22c, 24b, 24c,	
		13, 18	1½" x 2½"
	2½"	4a, 7a, 11,	2½" x 2½"
		20, 22a, 24a	
	3½"	3a, 8a,	3½" x 3½"
		21a, 25a	
		15	2½" x 3½"

ASSEMBLY

Refer to the piecing diagrams below and on the next page. To make the construction easier, we divided Unit A into 3 parts.

1. Assemble sections 2a, 3a, 4a, 5a, 7a, 8a, and 9a, using the 45 Flip (page 21).
2. Add pieces 3b, 4b, 7b, and 8b to the proper sections, using the Piggyback Flip (page 22).
3. Arrange these sections with pieces 1 and 6, and join to complete Unit A1.

Unit A1

4. Assemble sections 11a, 13a, 14a, 15a/b, 17a/b, 18a, and 20a, using the 45 Flip.

5. Arrange these sections with pieces 10, 12, 16, and 19, and join to complete Unit A2.

Unit A2

6. Assemble sections 21a, 22a/b/c, 24a/b/c, and 25a, using the 45 Flip.

7. Arrange these sections with piece 23, and join to complete Unit A3.

Unit A3

8. Sew Unit A2 to the bottom edge of Unit A1; sew Unit A3 to the bottom edge of Unit A2.

Unit B: Deer

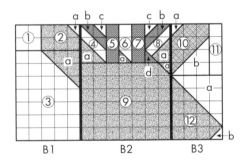

B1   B2   B3

CUTTING

Use the strips listed in the chart on page 76.

Fabric	Strip Width	Piece #	Dimensions
Background	1½"	2a, 4c, 8c, 10a, 12b	1½" x 1½"
		11	1½" x 4½"
	2½"	1	2½" x 2½"
		4, 8	2½" x 3½"
	3½"	6	1½" x 3½"
		10b	3½" x 3½"
	6½"	3	5½" x 7½"*
		12a	4½" x 4½"*
Blue #1	2½"	2	2½" x 3½"
		4a	2½" x 2½"
	4½"	3a	3½" x 3½"*

Continued next column

Fabric	Strip Width	Piece #	Dimensions
Blue #1		12	4½" x 5½"
	6½"	9	6½" x 7½"
Blue #2	2½"	8a	2½" x 2½"
		9a	1½" x 1½"*
	4½"	10	3½" x 4½"
Black	1½"	5, 7	1½" x 3½"
		6a, 8d	1½" x 1½"
	2½"	4b, 8b	2½" x 2½"

*Cut from the larger strip and trim to the proper size.

ASSEMBLY

Refer to the piecing diagram below. To make the construction easier, we divided Unit B into 3 parts.

1. Assemble sections 2a and 3a, using the 45 Flip.

2. Arrange these sections with piece 1, and join to complete Unit B1.

Unit B1

3. Assemble sections 6a and 9a, using the 45 Flip.

4. Sew piece 4a to the lower left corner and piece 4b to the upper right corner of piece 4, using the 45 Flip. Add piece 4c to the upper right corner, using the Piggyback Flip.

5. Sew piece 8a to the lower right corner and piece 8b to the upper left corner of piece 8. Add piece 8c to the upper left corner, using the Piggyback Flip; then add piece 8d to the lower left corner, using the 45 Flip.

6. Arrange all the sections with pieces 5, 7, and 9; join to complete Unit B2.

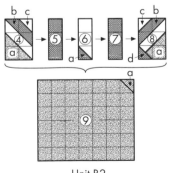

Unit B2

7. Assemble sections 10a/b and 12a/b, using the 45 flip.

8. Arrange these sections with piece 11 and join to complete Unit B3.

Unit B3

9. Sew Unit B2 to the right edge of Unit B1; then add Unit B3 to the right side of B1/2.

Unit C: Deer

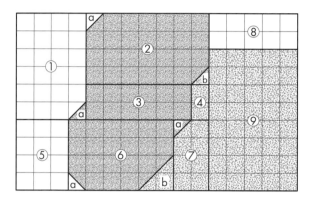

CUTTING

Use the strips listed in the chart on page 76.

Fabric	Strip Width	Piece #	Dimensions
Background	1½"	2a, 6a	1½" x 1½"
	2½"	8	2½" x 5½"
	3½"	5	3½" x 4½"
	6½"	1	4½" x 6½"
Blue #1	2½"	1a, 7a	1½" x 1½"*
	4½"	2	4½" x 7½"
	6½"	6	4½" x 6½"
		3	2½" x 6½"
Blue #3	2½"	2b	1½" x 1½"*
		4	1½" x 2½"
		6b	2½" x 2½"
		7	2½" x 4½"
	5½"	9	5½" x 8½"

*Cut from the larger strip and trim to the proper size.

ASSEMBLY

Refer to the piecing diagram below.

1. Assemble sections 1a, 2a/b, 6a/b, and 7a.
2. Arrange these sections with pieces 3, 4, 5, 8, and 9, and join to complete Unit C.

Unit D: Deer

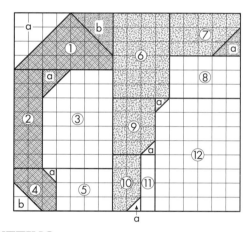

CUTTING

Use the strips listed in the chart on page 76.

Fabric	Strip Width	Piece #	Dimensions
Background	1½"	4a, 9a, 10a	1½" x 1½"
		11	1½" x 4½"
	2½"	4b	2½" x 2½"
	3½"	5	3½" x 4½"
		8	3½" x 5½"
	6½"	1a	4½" x 4½"*
		3	5½" x 7½"*
		12	6½" x 8½"
Blue #1	2½"	7a	2½" x 2½"
	4½"	1b	3½" x 3½"*

Continued next page

Fabric	Strip Width	Piece #	Dimensions
Blue #2	2½"	2	2½" x 7½"
		3a	2½" x 2½"
	4½"	1	4½" x 7½"
		4	3½" x 3½"*
Blue #3	2½"	10	2½" x 4½"
		12a	1½" x 1½"*
	5½"	6	4½" x 6½"*
		7	3½" x 5½"
		9	3½" x 4½"*

*Cut from the larger strip and trim to the proper size.

ASSEMBLY

Refer to the piecing diagram below.
1. Assemble sections 1a/b, 3a, 4a/b, 7a, 9a, 10a, and 12a, using the appropriate fabrics (as shown in the unit illustration on the facing page) and the 45 Flip.
2. Arrange these sections with pieces 2, 5, 6, 8, and 11, and join to complete Unit D.

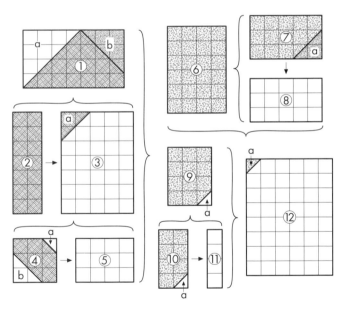

Unit E: Deer

For Unit E, cut 1 rectangle of background fabric, 15½" x 20".

Unit F: Deer Track Symbol

Note: If you prefer not to include the Deer Track symbol, eliminate the black squares, 9c and 9d.

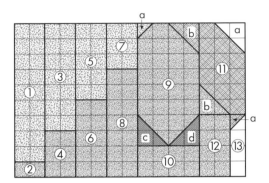

CUTTING

Use the strips listed in the chart on page 76.

Fabric	Strip Width	Piece #	Dimensions
Background	1½"	13	1½" x 4½"
	2½"	11a	2½" x 2½"
Blue #1	2½"	2	1½" x 2½"
		4	2½" x 3½"
		6	2½" x 5½"
		8	2½" x 7½"
		11b	2½" x 2½"
	4½"	9	4½" x 8½"
		10, 12	2½" x 4½"
Blue #3	2½"	1	2½" x 9½"
		3	2½" x 7½"
		7	2½" x 3½"
		9a	1½" x 1½"*
	5½"	5	2½" x 5½"
Blue #4	3½"	9b	2½" x 2½"*
		13a	1½" x 1½"*
	3½"	11	3½" x 6½"
Black	2½"	9c, 9d	2½" x 2½"

*Cut from the larger strip and trim to the proper size.

ASSEMBLY

Refer to the piecing diagram below.

1. Assemble sections 9a/b/c/d, 11a/b, and 13a, using the 45 Flip.
2. Arrange all the sections with pieces 1, 2, 3, 4, 5, 6, 7, 8, 10, and 12, and join to complete Unit F.

Unit G: Deer

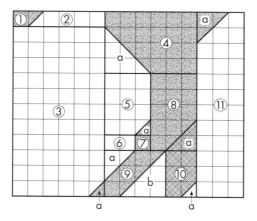

CUTTING

Use the strips listed in the chart on page 76.

Fabric	Strip Width	Piece #	Dimensions
Background	1½"	2	1½" x 5½"
		10a	1½" x 1½"
	2½"	6	1½" x 2½"
		9a	2½" x 2½"
	3½"	4a, 9b	3½" x 3½"
		5	3½" x 4½"
	6½"	3	6½" x 11½"
	15½"	11	3½" x 12½"*
Blue #1	2½"	1	1½" x 2½"
		3a, 5a, 7	1½" x 1½"*
		11a	2½" x 2½"
	4½"	9	3½" x 4½"
	6½"	4	4½" x 6½"
		8	3½" x 5½"*
Blue #2	2½"	8a	2½" x 2½"
		10	2½" x 3½"

*Cut from the larger strip and trim to the proper size.

ASSEMBLY

Refer to the piecing diagram on the next page.

1. Assemble sections 3a, 4a, 5a, 8a, 9a/b, 10a, and 11a, using the 45 Flip.
2. Sew piece 1 to piece 2, using the right 45 Joint.

3. Arrange all the sections with pieces 6 and 7, and join to complete Unit G.

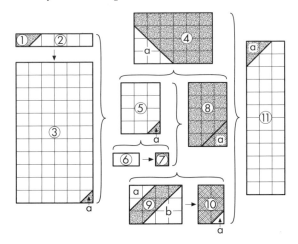

Quilt Top Assembly

1. Arrange all the units as shown in the quilt plan on page 75.
2. Sew the units together in vertical rows, pressing seams in opposite directions from row to row. Sew the rows together.
3. For side borders, cut 2 strips of background fabric, one 4½" x 42" and the other 9½" x 42". Measure the quilt top for borders as shown in "Adding Borders" on page 23. Trim the strips to fit. Sew the 4½"-wide border to the left side and the 9½"-wide strip to the right side of the quilt top.
4. From background fabric, cut 2 strips, each 2½" x 42", for the inner bottom border. Sew the strips together to make a strip that is long enough for the border. Measure the quilt for the bottom border, trim the strip to size, and sew it to the bottom edge of the quilt.
5. From blue #1, cut 22 rectangles, each 2½" x 4½", for the deer track border. Cut 44 squares, each 2½" x 2½", from black fabric. Assemble 22 deer track sections, using the 45 Flip.

6. Sew 11 deer track sections together; repeat with the remaining 11 deer track sections.

Make 2

7. From background fabric, cut a 4½" x 42" strip. Sew 1 section of 11 deer tracks to the end of the border strip. Measure, trim, and sew the border to the right side of the quilt top as shown, matching the bottom edge of the quilt top with the bottom edge of the deer track units. Refer to the illustration below.

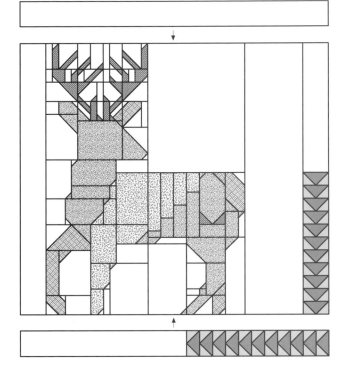

8. From background fabric, cut 2 strips, each 4½" x 42". Sew the remaining deer track section to the right end of 1 border strip. Measure the quilt and trim the border to fit, reserving the piece you trimmed off for the top border. Sew the border to the bottom edge of the quilt top as shown.
9. Sew the reserved border piece to the remaining strip. Measure the quilt top and trim the top border to fit. Sew it to the top edge of the quilt.

Finishing

1. Layer the quilt with backing and batting; baste.
2. Quilt as desired and bind the edges. We quilted trees and leaves in the background, and we stipple quilted the head and hindquarter sections of the deer.

In the Presence of the Arrow

Wapiti is a Shawnee word that means white rump, one of the most obvious characteristics of the elk. Because of his handsome coat, his shrill bugle of courtship, and his prowess as "harem master," both the Shawnee and the Sioux looked on the elk as a symbol of love.

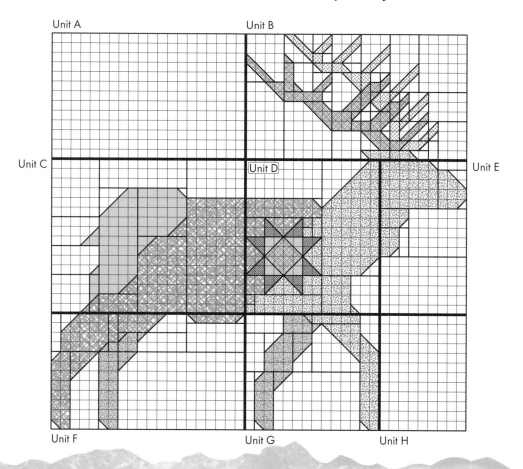

Quilt Size: 51" x 49"

Elk Image Size: 41" x 43"

Symbol: Navaho Great Star

Color Photo: Page 14

Materials: 44"-wide fabric

1½ yds. for background and outer border
½ yd. brown for body
½ yd. medium tan for body
¼ yd. white for body and star
¼ yd. dark tan for body
¼ yd. medium pink for horn and star
¼ yd. light pink for horn
⅛ yd. black for star
3 yds. for backing
⅝ yd. for binding
53" x 55" piece of batting

Strip Cutting

Cut the following strips across the fabric width (crosswise grain). For additional cutting directions, see the chart with each design unit.

Fabric	No. of Strips	Strip Width
Background	2	1½"
	2	2½"
	2	3½"
	1	4½"
	1	5½"
	1	6½"
	1	13½"
Brown	1	1½"
	1	2½"
	1	6½"
Medium tan	1	1½"
	1	2½"
	1	6½"
White	1	5½"
Dark tan	1	4½"
Medium pink	1	1½"
	1	4½"
Light pink	1	1½"
	1	3½"
Black	1	2½"

Unit Cutting and Assembly

Using the strips you just cut, cut the required number of pieces for each fabric listed in the unit cutting charts. In most cases you will simply crosscut the strips; occasionally you will need to trim pieces to the dimensions given in the chart.

Units A and H: Elk

1. From background fabric, cut a 13½" x 20½" rectangle for Unit A.
2. From background fabric, cut a 9½" x 12½" rectangle for Unit H.
3. Label and set both pieces aside for "Quilt Top Assembly" on page 89.

Unit B

Because of the complex piecing, you may prefer to piece Unit B last. To make the construction easier, we divided Unit B into 3 parts.

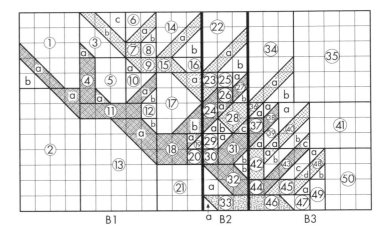

B1   B2   B3

Unit B1: Elk

CUTTING

Use the strips listed in the chart at left.

Fabric	Strip Width	Piece #	Dimensions
Background	1½"	6b, 8, 9a, 10b, 12, 13b, 19	1½" x 1½"
	2½"	1b, 3c, 6, 10, 14b,	2½" x 2½"
		16	1½" x 2½"
	3½"	3, 14, 21	3½" x 3½"
		5	2½" x 3½"
		17	3½" x 4½"
	4½"	2	4½" x 8½"
	5½"	13	5½" x 6½"
		1	4½" x 5½"
Medium pink	1½"	3a, 5a, 19a, 20	1½" x 1½"
		4	1½" x 3½"
		11	1½" x 4½"
	4½"	1a, 13a	3½" x 3½"*
		2a, 10a, 17b, 18	2½" x 2½"*
Light pink	1½"	7	1½" x 1½"
		9, 15	1½" x 2½"
	3½"	3b, 14a	3½" x 3½"
		6a, 17a	2½" x 2½"*

*Cut from the larger strip and trim to the proper size.

ASSEMBLY

Refer to the piecing diagram below.

1. Assemble sections 2a, 5a, 9a, 17a/b, and 19a, using the 45 Flip (page 21).
2. Construct 1a, 3a/b, 6a, 13a, and 14a, using the 45 Flip. Add pieces 1b, 3c, 6b, 10b, 13b, and 14b to the appropriate sections, using the Piggyback Flip (page 22).
3. Join pieces 15 and 16, using the left 45 Joint.

4. Arrange all the sections with pieces 4, 7, 9, 11, 12, 18, and 21, and join to complete Unit B1.

Unit B2: Elk

CUTTING

Use the strips listed in the chart on page 83.

Fabric	Strip Width	Piece #	Dimensions
Background	1½"	24a, 25	1½" x 1½"
		27a, 27b, 28a,	
		28b, 29, 31a,	
		31b, 32b, 33a	
	2½"	22b, 32a,	2½" x 2½"
	3½"	22	3½" x 4½"
Medium pink	1½"	24	1½" x 3½"
		26	1½" x 1½"
		28c, 30,	
		27	1½" x 2½"
	4½"	31	2½" x 2½"*
		32	2½" x 3½"
Light pink	1½"	23	1½" x 2½"
	3½"	22a	3½" x 3½"
		28	2½" x 2½"*
Brown	1½"	33	1½" x 3½"

*Cut from the larger strip and trim to the proper size.

ASSEMBLY

Refer to the piecing diagram on the next page.

1. Assemble sections 27a/b, 28a/b/c, 31a/b, 32a/b, and 33a, using the appropriate colors (as shown in the unit illustration on the next page) and the 45 Flip.
2. Sew piece 22a to piece 22, using the 45 Flip; then add piece 22b, using the Piggyback Flip.
3. Join piece 23 to piece 24, using the left 45 Joint; then add piece 24a to the lower right corner, using the 45 Flip.

4. Arrange all the sections with pieces 25, 26, 29, and 30, and join to complete Unit B2.

Unit B2

Unit B3: Elk

CUTTING

Use the strips listed in the chart on page 83.

Fabric	Strip Width	Piece #	Dimensions
Background	1½"	36a, 38a, 45a, 48a, 48b	1½" x 1½"
	2½"	39, 47, 49	1½" x 2½"
		34b, 40a, 40b, 43b, 43c	2½" x 2½"
	3½"	41, 50	3½" x 4½"
	5½"	35	5½" x 6½"
	6½"	34	3½" x 6½"
Medium pink	1½"	40c	1½" x 1½"
		37, 38, 44	1½" x 2½"
	4½"	43	2½" x 3½"*
Light pink	1½"	42, 48	1½" x 2½"
		36, 37a, 39a, 43a,	1½" x 1½"
		43d	1½" x 1½"
		45	1½" x 3½"
	3½"	34a,	3½" x 3½"
		40	2½" x 3½"
Brown	1½"	46	1½" x 3½"

*Cut from the larger strip and trim to the proper size.

ASSEMBLY

Refer to the piecing diagram below.

1. Assemble sections 36a, 37a, 38a, 39a, and 48a/b, using the 45 Flip.
2. Construct section 34a, and 40a/b, using the 45 Flip; then add pieces 34b and 40c to the appropriate sections, using the Piggyback Flip.
3. Sew pieces 43b and 43c to piece 43, using the 45 Flip; then add pieces 43a and 43d, using the Piggyback Flip.
4. Sew piece 44 to piece 45, using the right 45 Joint. Add piece 45a to the right side, using the 45 Flip. Sew piece 46 to piece 47, using the left 45 Joint.

Right 45 Joint   Left 45 Joint

5. Arrange all the sections with pieces 35, 41, 42, 49, and 50, and join to complete Unit B3.

Unit B3

6. Sew Unit B2 to the right edge of Unit B1; sew Unit B3 to the right edge of Unit B2 to complete Unit B. Refer to the Unit B illustration on page 83.

Unit C: Elk

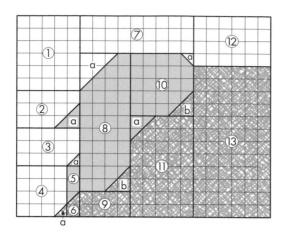

CUTTING

Use the strips listed in the chart on page 83.

Fabric	Strip Width	Piece #	Dimensions
Background	1½"	10a	1½" x 1½"
	3½"	7	3½" x 9½"
		8a	3½" x 3½"
		2, 3	3½" x 5½"
	4½"	4	4½" x 4½"
	5½"	1	5½" x 6½"
	6½"	12	6½" x 4½"
Medium tan	1½"	4a	1½" x 1½"
		6	1½" x 2½"
	2½"	8b, 10b	2½" x 2½"
		9	2½" x 4½"
	6½"	11	5½" x 8½"*
		13	6½" x 12½"
White	5½"	2a	2½" x 2½"*
		3a	1½" x 1½"*
		5	1½" x 3½"*
		8	4½" x 11½"*
		10	5½" x 5½"
		11a	2½" x 3½"*

*Cut from the larger strip and trim to the proper size.

ASSEMBLY

Refer to the piecing diagram above right.
1. Assemble sections 2a, 3a, 4a, 8a/b, 10a/b, and 11a, using the appropriate colors (as shown in the unit illustration above) and the 45 Flip.

2. Sew piece 5 to piece 6, using the left 45 Joint.

3. Arrange all the sections with pieces 1, 7, 9, 12, and 13, and join to complete Unit C.

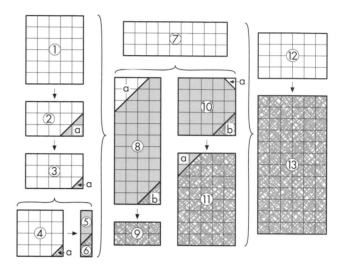

Unit D: Navaho Great Star Symbol

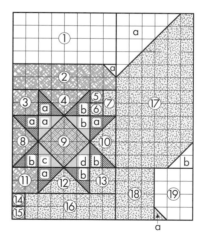

Note: If you choose not to use the Symbol block, do not cut pieces 3–16. Replace them as follows. Cut 1 square, 8½" x 8½", from tan fabric, and 1 rectangle, 8½" x 10½", from brown fabric. Sew tan square to upper left corner of brown rectangle, using the 45 Flip.

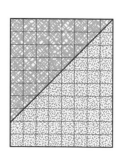

CUTTING

Use the strips listed in the chart on page 83.

Fabric	Strip Width	Piece #	Dimensions
Background	1½"	2a	1½" x 1½"
	2½"	17b	2½" x 2½"
	3½"	19	3½" x 4½"
	4½"	1	4½" x 8½"
	5½"	17a	5½" x 5½"
Brown	1½"	6, 15, 19a	1½" x 1½"
		7	1½" x 2½"
	2½"	10, 12	2½" x 4½"
		13	2½" x 2½"
		16	2½" x 7½"
	6½"	17	6½" x 12½"
		18	3½" x 4½"
Medium tan	1½"	5, 14	1½" x 1½"
	2½"	2	2½" x 8½"
		3, 11	2½" x 2½"
		4, 8	2½" x 4½"
White	5½"	9a, 9b, 9c, 9d	2½" x 2½"*
Medium pink	4½"	9	4½" x 4½"
Black	2½"	4a, 4b, 8a, 8b, 10a, 10b, 12a, 12b	2½" x 2½"

*Cut from the larger strip and trim to the proper size.

ASSEMBLY

Refer to the piecing diagram above right.
1. Assemble sections 2a, 4a/b, 8a/b, 9a/b/c/d, 10a/b, 12a/b, 17a/b, and 19a, using the appropriate colors (as shown in the unit illustration on the facing page) and the 45 Flip.

2. Arrange all the sections with pieces 1, 3, 5, 6, 7, 11, 13, 14, 15, 16, and 18, and join to complete Unit D.

Unit E: Elk

CUTTING

Use the strips listed in the chart on page 83.

Fabric	Strip Width	Piece #	Dimensions
Background	1½"	1a, 3b, 4a, 5a	1½" x 1½"
	2½"	3a	2½" x 2½"
	3½"	2, 6	1½" x 3½"
	5½"	7	5½" x 6½"
	6½"	8	6½" x 9½"
Brown	2½"	4, 5	2½" x 3½"
	6½"	1	5½" x 6½"
		3	3½" x 4½"*

*Cut from the larger strip and trim to the proper size.

ASSEMBLY

Refer to the piecing diagram below.

1. Assemble sections 1a, 3a/b, 4a, and 5a, using the 45 Flip.
2. Arrange the completed sections with pieces 1, 2, 6, 7, and 8, and join them to complete Unit E.

Fabric	Strip Width	Piece #	Dimensions
Medium tan		7a	1½" x 1½"
		9	1½" x 6½"
	2½"	11	2½" x 8½"
	6½"	5	2½" x 5½"*
		2	4½" x 5½"*
		12a	3½" x 3½"*
Dark tan	4½"	2b, 4,	1½" x 1½"*
		8a, 14a	
		7	2½" x 2½"*
		13	2½" x 8½"*

*Cut from the larger strip and trim to the proper size.

ASSEMBLY

Refer to the piecing diagram below.

1. Assemble sections 2a/b, 7a, 8a, 9a/b, 11a/b, 12a, 13a, and 14a, using the appropriate colors (as shown in the unit illustration at left) and the 45 Flip.
2. Sew piece 5 to piece 6, using the right 45 Joint.

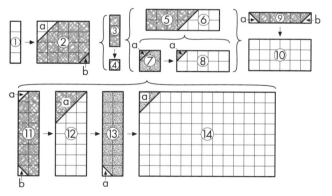

3. Arrange all the sections with pieces 1, 3, 4, and 10, and join to complete Unit F.

Unit F: Elk

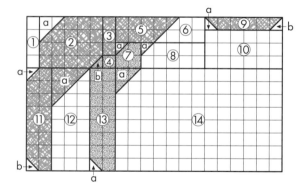

CUTTING

Use the strips listed in the chart on page 83.

Fabric	Strip Width	Piece #	Dimensions
Background	1½"	1	1½" x 4½"
		9a, 9b,	1½" x 1½"
		11a, 11b, 13a	
	2½"	2a	2½" x 2½"
		6	2½" x 4½"
		8	2½" x 5½"
	3½"	12	3½" x 8½"
	6½"	10	3½" x 6½"
	13½"	14	8½" x 13½"
Medium tan	1½"	3	1½" x 3½"

Continued next column

Unit G: Elk

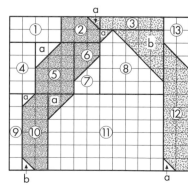

CUTTING

Use the strips listed in the chart on page 83.

Fabric	Strip Width	Piece #	Dimensions
Background	1½"	9	1½" x 6½"
		10a, 10b,	1½" x 1½"
		12a	
	2½"	1, 4, 13	2½" x 4½"
		5a	2½" x 2½"
	3½"	7	2½" x 3½"
	5½"	8	5½" x 5½"
	6½"	11	6½" x 9½"
Brown	1½"	2a	1½" x 1½"
		3	1½" x 5½"
	2½"	12	2½" x 10½"
	6½"	8b	4½" x 4½"*
Dark tan	4½"	2, 6	2½" x 3½"*
		5	3½" x 4½"
		8a	1½" x 1½"*
		10	2½" x 6½"*
		11a	2½" x 2½"*

*Cut from the larger strip and trim to the proper size.

ASSEMBLY

Refer to the piecing diagram above right.
1. Assemble sections 2a, 5a, 8a/b, 10a/b, and 11a, using the appropriate colors (as shown in the unit illustration on the facing page) and the 45 Flip.
2. Sew piece 6 to piece 7, using the left 45 Joint. Sew piece 12 to piece 13, using the right 45 Joint. Add 12a to the lower left corner.

Left
45 Joint

Right
45 Joint

3. Arrange all the sections with pieces 1, 3, 4, and 9, and join to complete Unit G.

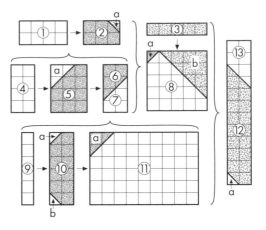

Quilt Top Assembly

1. Arrange all the completed units as shown in the quilt plan on page 82.
2. Sew the units together in horizontal rows, pressing seams in opposite directions from row to row. Sew the rows together.
3. For the side borders, cut 2 strips of background fabric, each 4½" x 42". Measure the quilt top for borders as shown in "Adding Borders" on page 23. Trim the strips to fit and sew them to opposite sides of the quilt top.
4. From background fabric, cut 3 strips, each 4½" x 42". Cut 1 strip in half crosswise and sew 1 short piece to each of the remaining strips. Measure the quilt and trim the border strips to fit. Sew the strips to the top and bottom edges of the quilt top.

Finishing

1. Layer the quilt with backing and batting; baste.
2. Quilt as desired and bind the edges. We quilted the background and the elk's hindquarters with straight lines and also used meandering lines for part of the background. We stipple quilted the front of the elk's body and his front legs.

Working with the Designs

Create a design with multiple animals by repeating elements of one animal. Use the "counted patchwork" principle to adjust the background pieces for the additional shapes.

One way to design these adaptations is to choose a quilt plan, and then make several photocopies of it. (You have permission to photocopy the quilt plan for this purpose only.) Using one of the photocopies, cut out a section of the animal shape you want to repeat. Attach the cut-out to a graph of the original quilt plan. Add more animal cut-outs as desired. After you have designed your quilt you can follow the original piecing diagram. Adjust areas where one section overlaps another and where you altered the design, such as removing antlers from the deer.

In the example below, we used the deer pattern on page 75. We copied the quilt plan and cut out the shapes we wanted. Notice that we eliminated the antlers to make the new deer female.

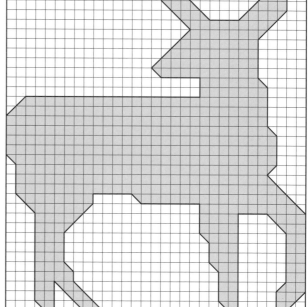

Add a third shape, and reverse this one.

We attached the cut-outs to the quilt plan to make our new design. See "Sunrise" on page 15.

Design Ideas

There are other ways to be creative with the animal designs.

❖ Create dimension with value. The animals in front are darkest; the ones in back are lighter.

❖ Reverse the image to make one animal face in a different direction.

❖ Eliminate the horns to create a female mate for deer or elk.

❖ In the wild, there are usually more females than males; repeat this theme in your quilt.

❖ Alter the original shape slightly, as we did with the cougar pattern ("Spirit of the Mountains" on page 9). We made one cougar seated and one lying down.

All Ten Together

After we designed all ten animals, we decided to combine them in "Peaceable Kingdom" on page 16. No directions are given for this quilt, but you can refer to each animal pattern to determine which pieces to cut. Sew each animal individually, but pay attention to the animal behind it and to the background. One of the most difficult parts of making all ten animals is choosing fabrics for each one. Some of the color and print choices we made were better than others. There is a "humility block" in the design, one we would change if we could. Can you find the humility block in the quilt photo?

You may want to enlarge the design on a photocopy machine to make it easier to see.

Finishing Your Quilt

Remember to square your quilt once again after you finish piecing it. See page 23.

Backing

Measure the center of the quilt top both vertically and horizontally. Cut the backing and batting 4" longer and 4" wider than the quilt top. Most backs are larger than the 45"-wide fabric, so be creative by adding strips. Use fabric strips leftover from piecing the animal; some of the scrap pieces left from the 45 Flips, 45 Joints, and Piggyback Flips; or something entirely unrelated. Continue your story on the quilt back.

Basting

We use a 36" x 72" work table to baste wall-size and full-size quilts. Mark the center of each end of the table. Mark the center of each side of the backing, batting, and quilt top.

Lay the backing fabric wrong side up on the table. Align the center marks of the backing with the center marks on both ends of the table. Smooth the fabric and clip it to the sides of the table with large binder clips. Smooth the batting in place on top, aligning all center marks.

Lay the pieced quilt top on the batting with the right side up; align all center marks. Smooth the layers from the center to the outer edge. Pin with 1" safety pins or baste through the center of the

sandwich horizontally, vertically, and in an X as shown in the illustration below.

Pin

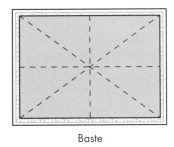

Baste

Marking and Quilting

Once your beautiful creature is pieced, bordered, and sandwiched, you must decide how to quilt it. Use the quilting patterns we suggest, or design your own. Consider forms in nature that relate to the animal you have created. Choose a specific design element, or use a free-motion, allover quilting design.

To mark quilt tops for quilting, we use silver, yellow, and white pencils, wash-out pencils, or any other marker that we know will wash out. Long quilt rulers and even a 48"-long carpenters' rule are handy for drawing straight lines. Use plates, cups, or cans to make circular designs.

Use cotton thread that matches the fabric color, matching the bobbin thread to the backing and the top thread to the top. On multicolored prints, we have found that taupe thread blends nicely.

In our quilts, we first outline-quilt around the animal and the design elements within the animal. This secures the quilt sandwich and allows us to proceed with creative quilting without worrying that the layers will slip.

We use machine stipple quilting extensively. Stippling is a random, continuous design that fills large areas and creates wonderful texture. Space it close together in a small area, or space it farther apart in a larger area for a different appearance.

Stippling

The best way to achieve a satisfactory result is practice and more practice. Refer to *Machine Quilting Made Easy* by Maurine Noble for more information about machine quilting and some great practice exercises.

Adding a Sleeve

Add a sleeve for hanging before you attach the binding. Measure across the top of your quilt and subtract 2". Cut an 8½"- wide fabric strip to match this measurement. Make a narrow double hem at each end of the sleeve and stitch in place. Fold the sleeve in half, wrong sides together, keeping the raw edges even. The sleeve should be 4¼" wide. Match the center of the quilt to the center of the sleeve; pin the sleeve to the top edge of the quilt.

Binding

As you prepare to bind your quilt, square it one more time if necessary, trimming away excess batting and backing.

1. We cut 2½"-wide strips across the straight grain of the fabric. To determine the amount of fabric needed for binding, measure all four sides of the quilt and add 12". If the perimeter measurement is 168", add 12" to equal 180". Divide 180" by 40" (the usable width of 45"- wide fabric) to determine the number of strips you need. In our example, this equals 5 strips. Five strips, each 2½" wide, require 12½" of fabric, or ½ yard to be safe.

2. Join the strips, using the 45 Joint method on page 22 to make 1 long strip of binding.

Joining Straight-Cut Strips

3. Press seam allowances to one side; press the binding in half, wrong sides together, to make a strip that is 1¼" wide. Open the strip at the left end and fold the corner to form a 45° angle. Press. Fold in half again.

4. Place the binding right sides together with the quilt, keeping raw edges even. Begin sewing 6" from the folded end of the binding. Use a ⅜"- wide seam allowance and do not stretch the binding as you sew. We find it helpful to use a walking foot to apply binding. Sew toward the corner, stopping ⅜" from the edge. The needle should be in the down position.

5. Turn the quilt 90° so that you are ready to stitch down the next side. Backstitch to the edge of the quilt. Remove the quilt from the sewing machine and fold the binding to create a mitered corner. Align the top fold of the binding with the top edge of the quilt; keep the raw edges on the next side of the quilt even.

45° angle

Quilt top

6. Stitch the next side, beginning at the edge. Repeat for all four corners.

Quilt top

7. Where the end of the binding meets the beginning, trim the binding to allow 2" to overlap. Unfold the binding and lay the end inside the fold. Refold and continue stitching to the end.

Quilt top

8. Turn the binding to the back of the quilt and hand stitch in place, mitering the corners.

Quilt back

Quilt back

9. Hand-stitch the bottom edge of the sleeve, being careful that your stitches catch only the backing and don't show on the front of the quilt.

About the Authors

Judy Gillaspy Zehner has spent most of her life on a ranch that has been in her husband David's family for three generations. Ranch work and raising three children left little time for hobbies. After the children were grown, however, sewing and quilting filled Judy's life, culminating in the opening of a quilt shop named "Traditions." Judy has taught, lectured, and shared her skills with children and adults throughout northwestern Colorado.

Kim Zehner Mosher grew up on the same ranch and learned to sew as a child, but she did not become interested in quilting until Traditions opened. She now shares her talent with friends and associates, teaching classes and conducting workshops. Kim is the mother of two daughters and works as a Certified Medical Assistant. She lives in Steamboat Springs, Colorado, with her husband, Lucky, and their children.

Judy and Kim collaborate on wildlife patterns, and their "Counted Patchwork" technique is the result of these efforts. They both belong to the Delectable Mountains Quilter's Guild in the beautiful Yampa Valley of Colorado.

That Patchwork Place Publications and Products

4", 6", 8", & metric Bias Square® • BiRangle™ • Ruby Beholder™ • ScrapMaster • Rotary Rule™ • Rotary Mate™ • Bias Stripper™ Ruler
Shortcuts to America's Best-Loved Quilts (video)

Eighth Edition

Atlas
of the Pacific Northwest

Edited by
Philip L. Jackson &
A. Jon Kimerling

OSU Press

Third edition © 1962
Fourth edition © 1968
Fifth edition © 1973
Sixth edition © 1979
Seventh edition © 1985
Eighth edition © 1993

Oregon State University Press, Waldo 101, Corvallis OR 97331-6407

Library of Congress card catalog number: Map 62-50
ISBN 0-87071-416-3 (cloth), 0-87071-415-5 (paper)
Printed in the United States of America

Contents

Maps and Graphs

Acknowledgments

This eighth edition of the *Atlas of the Pacific Northwest* is born from classic research traditions and computer assisted production technology. It seems, however, that there is still no substitute for vision, enthusiasm, and hard work when it comes to producing an up-to-date reference book and teaching aid. The vision, displayed in the first six editions, is that of Richard M. Highsmith, Jr. Over forty years ago, Dick Highsmith saw the need for comprehensive regional information about the resources and human activities of the Pacific Northwest, and we have followed that theme. For their enthusiasm and hard work, we are indebted to the chapter authors and the staff at the OSU Press. Most authors are faculty in the Geosciences Department at Oregon State, but we also welcome the contributions of William Beyers, Chair of the Geography Department at the University of Washington; Steven Kale and Alexander Sifford, III, with the Oregon Department of Transportation; James Good, Marine Resources Program, College of Oceanic and Atmospheric Sciences at OSU; and faculty emeriti Granville Jensen, Ray Northam, and Robert Frenkel. OSU Press director Jeff Grass, managing editor Jo Alexander, and editorial assistant Gayle Stevenson deserve great credit for seeing the *Atlas* to completion.

A focus on the geography of resources and human activities is retained here, with expanded coverage of marine and ocean resources, and timber, water, land, and energy resources to reflect current regional issues. The chapter on population has been revised to better illustrate recent migration flows, spatial patterns of population change, and minority characteristics. Also expanded is the chapter on manufacturing and industries, which provides a comprehensive look at economic production, employment, and markets. There are 113 new maps and charts, and several maps have been redesigned for graphic clarity.

The majority of the eighth edition's new graphics were electronically composed personally by Jon Kimerling in the Geosciences Department's computer lab. Graphics for the agriculture chapter were composed by Greg White of C & G White Cartography. Greg White also finalized a draft diagram by Chuck Rosenfeld modeling regional plate tectonics.

Professor Jackson was responsible for overall editorship including organization, content, and text editing. Professor Kimerling was responsible for cartographic design and graphics production.

Philip L. Jackson
A. Jon Kimerling

Photograph Acknowledgments

The editors and publishers of the *Atlas of the Pacific Northwest* would like to thank the following for permission to reproduce the photographs:

Jon Kimerling (pages 2, 4, 12, 15, 27, 43, 51, 63, 81, 86, 89, 90, 91, 141); Knight Library, University of Oregon (page 9); Oregon Sea Grant, photographs by Jim Larison (pages 29, 73, 121), photograph by Jeff Anderson (page 115); Oregon State Highway Division (page 33); U.S. Department of Interior, National Park Service (page 40); Philip Jackson (pages 46, 68, 151); Bureau of Reclamation, photograph by J.D. Roderick (page 76); Forestry Media Center, photograph by Ed Jensen (page 103); David Simons (page 142); Idaho Department of Commerce & Development (page 143)

The Region

The Pacific Northwest, as we define it, consists of the states of Idaho, Oregon, and Washington. Physically, parts of the region differ markedly from each other—the sagebrush desert landscape of eastern Oregon and Washington, the Rocky Mountains and lava fields of Idaho, the rugged coastline and sand dunes of the Oregon coast, the wheatlands of eastern Washington, the alpine landforms of the Wallowa Mountains of Oregon, Washington's northern Cascades, and the Olympic Range, the rainforests of the Olympic peninsula. The climate of the region also varies widely, including the mild wet coastal region, the dry sunny summers and wet mild winters of the western lowlands, and the wide temperature ranges and low precipitation totals of the intermontane region. Lifestyles, values, and politics differ widely, too.

The western portions of Washington and Oregon have more in common than the western and eastern parts of either state. Similar differences are apparent between northern Idaho and the more populous Snake River Plain. In Oregon and Washington, most economic development has occurred and most government institutions are located in the lowlands between the Coast Range and the Cascade Mountains. In Idaho, the Snake River Plain and the Boise region in particular have achieved governmental and economic dominance, creating a dichotomy between mountain and valley which parallels that between east and west in the coastal states.

Politically, too, the region is a mixed bag. Traditional conservative values, emphasizing independence and individual freedom, hard work and patriotism, are strong and widespread, reflecting the original pioneer spirit of early settlers and the geographical and cultural isolation of the region. For a while, particularly in the 1970s, the region had a more liberal reputation, particularly on environmental issues and "livability." Oregon was perceived as leading the nation in environmental legislation, largely as a result of the 1972 Bottle Bill, requiring a returnable deposit on certain bottles and cans, and the statewide land-use

PACIFIC NORTHWEST COUNTIES

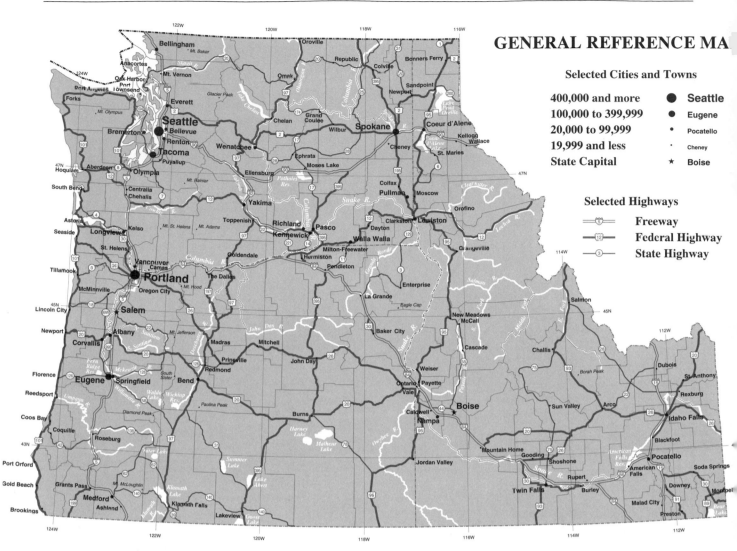

GENERAL REFERENCE MA

Selected Cities and Towns

400,000 and more	● **Seattle**
100,000 to 399,999	● Eugene
20,000 to 99,999	• Pocatello
19,999 and less	· Cheney
State Capital	★ Boise

Selected Highways

5	Freeway
12	Federal Highway
3	State Highway

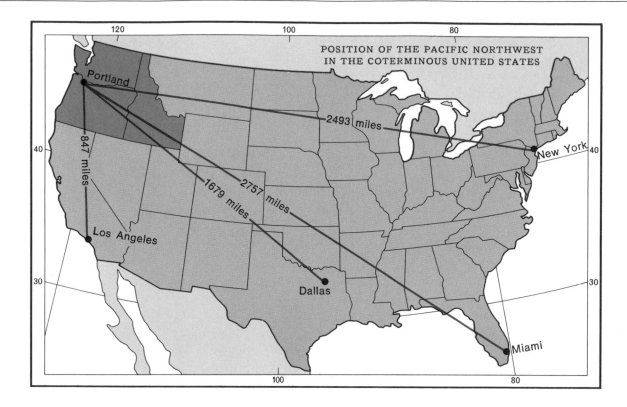

POSITION OF THE PACIFIC NORTHWEST
IN THE COTERMINOUS UNITED STATES

planning laws implemented in the following year. The intent of Oregon's program is to balance conservation and development—to slow the rate of conversion of resources and environmentally sensitive lands by a rational, democratic planning process. While the program has generally been successful in meeting these goals, recent political pressure has been focused on loosening land-use controls to allow limited development on "secondary resource lands." Both Washington and Idaho have environmental quality legislation, and within the past several years Washington has made a major commitment to strengthening its land, air, and water quality standards. The classic debate over land-use regulation and private property rights continues to be politically important.

Better than most areas of the nation, the Pacific Northwest has weathered a prolonged national economic recession, and now shows modest growth. In the face of potential job cutbacks in military spending following the end of the Cold War and in timber-related industries due to harvest limitations on federal lands, sustained economic progress will likely depend on the strength of natural resource advantages, economic diversity, innovation, ties to broad national and international markets, and to an investment in education.

The recent regionwide drought has heightened concerns about balancing water availability for domestic supplies, power production, fisheries, and agriculture. Water management in the summer-dry and drought-cycle climates of the Pacific Northwest will continue to provide engineering and political challenges to cope with growing population concentrations and regional water demands.

The region's economic base has traditionally relied on primary production, especially forest products and agriculture. Commercial timberlands cover 36 percent of the region's land area, producing about half the nation's softwood lumber and plywood, much of it on public lands. The region has been the scene of an ongoing struggle over the future of both the remaining old-growth timber and the livelihood of timber-dependent communities, with environmental groups invoking the Endangered Species Act and using court injunctions to halt logging. Similar struggles over the survival of various anadromous species in the rivers of the region threaten to have even more far-reaching effects.

About 32 percent of land area is in farms, of which 59 percent is used for livestock grazing and the remainder as cropland. The leading agricultural commodities by value are cattle, calves, and wheat, but specialty crops—including filberts, potatoes, apples, pears, grass seed, and mint—are locally important. With economic problems facing both the forest products industry and farming in the region, diversifying the economy to include high-tech industries is seen as the hope for the future.

Much of the region is stunningly beautiful and remarkably unspoiled. Population density is low, despite four decades of net immigration. Though the total land area of the Pacific Northwest is approximately 250,000 square miles, representing 6.8 percent of the area of the U.S. (including Alaska), the region's population represents only 3 percent of the national total. Within the region, population is unevenly distributed, due in part to the high proportion of land in public ownership. More than half the population lives in the Seattle area or the Willamette Valley.

Geographically, the entire Pacific Northwest is isolated within the United States. Portland, for instance, is 2,883 miles from New York by road, and less than twice this distance from Tokyo, Moscow, and Paris. Links to the Pacific Rim are likely to become increasingly important as the citizens of this region continue to look west for new opportunities.

THE PACIFIC NORTHWEST IN THE WORLD

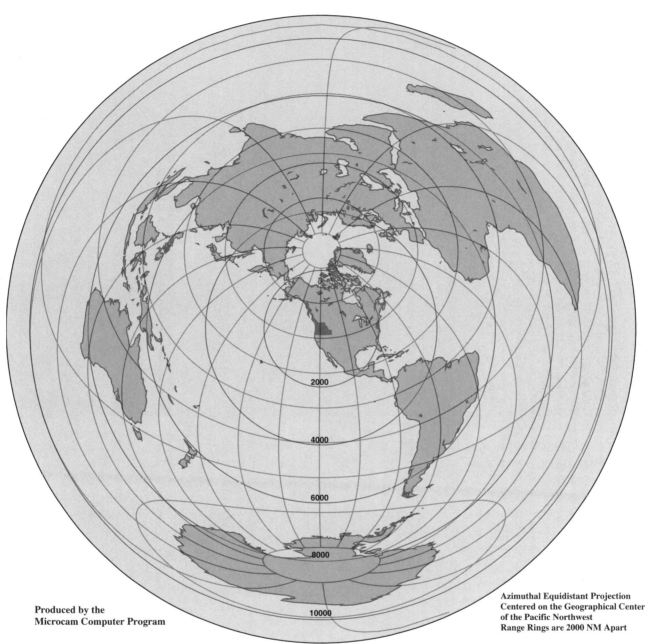

2000

4000

6000

8000

10000

**Produced by the
Microcam Computer Program**

**Azimuthal Equidistant Projection
Centered on the Geographical Center
of the Pacific Northwest
Range Rings are 2000 NM Apart**

MAP
of the
UNITED STATES
TERRITORY OF OREGON
West of the Rocky Mountains

Exhibiting the various Trading Depots or Forts
occupied by the British Hudson Bay Company con-
nected with the Western and northwestern Fur Trade.

Compiled in the Bureau of Topographical
Engineers from the latest authorities under
the direction of Col. J.J. Abert by
Wash: Hood.
1838.
M.H.Stansbury del.

The prolongation of the 49th parallel of latitude from the Rocky
Mountains to the Pacific has been assumed as the Northern Boundary
of the U.States possessions on the N.W. coast, in consequence of
the following extract from the Hon. H.Clays letter to Mr.Gallatin
dated June 19th 1826. (see Doc. 199. 20th Cong.1.sess.Ho. of R.) You are
then authorized to propose the annulment of the third article of the
Convention of 1818. and the extension of the line on the parallel of
49 from the eastern side of the Stony Mountains where it now
terminates, to the Pacific Ocean as the permanent boundary
between the territories of the two powers in that quarter. This is
our ultimatum and so you may announce it.

The Posts of the British Hudsons Bay Company are marked thus. O

Historical Geography

MARY LEE NOLAN

Native Americans

The first inhabitants of the Pacific Northwest were probably descended from small groups of Siberian hunters who reached North America over the Bering land bridge during the last Ice Age. Because a direct route from Alaska to the Pacific Northwest was blocked by continental glaciers, these peoples probably followed an ice-free corridor. Later migrants may have traveled by water, reaching Puget Sound by way of the inside passage extending from Alaska down the coast of British Columbia to Puget Sound.

Archeologists have identified two early Indian cultures in the region; the Old Cordilleran, known from sites in the river valleys of Oregon and Washington, and a Desert culture, which extended throughout the Great Basin, and is evidenced at Fort Rock Cave and other places in southeastern Oregon. Artifacts and radio-carbon dating suggest that these cultures may date back eleven thousand years or more. The ancient Desert culture, which once was found in much of arid and semi-arid western North America, persisted in eastern Oregon into historic

times. The Old Cordilleran culture seems to have been the parent culture for later peoples of the Northwest coastal and plateau areas. The coast, the interior plateaus, and the desert offered quite different environmental conditions to their hunter-gatherer inhabitants and these subsistence differences were reflected in other aspects of native culture.

Coastal Peoples

The coastal Indians occupied a cool, rainy land cut off from the interior by hills and mountains and deeply cut by bays and estuaries. The natural forest cover of fir, spruce, cedar, and some deciduous tree species provided resources for buildings, canoes, clothing, tools, and ceremonial objects. The ocean, the bays, and the rivers were rich in fish including salmon, halibut, cod, herring, and smelt. Olachen or candle-fish provided oil for cooking and illumination. Seals, porpoises, otters, and whales rewarded the sea hunters and mussels, clams, and other mollusks were abundant along the beaches

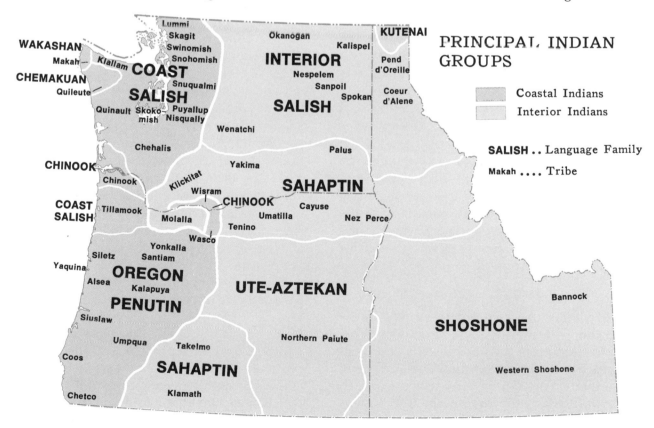

and tidal flats. Waterfowl were plentiful along the shores, and game, including deer, elk, and bear roamed the interior hills. Along with this bounty were vegetable foods including sea weed, berries, and numerous other edible and medicinal plants.

Natives of the Washington and Oregon coasts included various branches of the Wakashan, Chemakuan, Chinook, Oregon Penutin, and Coast Salish peoples. During the period of initial European contact, these peoples had a prosperous economy based on fishing and sea-mammal hunting. They used a variety of angling devices, traps, and harpoons and were noted for their large, handsomely made dugout canoes. Polished stone, bone, and antler, which were originally used as woodworking tools, were replaced with metal tools when these became available through trade with Europeans and Euro-Americans in the eighteenth and nineteenth centuries.

People lived in large wood plank houses arranged along the coast in autonomous villages composed of relatives. Rigid social differences were based on heredity and wealth, and slaves were kept to do menial tasks. First salmon rites were celebrated to insure the continuation of bountiful salmon migrations, and the stored food supply made possible by the annual salmon harvest made these coastal natives as economically secure as many agricultural peoples. In this society of relative abundance, the accumulation, display, and redistribution of wealth was of great importance. For the most part, this took the form of the "potlatch," a ceremony at which the host gave away material possessions, but gained great prestige.

Initial contacts with Europeans increased the material wealth of most coastal peoples, although European diseases took a toll of the population. Tribes to the north managed to keep fur-trading posts out of their territories through most of the nineteenth century, thus preserving many of their customs to a greater extent than was possible for the more southerly peoples.

Desert Peoples

In sharp contrast to the abundance enjoyed by the coastal peoples were the sparse resources utilized by the inhabitants of the northeasterly portion of the Great Basin that lies in southeastern Oregon and southern Idaho. Much of the region is marked by a basin and range topography and has a pattern of interior drainage characterized by large, shallow basin lakes, some of which retain water only after rainy periods. The dry climate and relative sparsity of food resources favored the development of a semi-nomadic life style based on collecting drought-adapted plants and hunting small game. Milling stones were used to grind the small, tuff-coated seeds that were important for subsistence. Arrow heads were made of chipped stone and awls were made of bone. Local plant fibers, including reeds from lake shores, were used to make baskets, mats, and sandals.

In historic times, peoples of the northeasterly portion of the Great Basin were Ute-Aztecans that included the Northern Paiute, and the Shoshone that included the Western Shoshone and Bannock. Populations remained small and people ranged for food in small family groups except during periods of relative abundance when encampments were established near lake shores and water holes. The problems of life in such an environment were eased during the nineteenth century when several tribal groups obtained horses from neighboring peoples.

Plateau Peoples

The Interior Plateau area of the Pacific Northwest is bounded on the east by the high crests of the Rocky Mountains and on the west by the slopes of the Cascades and British Columbian Coast Ranges. It extends northward to the Canadian border and its southern boundary merges with the drylands of the Great Basin in central Oregon and southern Idaho. The southern part of the Plateau is a lava-floored basin 4,000 to 5,000 feet in elevation surrounded by mountains on the west, north, and east. The plateau surface is cut by deep canyons, so that elevations range from near sea level on some canyon floors to 10,000 feet or more on the slopes of nearby mountains. The Columbia-Snake river system provides drainage for most of the plateau.

The varied environments of the Interior Plateau were occupied by peoples whose cultures displayed aspects of the Desert tradition to the south, the Plains Indian tradition to the east, and the Coastal tradition to the west. Settlement tended to be concentrated along the river valleys where there was ample water and an abundance of fish. Salmon, which moved far inland from the ocean to spawn and die, were of particular importance. Many of these peoples followed a pattern of seasonal migration, spending the hotter summer months collecting camas roots and other plants high in the mountains and retreating to the canyon floors during the winter. Although fish was a staple, game was generally a more important part of the diet than among the coastal Indians.

The two principal linguistic groups were the Interior Salish peoples whose territories extended from British Columbia down to south central Washington and the Sahaptin peoples who lived along the Columbia River and southward. Major Salish tribes include the Okanogan, the Kalispel, and the Spokan. The Yakima, Umatilla, Cayuse, Nez Perce, and Klamaths were among the Sahaptin peoples. Chinook-speaking people lived along the Columbia as far east as the rapids at The Dalles. Toward the northeast, the Kutenai represented a different language group.

The Sahaptin peoples were exposed to the influence of the Plains Indians earlier than the more northerly groups. Aspects of Plains Indian culture originally derived from European contact, such as horses and guns, spread from Plains tribes such as the Blackfoot to the Nez Perce, and from them to groups living further west. Salish tribes were initially exposed to aspects of European culture indirectly in the form of items such as copper and glass beads that were traded inland from the coast.

European Coastal Explorations

The first Europeans to sight Pacific Northwest shores were sixteenth-century Spaniards exploring northward from Mexico. In 1542, two small ships under the command of Juan Rodriquez Cabrillo sailed along the west coast of the Baja California Peninsula. Cabrillo discovered San Diego Bay, but died of an infected leg in January 1542. His lieutenant, Bartolome Ferrelo, continued northward as far as the 42nd parallel (to Cape Ferrelo), where he turned back due to storms.

In 1578, Francis Drake's ship, the *Golden Hind*, sailed through the Straits of Magellan and continued northward up the west coast of the Americas, plundering Spanish shipping en route. Reaching Drake's Bay on the California coast in July 1579, the English adventurer landed and claimed ownership for England of "New Albion," a name used by cartographers for the area north of California for more than two centuries thereafter.

Spanish explorations continued through the latter part of the sixteenth century. The Greek sailor, Apostolos Valerianos, known to history by his Spanish name of Juan de Fuca, seems to have visited the northwest coast in about 1592. His highly imaginative account of a passageway to an inland sea was published in England in 1622, but the Strait of Juan de Fuca, leading to Puget Sound, was not rediscovered until the late eighteenth century. During the remainder of the seventeenth century, however, Spain was preoccupied with her vast Central and South American colonies and attempted no further exploration along the Pacific coast. England's attention was focused on colonies along North America's Atlantic seaboard, and the native peoples of the Pacific Northwest remained largely unaffected by European activities.

The second half of the eighteenth century witnessed a renewed European interest in the region. In 1741 the Danish navigator, Vitus Bering, sailing for Russia, landed on the southeast Alaskan coast and the Aleutian Islands. By the 1760s, Russian vessels in search of sea otter and seal skins were cruising the coast of the Oregon Country. Russian activity stimulated a renewed Spanish interest.

EXPLORATION
BY SEA AND LAND
1542-1820

Meriwether Lewis &
━━+━━ William Clark 1805-1806
━━×━━ David Thompson 1811
━━·━━ Overland Astorians 1811-1812

Cape Flattery
Cape Alava
Destruction Island
Point Grenville
Gray's Harbor
Cape Disappointment
Point Adams
Fort Clatsop (1805)
Tillamook Bay
Cape Meares
Cape Foulweather
Cape Perpetua
Heceta Head
Cape Arago
Cape Blanco
Cape Ferrelo

San Juan Islands
Strait of Juan De Fuca
Whidbey Island
Puget Sound (1792)
Lake Pend Oreille
Kullyspell House (1809)
Spokane House (1810)

NEW GEORGIA

Nisqually House
Nisqually trail
Cowlitz R.
Fort Astoria (1811)
Lolo trail
Clearwater R.
Columbia R.
Umatilla R.
Willamette House (1811)
Wallace House (1811)
Pack trail
Willamette R.
Fort Umpqua
Fort Henry (1810)
Boise R.
NEW ALBION
Snake R.
Owyhee R.
Bear R.
Bear Lake

The Tonquin *crossing the Columbia River bar on March 25, 1811.*

Juan Perez, sailing for Spain in 1774, made landfall on the west coast of Vancouver Island where he was well received by Indians. On this voyage he sailed close enough to the Washington coast to see Mount Olympus, which he named Santa Rosalia. In 1775, two more Spanish ships, the *Sonora* and the *Santiago,* sailed northward along the coast. The *Santiago*'s captain, Bruno Hezeta, went ashore at a place on the Washington coast later named Point Grenville by the English, and claimed the land for the crown of Spain. Later Spanish voyages to the region were made by Manuel Quimper, who explored the Strait of Juan de Fuca during the summer of 1790, and Francisco de Eliza who sailed through the San Juan Islands in the summer of 1791.

Meanwhile, in 1778, the English captain James Cook sailed to the region with instructions to chart the coast from Oregon to the Arctic and to determine if a Northwest Passage to the Atlantic existed. Although the Cook expedition found no Northwest Passage, they continued their journey to become the first Europeans to land on the Sandwich Islands, now known as the Hawaiian Islands. Continuing to China, crew members found that furs, which they had purchased from the Indians in British Columbia, could be sold at great profit in the Orient. The publication of Cook's journals and charts in 1784 stimulated interest in the region and several English trading expeditions set out in the latter years of the decade. In 1787, Frances Hornby Trevor, the young wife of Captain Charles Barkley, became the first European woman to visit the Pacific Northwest.

The first Anglo-Americans in the region were Robert Gray in the *Lady Washington*, and John Kendrick in the *Columbia Rediviva*. These merchants from the newly formed United States arrived from Boston in 1788 eager to establish themselves in the lucrative Pacific fur trade. During the month of August, Gray traded along the Pacific coast just south of the Oregon border with California. He then continued northward to the site of present-day Lincoln City, where he established a friendly relationship with natives who were happy to exchange sea-otter skins for metal tools.

The next year, 1789, Gray sailed for China with a cargo of furs that brought only a modest return due to a glutted market. He returned home via the Indian and Atlantic oceans, becoming the first citizen of the United States to circumnavigate the globe. By 1792, Gray was back in Pacific Northwest waters in command of the *Columbia Rediviva*. This second voyage was noteworthy because Gray located the mouth of the Great River of the West, took his ship across the dangerous bar at its mouth, and named the river "Columbia" after his vessel. This exploit helped the United States' claim to the region.

Overland Expeditions

The first overland explorations of northwestern North America, sponsored by the fur-trading North West Company of Montreal, were undertaken by Alexander Mackenzie during the late eighteenth century. In 1789, Mackenzie reached the Arctic Ocean along a route that led from Fort Chipewyan, Alberta, to Great Slave Lake and from there down the north-flowing river that bears his name. Four years later, he crossed the Rocky Mountains with six French Canadians and two Indians. After following the Fraser River along part of its course, he headed overland and reached the Pacific Ocean at Dean Channel, British Columbia, on July 21, 1793. Mackenzie is credited with being the first person of European descent to cross the continent north of Mexico.

In 1803 the United States acquired the Louisiana Territory from France. This enormous region extended from the Mississippi River to the crests of the Rocky Mountains. Even before the Louisiana Purchase, President Thomas Jefferson put Meriwether Lewis and William Clark in charge of an expedition to explore westward up the Missouri River to its source. Lewis and Clark were instructed to make careful records of plants and animals, minerals, and general geography, and to search for a water route to the Pacific. The expedition leaders set out for the western frontier in July 1803. They recruited a band of 48 young frontiersmen and wintered near St. Louis, Missouri. In the spring of 1804, they started up the Missouri.

Expedition members spent the winter of 1804-5 among the Mandan Indians at Fort Mandan in what is now North Dakota. In a nearby Minnetarre village, Lewis and Clark recruited a French Indian interpreter named Charbonneau who was accompanied by his Shoshone wife, Sacajawea, and the couple's infant son. The expedition started out once more in April 1805, and traveled to the upper branches of the Missouri. From Sacajawea's people, expedition members acquired horses for the overland journey across the Rocky Mountains on the Lolo trail route through what is now northern Idaho. In September 1805, they reached the Columbia River, built canoes, and continued downstream. In mid-November the Lewis and Clark Expedition reached the shores of "that ocean, the object of all our labours, the reward of all our anxieties."

The explorers established winter camp at Fort Clatsop near the Columbia River and the sea, and endured an extremely rainy winter before beginning the return trip to the United States in late March 1806. They reached St. Louis in September, 1806, laying a further foundation for United States claims to the Pacific Northwest.

The Fur Traders

As soon as reports of the Lewis and Clark journey down the Columbia River reached the United States in 1806, fur traders flocked into St. Louis. The first trapping and trading trips were made into the Rocky Mountains. Then, in 1810, a German-born entrepreneur named John Jacob Astor created the Pacific Fur Company and sent two expeditions to the Pacific Northwest. Thirty-three traders left the east coast by ship in September 1810 and reached the Columbia River in 1811. Near the mouth of the river, in what is now the state of Oregon, the traders built a blockhouse and named the place Fort Astoria. Another group, known as the Overland Astorians, left St. Louis in March 1811 and, after an arduous journey, reached Fort Astoria early in 1812. These traders, led by Wilson Price Hunt, included Americans, French Canadians, and Scots.

Donald McKenzie, one of the overlanders, led a party from Astoria to explore the Willamette Valley as far south as the confluence of the McKenzie and Willamette rivers. Two of the party, Etienne Lucier and Joseph Gervais, eventually became the first independent farmers in the Pacific Northwest.

In June 1812, a group of "returning Astorians" headed back east with a load of pelts. This party, led by Robert Stuart, crossed the continental divide in Wyoming, probably just to the south of South Pass. They continued along the Platte River, thus pioneering the route that would become the

Fort Vancouver

famous Oregon Trail traveled by pioneers in the mid-nineteenth century. According to a report in the St. Louis *Missouri Gazette* in 1813, "By information received from these gentlemen, it appears that a journey across the continent of North America might be performed with a waggon, there being no obstruction on the whole route that any person would dare call a mountain in addition to its being much the most direct and short one to go from this place to the mouth of the Columbia River."

In 1813, news of the War of 1812 between the United States and Great Britain reached Astoria along with word that a British warship had been dispatched to take the trading post. Knowing that resistance would be useless, the Astorians sold their enterprise to the British North West Company for a small sum, thus leaving the Oregon Country in the hands of the British fur traders. The war ended in 1814, and in 1818 Great Britain and the United States signed a joint occupation treaty to the effect that the region west of the Rockies, north of Mexico and south of Russian Alaska would be "free and open to the vessels, citizens and subjects of both [countries] for ten years."

In 1821 the North West Company was merged with the Hudson's Bay Company and the resulting company was given a 21-year monopoly in the Oregon Country. Administrator George Simpson assumed control of the Columbia Department of the Hudson's Bay Company in 1822 and traveled to the region overland in 1824. He ordered his men to build a large stockade at Fort Vancouver near the confluence of the Willamette and Columbia rivers. Fur traders were encouraged to plant crops and raise livestock during the summer months when there was no trapping to be done. Simpson appointed Dr. John McLoughlin as the Chief Factor at Fort Vancouver. McLoughlin, a native of Scotland, was a man of great ability who had learned the fur-trading business in eastern Canada. McLoughlin established new trading areas and encouraged retiring employees to settle in the Willamette Valley. By 1836, at least thirty French-speaking Canadian and *métis* families had settled in the French Prairie area along the Willamette River.

Supply ships and trading vessels sometimes stopped at the Sandwich (Hawaiian) Islands on voyages to and from the Pacific Northwest, and a substantial number of Hawaiian islanders, then called Owyhees, also came to the region during the 1830s and 40s, adding to the diverse population blend of Scots and French Canadians. Most of the men of European descent married Indian or part-Indian women.

After the renewal of the joint occupancy treaty in 1828, Americans from the United States began to take a greater interest in the Oregon Country. Nathaniel Wyeth, a Massachusetts merchant, tried to establish a commercial operation on the banks of the Columbia in 1832, but returned to New England after his supply ship failed to arrive. He returned in 1834 with Jason Lee and four other Methodist missionaries, who established a mission and school in the Willamette Valley. Wyeth, however, could not compete with the Hudson's Bay Company and eventually sold out to McLoughlin.

In 1836, two missionary wives, Narcissa Whitman and Eliza Spalding, accompanied their husbands, Marcus and Henry, to the Oregon Country. The Whitman-Spalding party began the journey with wagons and driven cattle. The last wagon broke down before they reached Fort Hall on the Snake River, but Dr. Whitman had it rebuilt as a cart which continued the journey as far as Fort Boise. The Spaldings settled among the Nez Perce people near Lapwai, Idaho, and the Whitmans established their mission among the Cayuse near present-day Walla Walla, Washington.

Marcus and Narcissa Whitman had established their mission in order to introduce Christianity and agriculture to the Cayuse Indians. As a farming enterprise, the mission was successful and the tracks of wagon wheels engraved on the mission grounds provide evidence of the couples' important role in aiding the early pioneers bound for the Willamette Valley. The Cayuse, however, were a nomadic hunting and fishing people not inclined toward agriculture and strong in the faith of their own religion. The Indians were also disturbed by the ever-growing number of white settlers passing through their territory. In 1847, a measles epidemic decimated the native population but spared the whites who had greater resistance to this European disease. Believing that the Whitmans were to blame, angry young Indians killed Marcus and Narcissa along with several other people who were staying at the mission. This tragic event spurred Congress to grant territorial status to the Oregon Country and take stronger measures to protect settlers from the Indians.

IMMIGRATION ROUTES AND
EARLY SETTLEMENTS 1820-1860

Along the Oregon Trail

By the early 1840s, the westward thrust of United States settlement reached beyond the Mississippi River to the edge of the eastern forests. There, on the margin of the prairies, the pioneers hesitated. They were sons and daughters of a people who had moved westward for two centuries, but the land where grass replaced the trees was alien to them. Settlers in the Mid West believed they were on the edge of the Great American Desert, a region more suited for nomadic Indians than pioneer farmers. However, publicity generated by the Whitmans and other missionaries, as well as a variety of promoters with other interests, advertised that beyond the prairies, plains, and mountains lay the fertile, well-watered lands of the Oregon Country.

Although American claims to the Pacific Northwest were disputed by Great Britain, perhaps the region could become part of the United States if pioneer settlers followed the westward call of what was termed the nation's "Manifest Destiny" and simply occupied the land. In addition to nationalistic fervor, the migrants were motivated by economic depression in the United States, and the promise of free land in Oregon. Even more potent, perhaps, was the frontier farmer's dream of better lands and a better life beyond the edge of settlement.

The Platte River road had been traveled by wagon since the early 1830s and three wagons survived the journey as far as the Columbia River in 1840. One was floated down the river to the Willamette Valley in 1841. Also in 1841, the Bidwell-Bartleson party took wagons along the Oregon Trail as far as Fort Hall. More than one hundred people with sixteen to eighteen wagons left the Missouri frontier under the leadership of Dr. Elijah White in 1842 and took their wagons to the Snake. The next year, numerous wagons were taken to The Dalles near the eastern end of the Columbia Gorge, then floated and portaged down the Columbia River. In this "Great Migration," which began 1843, approximately 875 men, women, and children set out from Independence, Missouri, to follow the Oregon Trail.

It was nearly two thousand miles from Independence to Fort Vancouver on the Columbia River. By the end of the nineteenth century approximately 350,000 people had moved westward along this route, participating in one of the epic migrations in human history. For some, the journey

Continued on page 17

INDIAN LAND CESSIONS

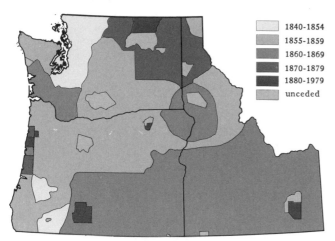

	1840-1854
	1855-1859
	1860-1869
	1870-1879
	1880-1979
	unceded

INDIAN RESERVATIONS

EVOLUTION OF THE PACIFIC NORTHWEST STATES

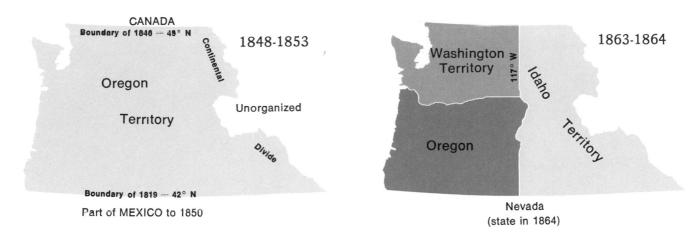

1848-1853

CANADA
Boundary of 1846 — 49° N
Continental

Oregon

Territory

Unorganized

Divide

Boundary of 1819 — 42° N

Part of MEXICO to 1850

1863-1864

Washington
Territory

117° W

Idaho

Territory

Oregon

Nevada
(state in 1864)

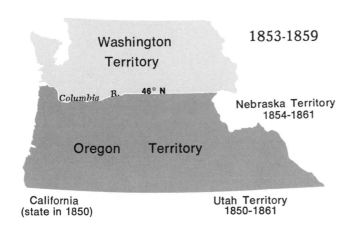

1853-1859

Washington
Territory

Columbia R. 46° N

Nebraska Territory
1854-1861

Oregon Territory

California
(state in 1850)

Utah Territory
1850-1861

1864-1868

Washington
Territory

116° W Montana

Territory

Idaho Territory

Oregon

1859-1863

Washington

Oregon
State
(1859)

Snake R.

117° W

Dakota Territory
1861-1863

Territory

Nevada Territory
1861-1864

Utah Territory

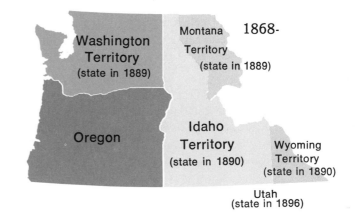

1868-

Washington
Territory
(state in 1889)

Montana
Territory
(state in 1889)

Oregon

Idaho
Territory
(state in 1890)

Wyoming
Territory
(state in 1890)

Utah
(state in 1896)

PUBLIC LAND SURVEY

Township Survey Date

N.A. 1851-1865

1866-1885

1886-1905

1906-

Surveyed From
Boise Meridian

Surveyed From
Willamette Meridian

N.A.—not applicable

ended in the fertile lands of Oregon's Willamette Valley where they found the homes they were seeking. Their presence helped support American claims to the region and the Oregon Territory was annexed by the United States in 1846. Other pioneers left the Oregon Trail beyond the Rockies and headed southward toward the golden promise of California, a region won from Mexico in 1848. For the Mormons, many of whom took a parallel trail pushing their worldly goods in hand carts, the end of the journey lay in the valley of the Great Salt Lake. There in what became the state of Utah, they built a unique way of life based on their religious beliefs.

But for some it was a journey to death. Thousands were buried in the trail, their graves marked only by the wagon ruts. By burying their dead in the trail and rolling wagons over the graves, the emigrants sought to prevent desecration of the graves by wild animals. Disease, particularly dysentery and the dread Asian Cholera, claimed the most victims along the trail. Accidents also took a toll, but most of the hardy pioneers—probably 90 percent of those who set forth—arrived safely at their chosen destinations, carved their new homes from the wilderness, and told tales of hardship and

high adventure for the rest of their lives. During the early years of the migrations, fear of Indians proved exaggerated. Most either ignored the emigrants or were friendly.

Tens of thousands of pioneers poured down into the inviting Willamette Valley and filled it with farms, towns, and their descendants. For the native inhabitants, however, the invasion of a large Euro-American population was virtually catastrophic. In words attributed to Chief Sealth, "There was a time when our people covered the land as the waves of a wind-ruffled sea cover its shell-paved floor, but that time long since passed away with the greatness of tribes that are now but a mournful memory . . . . When the last Red Man shall have perished, and the memory of my tribe shall have become a myth among the white man, these shores will swarm with the invisible dead of my tribe, and when your children's children think themselves alone in the field, the store, the shop or in the silence of the pathless woods, they will not be alone . . . . At night when the streets of your cities and villages are silent and you think them deserted, they will throng with the returning hosts that once filled them and still love this beautiful land. The White Man will never be alone."

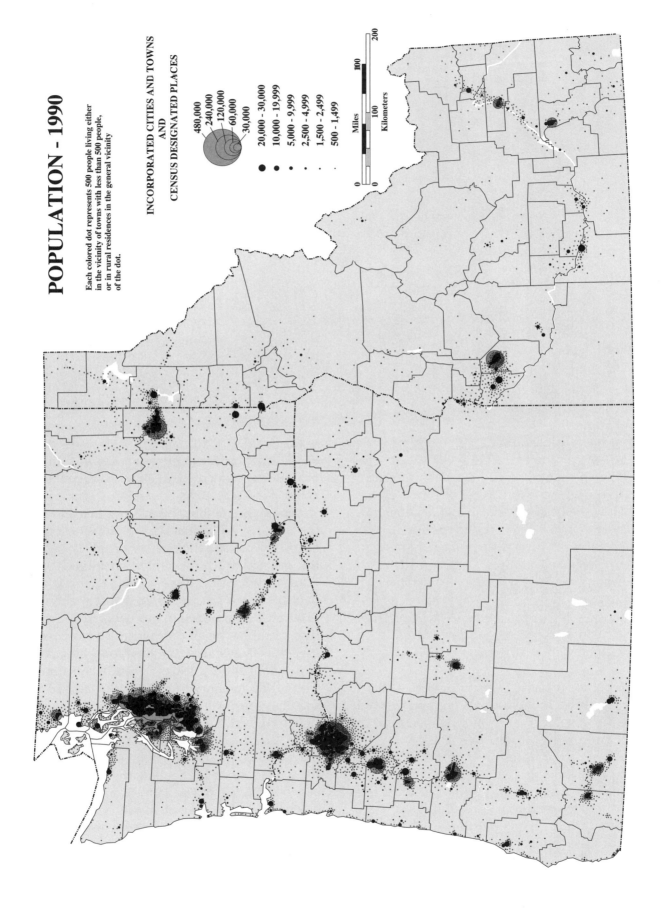

POPULATION - 1990

Each colored dot represents 500 people living either in the vicinity of towns with less than 500 people, or in rural residences in the general vicinity of the dot.

INCORPORATED CITIES AND TOWNS
AND
CENSUS DESIGNATED PLACES

480,000
240,000
120,000
60,000
30,000

20,000 - 30,000
10,000 - 19,999
5,000 - 9,999
2,500 - 4,999
1,500 - 2,499
500 - 1,499

Miles
Kilometers

Population
GORDON MATZKE

The Pacific Northwest has always been a region of population growth; the census has not shown a population decline since the first counts began in 1850. Oregon initially dominated the census statistics, but lost its relative prominence to Washington in 1890 (see graph below). The relative position of the three states has not varied since then, while overall growth continued at a faster rate than average for the nation. Washington, the nation's eighteenth most populous state, has five times more people than Idaho, while Oregon occupies a middle position between them.

PROPORTIONAL POPULATION BY STATE
1850 - 1990

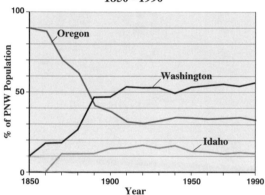

Population Change 1980-1990

The last census (1990) showed the region once again outpacing the national rate of population growth. As shown in the map on page 21, by 1990 the region was experiencing a net inflow of people from all regions of the U.S. and overseas, although California was the dominant source area. Jointly, the Pacific Northwest states now hold about 3.5 percent of the total United States population.

The overall population statistics show the Pacific Northwest as a growth area. However, this was only because of the state of Washington's strong performance, since both Idaho and Oregon lagged behind national average growth rates and experienced substantial outmigration for much of the decade. In addition, many counties (36) simultaneously experienced population declines. As shown in the map on page 20, a few coastal counties and a large number of the interior counties declined, some quite precipitously.

In the last fifty years, the most rapidly growing focus has been in the Seattle area. In contrast, the Washington coast, mountain mining and timber communities, and vast stretches of the dryland interior have stagnated or reversed their population growth and are characterized by dying small towns. As shown in the first map on page 22, many small communities are losing population even while larger centers are growing.

Population Distribution

The population of the Pacific Northwest is very unevenly distributed in favor of a few urban-dominated locations in the Puget Lowland and the Willamette Valley which together hold more than half of the region's population (see map on facing page). The Puget Sound counties are home to 35 percent of Pacific Northwest population and the Willamette Valley to another 20 percent.

The Pacific Northwest is distinguished from the rest of the U.S. by the fact that its coastal counties are not big population centers, being home to only 4 percent of the total population of the region. Major port facilities, and associated commercial development, are situated some distance from the coastline in Seattle and Portland. Although Oregon's coast has shown considerably more growth than Washington's, it is still lacks a major urban center and a stable economic base.

The vast interior of the region has only a few population concentrations of which the biggest is Spokane; other notable areas include Boise and the Tri-cities (Richland, Pasco, and Kennewick, Washington). Smaller city patterns have developed along the Yakima and Snake river valleys similar to those in the western part of the region.

Table 1. Pacific Northwest vs. other states by rank order of population size			
	RANK OF STATE IN SELECTED YEARS*		
	1890	1980	1990
Idaho	45	41	42
Oregon	38	30	29
Washington	34	20	18
1 = most populous and 50 = least populous state.			

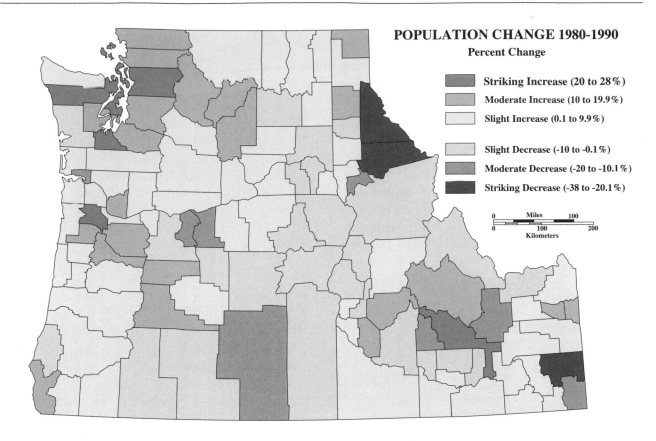

POPULATION CHANGE 1980-1990
Percent Change

Striking Increase (20 to 28%)
Moderate Increase (10 to 19.9%)
Slight Increase (0.1 to 9.9%)

Slight Decrease (-10 to -0.1%)
Moderate Decrease (-20 to -10.1%)
Striking Decrease (-38 to -20.1%)

Racial Minorities

The Pacific Northwest is an overwhelmingly (91 percent) white region compared to the rest of the United States (76 percent). However, the growth rates of minorities in the Pacific Northwest far exceeded those of the majority white population from 1980 to 1990. This was especially true for the Asian population which grew as the region strengthened its economic and cultural ties with the Pacific Rim. Equally important were changes in the immigration laws which allowed for a shift in immigrant source areas toward Asia and Latin America.

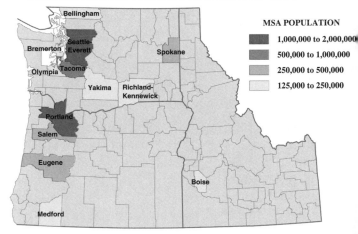

METROPOLITAN STATISTICAL AREAS - 1990

MSA POPULATION
1,000,000 to 2,000,000
500,000 to 1,000,000
250,000 to 500,000
125,000 to 250,000

Table 2. Comparative population growth U.S. vs. Pacific Northwest

	POPULATION SIZE		
	1980	1990	%
Idaho	944,000	1,006,749	+6.7
Oregon	2,633,105	2,842,321	+8.0
Washington	4,132,156	4,866,692	+17.8
Pacific NW	7,709,261	8,715,762	+13.1
U.S.	226,505,000	248,710,000	+9.8

Table 3. Size and growth rates of minorities in the Pacific Northwest, 1980-90

Pacific Northwest total	8,715,762	13%
Blacks	199,349	27%
Native Americans	133,759	36%
Asians	289,592	118%
Hispanic (all races)	320,424	44%

MIGRATION FLOWS 1990

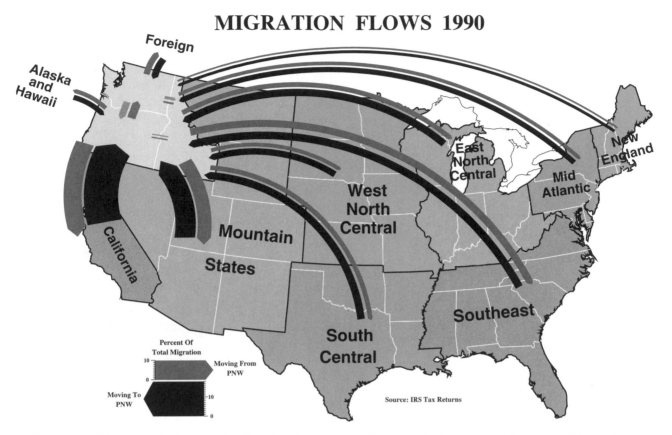

The nonwhite population in the Pacific Northwest shows substantial distributional variation between races (see map on page 22). Blacks are the most geographically concentrated of all nonwhite groups, with several important foci in the major urban areas of Oregon and Washington. In only two counties (Multnomah and Pierce) are they the most numerous minority group and nowhere do they represent a majority of the nonwhite population aggregated at the county level. Their urban focus is so great that three Idaho (Bear Lake, Butte, Clark), one Washington (Garfield), and two Oregon (Gilliam, Sherman) rural counties recorded no Black residents in 1990. Asians also show a strong urban distributional bias, but are spread out from the big cities to include both suburban and university communities as well. They represent the majority nonwhite population in seven Pacific Northwest counties and a plurality of nonwhite residents in ten others.

Indians and Hispanics, although represented in urban areas, are the dominant nonwhite minorities in Pacific Northwest rural counties. Although Native Americans are the smallest nonwhite population in the region, they are the most numerous minority in more counties than any other group;

there are Indian nonwhite majorities in 35 counties and pluralities in another 15. Hispanics are similarly widespread. Considering only those classifying themselves as "Other Race" in the 1990 census,* Hispanics were the nonwhite majority in 36 counties and held a plurality in eight others. Whereas the Native American distribution reflects a constriction from their former more nearly ubiquitous arrangement, the pattern of Hispanic distribution strongly reflects the historic attraction of seasonal work opportunities in agricultural areas. The Mexican-based migrant-labor stream resulted in permanent settlement in places like the apple-growing areas of central Washington, the diversified farms of the Willamette valley, and the Snake River borderland of Idaho and Oregon.

*Since the term Hispanic has a linguistic connotation, Hispanics can be of any race. Most claimed to be White in the 1990 census, but 97 percent of the Pacific Northwest residents who classified themselves as "Other Race" also said they were Hispanics.

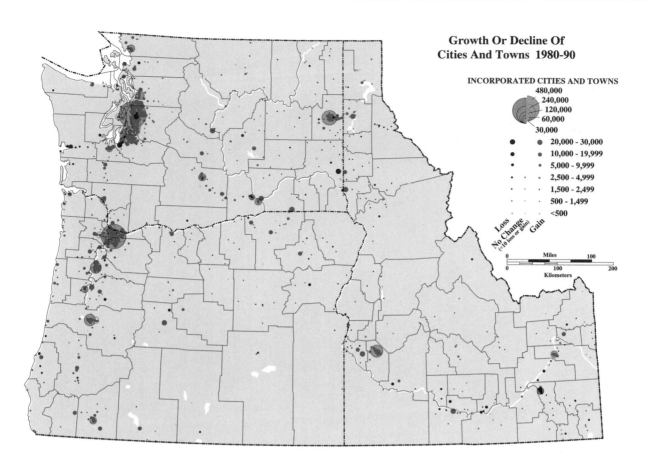

Growth Or Decline Of Cities And Towns 1980-90

INCORPORATED CITIES AND TOWNS

480,000
240,000
120,000
60,000
30,000

● 20,000 - 30,000
● 10,000 - 19,999
· 5,000 - 9,999
· 2,500 - 4,999
· 1,500 - 2,499
· 500 - 1,499
<500

Loss   No Change   Gain
(<10 loss or gain)

Miles
Kilometers

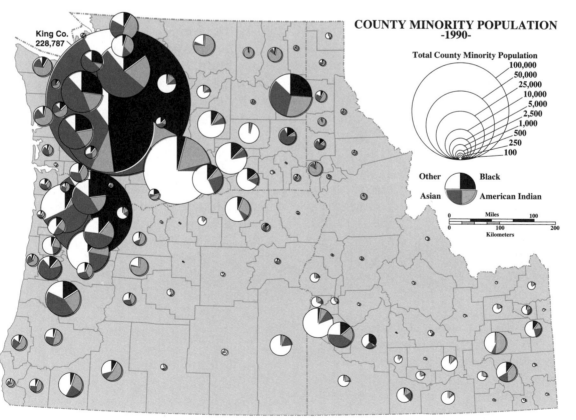

COUNTY MINORITY POPULATION
-1990-

King Co.
228,787

Total County Minority Population

100,000
50,000
25,000
10,000
5,000
2,500
1,000
500
250
100

Other   Black

Asian   American Indian

Miles
Kilometers

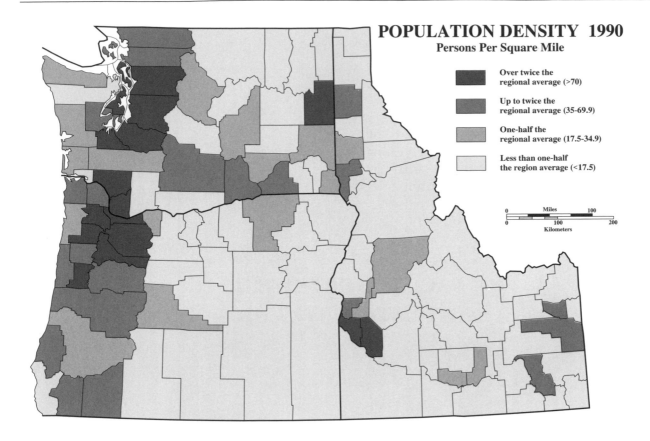

POPULATION DENSITY 1990
Persons Per Square Mile

Over twice the
regional average (>70)

Up to twice the
regional average (35-69.9)

One-half the
regional average (17.5-34.9)

Less than one-half
the region average (<17.5)

Population Density

Average population density for the Pacific Northwest rose to 35 per square mile in 1990. The individual state densities were 63 per square mile in Washington (28th in U.S.), 30 p.s.m. in Oregon (40th in U.S.), and 12 p.s.m. in Idaho (44th in U.S.). Despite population growth, these densities were lower than the national 1990 average density of 70 persons per square mile. A visitor from the eastern U.S. or Europe might be struck by the vast stretches of totally unpopulated land in the region resulting from settlement prohibitions on the extensive public land holdings.

Population density at the county level (see map above) shows extreme levels of intraregional variation. The densely settled counties are few and located primarily on the Puget Sound-Willamette Valley axis with outliers only in the Boise and Spokane areas. Huge areas of eastern Oregon and Washington and most of Idaho are settled at very low density.

Age-Sex Composition

The Pacific Northwest age-sex composition is similar to the general pattern throughout the United States. The 1990 census shows that the "baby boomers" born between 1945 and 1965 are the most numerous age group, while younger age classes show the "baby bust" consequences of smaller family sizes after 1965. Boys are slightly more numerous than girls at birth, but females substantially outnumber males as differential mortality takes its toll in the older age groups. This pattern is clearly seen in the population pyramid for whites (see page 24).

Minority populations in the Pacific Northwest show a somewhat different arrangement. Native Americans suffer from significantly higher mortality rates at all ages, and have a much higher birth rate than the general population. As a result, the elderly comprise a smaller proportion of the population and the youngest age groups are larger. The Black population composition is similar to the Native American except that there is a strong male dominance in all but the oldest age classes. This probably reflects a population strongly influenced by sex-skewed migration streams. The

23

Black population is growing from in-migration, and there is commonly a male bias in long-distance migration within the U.S. For example, U.S. military personnel are predominantly male and include a disproportionately large Black population.

The Asian population also shows the influence of recent migration in its population pyramid. The elderly age classes are small and there is a skewing toward female dominance at a much earlier age than would be the norm in a population not influenced by migration.

PACIFIC NORTHWEST
POPULATION PYRAMIDS
-1990-

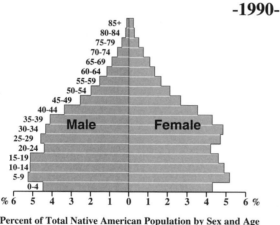

Percent of Total Native American Population by Sex and Age

Native American

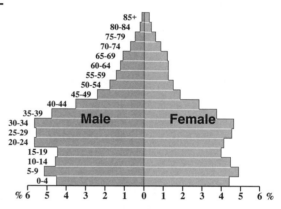

Percent of Total Black Population by Sex and Age

Black

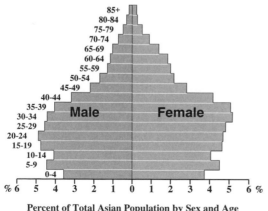

Percent of Total Asian Population by Sex and Age

Asian

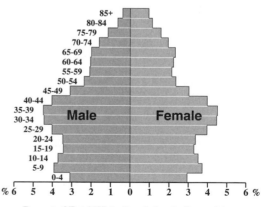

Percent of Total White Population by Sex and Age

White

Transportation

RAY M. NORTHAM

The Pacific Northwest is approximately 1,000 miles from Los Angeles, 2,000 miles from Chicago, and 3,000 miles from New York. Therefore, transportation links with major population and economic centers of the nation must overcome considerable friction of distance. Even within the region there are relatively long distances between regional transportation centers, yet systems of transportation involving a variety of modes have been developed and serve the region well.

Terrain has been a limiting factor in the development and operation of transportation routes and terminals. The mountainous topography of the region has led to a distinct channeling of land transportation routes through a limited number of natural corridors. The strategic importance of Stevens, Snoqualmie, Chinook, Santiam, and Willamette passes for railroads and/or highways is noteworthy. Probably of greater strategic significance, however, is the Columbia River Gorge—the only water-level route through the Cascades. This gap in the mountains provides a transportation

corridor between the intermontane areas, the western valleys, and the Pacific shoreline that is utilized for rail, highway, and inland waterway transportation. It provides a vital link between the Columbia Basin and Portland. Use of a water-level route is more energy efficient than the use of high mountain passes where greater motive power is needed to overcome steep grades and circuitous routes.

Passenger Transportation

Local and commuter transportation within the region relies overwhelmingly on the private automobile. Mass transit alternatives are generally available only in urban centers and are underutilized and heavily subsidized. Taxpayer subsidies to automobile transportation in the form of urban highway construction and maintenance costs are, however, also high.

Auto and truck travel dominate regional as well as local passenger transportation. Eighty-nine percent of all person-trips to destinations in

FEDERAL HIGHWAY SYSTEM

▬▬▬ Interstate Highway

───── Federal Aid Primary Highway

25

Washington are by automobile or truck; for Oregon and Idaho the figure is 90 percent.

In large part these figures reflect the lack of available alternatives to private automobiles and the low priority placed on investment in transportation alternatives. According to U.S. Department of Transportation figures, Idaho spends 92 percent of its total capital investment in transportation on highways, while the figures for Washington and Oregon are about 68 percent and 80 percent, respectively. Intercity bus services are available, but are criticized by users and potential users as slow and inconvenient. Nevertheless, intercity bus travel is the most fuel-efficient transportation mode available, providing 300-400 seat miles per gallon, compared to 200-350 for rail, 70-120 for automobiles, and 30-60 for air.

Air and particularly rail services are available from and to only a limited number of cities. Air transportation continues to take a larger share of this travel market, and this trend is likely to intensify if federal subsidies to the Amtrak rail system are reduced.

A number of major airlines operate scheduled passenger services from major air terminals in Seattle, Portland, Spokane, Boise, and Eugene. Connections are provided with other U.S. cities, with the Far East and Australia, and with western Europe using transpolar routes. Seattle dominates in passenger traffic, largely because it is the point of departure for overseas flights and for flights to Alaska. There is a high volume of passenger movement between major urban centers in the region, especially between Seattle, Portland, and Spokane.

Table 4. Washington mass transit systems, statewide operating statistics, 1990.

	A	B	C	D	E	F	G	H	I	J
Ben Franklin	128,798	1,784,493	2,43,729	104.6	18.9	1.4	1,231.3	37.59	1.98	7.4
Clallam	36,100	945,000	613,081	51.0	17.0	0.6	707.8	65.16	3.84	7.1
C-TRAN	145,000	2,675,000	3,041,000	146.4	21.0	1.1	990.4	53.77	2.56	16.6
Community	187,215	4,066,105	4,004,748	300.3	21.4	1.0	623.4	93.59	4.38	20.2
Cowlitz	15,922	218,967	304,132	13.0	19.1	1.4	1,224.8	54.07	2.83	5.6
Everett	81,624	1,054,703	1,480,351	64.0	18.1	1.4	1,275.4	46.20	2.55	8.1
Grays Harbor	85,589	1,532,564	1,256,534	73.0	14.7	0.8	1,172.5	37.30	2.54	7.6
Intercity	126,925	1,705,070	2,526,107	162.0	19.9	1.5	783.5	50.99	2.56	7.2
Island	17,064	482,000	353,094	24.0	20.7	0.7	711.0	54.12	2.62	—
Jefferson	13,119	349,743	196,056	18.0	14.9	0.6	728.8	58.70	3.93	7.8
Kitsap	76,501	1,117,782	2,376,390	96.0	31.1	2.1	796.9	52.21	1.68	19.3
Metro	1,831,029	30,054,460	95,410,000	2,807.7	52.1	3.2	652.1	91.27	1.75	21.0
Pacific	12,489	311,857	160,874	18.0	12.9	0.5	693.8	42.93	3.33	8.5
Pierce	430,414	6,069,086	10,383,804	424.0	24.1	1.7	1,015.1	58.83	2.44	13.5
Prosser	3,400	63,517	24,197	3.0	7.1	0.4	1,133.3	18.40	2.59	17.6
Pullman	10,684	142,525	692,145	9.7	64.8	4.9	1,101.4	61.18	0.94	28.7
Spokane	332,020	4,711,781	6,975,070	300.8	21.0	1.5	1,103.8	54.79	2.61	16.4
Twin	12,962	188,668	191,170	13.0	14.7	1.0	997.1	39.08	2.65	6.9
Valley	33,194	440,710	747,726	36.0	22.5	1.7	922.1	40.34	1.79	8.2
Whatcom	65,934	1,001,928	1,705,759	55.0	25.9	1.7	1,198.8	49.66	1.92	10.2
Yakima	44,014	511,929	1,246,966	38.5	28.3	2.4	1,143.2	51.97	1.83	11.3
Totals	3,689,997	59,427,888	136,128,933	4,758.0						

A = Passenger service hours. B = Passenger service miles. C = Passenger trips. D = Employees (FTEs).
E = Passenger trips/service hours. F = Passenger trips/service miles. G = Service hour/employee.
H = Operating cost/hours ($). I = Operating cost/trips ($). J = Farebox recovery ratio (%).

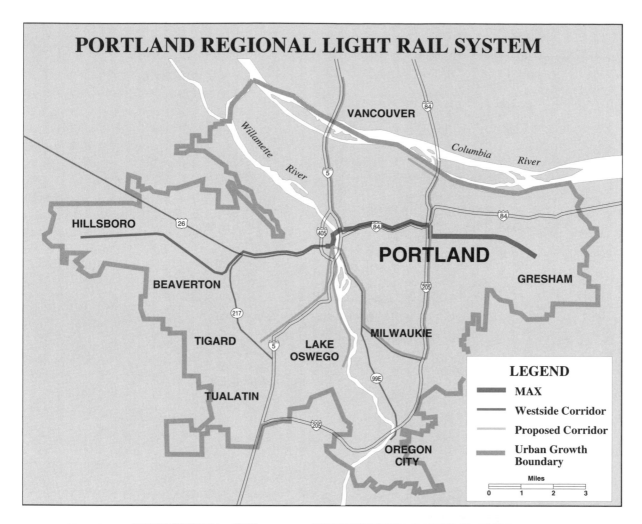

PORTLAND REGIONAL LIGHT RAIL SYSTEM

VANCOUVER

Willamette River

Columbia River

HILLSBORO

PORTLAND

BEAVERTON

GRESHAM

TIGARD

LAKE OSWEGO

MILWAUKIE

TUALATIN

OREGON CITY

LEGEND
— MAX
— Westside Corridor
— Proposed Corridor
— Urban Growth Boundary

Miles
0   1   2   3

**WATERBORNE
COMMERCE
-1986-**

Bellingham
Anacortes
Port Angeles
Everett
Seattle
Tacoma
Grays Harbor
Olympia
Longview
Astoria
Kalama
Vancouver
Portland
Kennewick
McNary Dam
The Dalles Dam
Lewiston
Coos Bay

RIVER CHANNEL DEPTH AND ANNUAL FREIGHT TONNAGE

Channel Depth
—— 8 feet
—— 14 feet
—— 27 feet
—— 37-40 feet

Port And Harbor Tonnage
· 1,000,000 to 5,000,000
● 5,000,000 to 10,000,000
● 10,000,000 to 20,000,000
● 20,000,000 to 30,000,000
○ Minor Port

RAIL LINES

—TONNAGE CARRIED—
> 20   Million
5-20   Tons
1-5   Annually

Seattle
Tacoma
Spokane
Portland
Eugene
Boise

A number of commuter flights connect several smaller cities in the region with large centers, particularly Seattle, Portland, Spokane, Boise, and Eugene, beyond the automobile commuting range. The volume of air passengers traveling to both domestic and overseas destinations has been increasing steadily, leading to expansions at major air terminals in the region.

Mass Transit

Mass transit involves the movement of passengers in large numbers by means of transportation that is publicly sponsored, most often in metropolitan areas. Motor busses are widely available in large and small cities, and in rural areas they may be used to transport merchandise and mail as well as people. There are twenty-three bus systems in the state of Oregon, twenty-two in Washington, but only four in Idaho. Although each is a regional system, the respective "hub" cities are Portland, Seattle, Spokane, and Boise.

A light rail line is under construction connecting downtown Portland and suburban communities on the east side of the Willamette River. This highly efficient mass transit line (MAX or Metropolitan Area Express) will be duplicated by a light rail line passing through a tunnel on the west side of Portland into the Tualatin Valley.

Freight Transportation

Railroads dominate interstate shipment between distant points, whereas truck transport is of major significance for shorter distance movements because of faster and more flexible service. Air carriers are also important for the movement of high-value, low-bulk freight while waterways move commodities of high-bulk, low-value per unit at relatively low cost.

About 23,442,000 tons of freight originated and was transported in Idaho for a total of 8,293 million ton/miles. More than three times as much freight was transported in Oregon—75,957,000 tons—for a total of 22,216 million ton/miles. The figures for Washington are higher: 81,559,000 tons of freight transported a total of 28,666 million ton/miles.

Transportation methods vary significantly between the states in the region. In part this reflects the availability of alternatives to trucking. Washington, where the most extensive rail and water transportation facilities are available, transports

more than half its freight by these means. In contrast, air freight retains a low percentage of overall tonnage in all three states.

Two air carriers dominate the movement of air freight in the region, one of which transports air freight exclusively. Air freight is especially important to Seattle and Portland and the volume of air freight moved through these major air terminals has been increasing steadily.

Inland waterway transportation is mainly on the Columbia River, with the predominant movements downstream of Portland-Vancouver where a channel depth of 35-40 feet is maintained with the aid of dredging, especially at the entrance to the Columbia River estuary. Upstream from Portland-Vancouver, barges are used, especially for grains from the intermontane plateaus. Barge movements occur as far upstream as Lewiston, Idaho, on the Snake River, taking advantage of a number of locks and slack-water reservoirs associated with the large dams built on the Columbia-Snake river system.

Important maritime trade consists of both coastwise and foreign shipping. This activity involves development and maintenance of deepwater ports that are accessible to both American and foreign-flag merchant ships. Regular dredging of inland ship channels must be conducted to maintain critical depths, especially of the lower Columbia River.

Table 5. Transportation trends, Oregon

	1990	2010 ESTIMATE	GROWTH RATE/YEAR (%)
Highway total	27 billion vehicle miles (vm)	34 to 44 billion vm	1.7 to 2.5
Highway metro	9 billion vm	15 billion vm	1.7 to 2.9
Transit total	65 million passengers/year (p/y)	108 million p/y	2.6
Transit metro	55 million p/y	97 million p/y	2.9
Intercity bus	0.66 million p/y	0.81 million p/y	1.0
Amtrak	0.56 million p/y	0.68 million p/y	1.0
Airplane	3.9 million p/y	10.8 million p/y	5.2
Truck	1.1 billion vm	1.8 billion vm	2.5
Rail	136 million tons	223 million tons	2.5
Pipeline	62 million barrels/year	76 million barrels/year	1.0
Ports—inland	11 million tons	18 million tons	2.5
Ports—export	21 million tons	34 million tons	2.5
Ports—import	3 million tons	8 million tons	5.0

SOURCE: Oregon Department of Transportation Strategic Planning Section, May 1992.

Ocean-going vessels utilize a number of ports in the Pacific Northwest in three different settings: (1) the Columbia River estuary; (2) Puget Sound/Strait of Juan de Fuca; and (3) coastal Oregon and Washington. Portland leads in total tonnage of foreign trade handled, mainly the export of grains from the Columbia Basin, followed by Seattle, Tacoma, Anacortes, Longview, Coos Bay, Everett, Grays Harbor, Port Angeles, and Vancouver. Seattle dominates in ocean-going barge traffic to Alaska, while Portland leads in barge and small ship construction and in ship repair.

Three railroads serve the region—Union Pacific, Burlington Northern, and Southern Pacific—concentrating on interstate shipment of bulky items such as lumber, wheat, and aggregate.

In all three states, the number of trucks used for personal rather than freight transportation has increased significantly in the past few decades. In Idaho this use rose from 42 to 60 percent and Oregon and Washington figures are comparable. Truck use for transportation of agricultural products—the second highest use—fell correspondingly from 35 to 18 percent in Idaho, from 21 to 15 percent in Oregon, and from 20 to 13 percent in Washington.

Most trucks are used for local transportation— 82 percent of trucks in Idaho are so used, as are 86 percent of those in Oregon and 72 percent in Washington. Similarly, 90 percent of all trucks in Idaho and Oregon and 92 percent of trucks in Washington drove at least 75 percent of their annual mileage within the state. The average truck in each state drove 10,000 miles in a year.

Pipelines provide another important mode of land transportation, especially in the movement of petroleum products and natural gas. This is an especially vital service since the Pacific Northwest is completely reliant upon external sources for these forms of energy.

Land use and ownership

JAMES R. PEASE

Land use in the Pacific Northwest is closely linked to both land ownership and soil quality. Privately owned lands are often managed for land uses that produce financial profit, making use of the most productive soils for intensive agriculture. Government-owned lands, however, are managed for uses that serve the public interest.

The predominant land cover throughout the region is forest, comprising 46.9 percent of the total land base. Approximately 79 percent of this forest land is managed as commercial timberland, which is defined as land capable of producing at least 20 cubic feet of wood per acre per year. As indicated in Table 7, much of this forest land is in public ownership.

The Forest Service (U.S. Department of Agriculture) controls 47 percent of the commercial timberland base, the Bureau of Land Management (U.S. Department of the Interior) 5 percent, state governments about 6 percent, and Indian reservations approximately 3.5 percent. The forest industry owns and manages 19 percent of the commercial timberland base. Another 18 percent of timberlands is in farm and other private ownership (see Commercial Timberland Resources, page 103). These forest areas are predominantly classified as soil capability class VI (see the map on page 37).

Grazing lands are the second major land use in the region, and are particularly important in Oregon and Idaho. As shown on the land use and land capability maps, the high lava plains of southeastern Oregon and southern Idaho outside of the Snake River plain support subhumid grassland and desert shrubland. Most of this area is administered under grazing permits by the Bureau of Land Management.

Irrigated and dry cropland accounts for significant land use in all three states, with 23.5 percent of nonfederal lands devoted to this use. Although

Continued on page 34

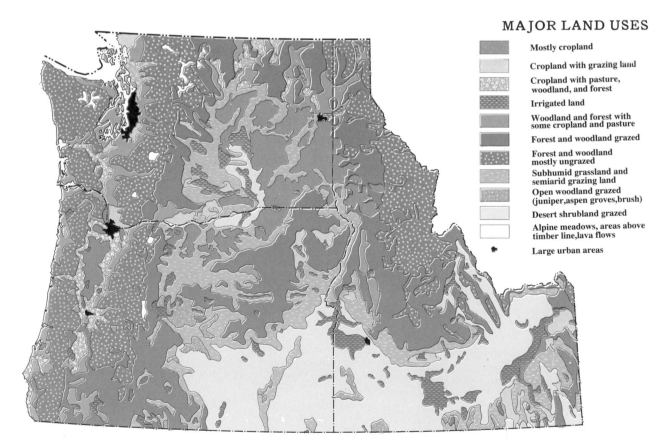

MAJOR LAND USES

- Mostly cropland
- Cropland with grazing land
- Cropland with pasture, woodland, and forest
- Irrigated land
- Woodland and forest with some cropland and pasture
- Forest and woodland grazed
- Forest and woodland mostly ungrazed
- Subhumid grassland and semiarid grazing land
- Open woodland grazed (juniper, aspen groves, brush)
- Desert shrubland grazed
- Alpine meadows, areas above timber line, lava flows
- Large urban areas

Table 6. Public land ownership

	OREGON		WASHINGTON[a]		IDAHO[b]	
	acres	%	acres	%	acres	%
Owned by federal government	29,668,753c	48.2	12,681,885	29.8	33,727,051	63.7
Owned by state government	1,662,059d	2.7	2,461,850	8.1	2,629,633	5.0
Total land area	62,126,720d	100.0	42,606,080	100.0	52,960,576	100.0

SOURCES:
[a] *Washington State Yearbook, 1889-1989,* 1989.
[b] *County Profiles of Idaho,* 7th edition, Idaho Department of Commerce, 1992.
[c] Table 4, *Public Land Statistics,* Volume 175, USDI Bureau of Land Management, 1991.
[d] *Oregon Bluebook, 1991-92,* p. 8.

Table 7. Land use in the Pacific Northwest

	PACIFIC NORTHWEST		OREGON		WASHINGTON		IDAHO	
	acres (000s)	%	acres (000s)	%	acres (000s)	%	acres (000s)	%
NONFEDERAL LANDS[a]								
Cropland	18,637.5	23.7	4,347.7	14.0	7,758.1	25.0	6,531.7	29.0
Irrigated land	6,873.8	8.5	1,751.5	6.0	1,623.8	5.0	3,498.5	15.0
Forest land	28,560.8	36.6	11,856.7	40.0	12,633.5	14.0	4,070.6	17.0
Pasture	4,690.3	10.4	1,915.9	6.0	1,420.5	5.0	1,353.9	7.0
Rangeland	21,322.4	27.1	9,152.4	31.0	5,574.1	19.0	6,595.9	30.0
Developed land (urban & transportation)	2,981.7	3.8	940.6	3.0	1,564.4	5.0	476.7	2.0
TOTAL	78,493,500	100	28,917.8	100	29,947.4	100	19,628.3	100
FEDERAL LANDS								
Commercial forest land[c]	28,587.0	36.9	13,811.0	43.2	5,214.0	40.2	9,562.0	29.4
Other forest land[c]	16,324.7	21.1	4,886.9	15.3	4,260.3	32.9	7,177.5	22.1
Rangeland[d]	30,485.8	39.3	13,135.8	41.0	1,667.6	12.9	15,682.4	48.2
National parks[b]	2,070.0	2.7	168.9	0.5	1,811.0	14.0	97.1	0.3
TOTAL	77,467.5	100	32,002.6	100	12,952.9	100	32,519.0	100

SOURCES:
[a] Summary Report, *1987 National Resources Inventory,* Statistical Bulletin 790, USDA Soil Conservation Service, 1989.
[b] *Public Land Statistics,* 1984.
[c] Table 3.4, *Forest Resource Report No. 23,* USDA Forest Service, 1981.
[d] Table 2.3, *Forest Resource Report No. 22,* USDA Forest Service, 1981.

NOTE: Figures may vary from Census, other sources, and other tables in this *Atlas* due to diffrences in definitions and data-gathering methods.

Table 8. Estimated acreage of agricultural land converted to urban uses, 1980-2000[a]

	TOTAL AGRICULTURAL LAND		TOTAL CROPLAND		IRRIGATED CROPLAND		PASTURE LAND	
	acres	%[b]	acres	%	acres	%	acres	%
Idaho	128,500	0.8	94,900	1.4	74,200	2.1	19,100	2.1
Oregon	76,000	0.4	43,000	0.9	18,100	1.1	15,900	1.7
Washington	159,500	0.9	92,200	1.1	64,200	3.5	32,100	5.9

SOURCE: Table IV-15, *Report No. 13*, Northwest Economic Associates, 1979.
[a] Based on medium population projections and the historical level of land conversion.
[b] Percentage of 1975-1977 base period nonfederal acreage.

Oregon's percentage of cropland (14.8) is less than that of Washington (25.8) and Idaho (32.8), two-thirds of Oregon's billion-dollar agriculture industry is provided by crop sales.

Changes in Land Use

While urban uses comprise only 2.1 percent of the regional land base, much land is being converted from agriculture to urban uses. One late 1970s projection estimated that 360,000 acres would be converted to urban uses between 1980 and the year 2000, based on historical conversion patterns, and that most of this conversion would occur on some of the region's most productive lands, including the Puget Sound Lowlands, the Willamette Valley, and the middle Snake River basin, because of historical urban settlement patterns. Table 8 shows estimated converted acreage and the type of agricultural land affected.

Table 9 indicates the change in prime farmland by land use between 1982 and 1987. Prime cropland decreased in all three states by 99,100 acres, while prime land in pasture increased by 18 percent (56,600 acres) in Oregon and farmland in

forest cover increased by 48 percent (1,800 acres) in Idaho. Regionally, prime farmland used for crops, range, and forest decreased while pasture increased by 10 percent.

Table 10 gives land-use change figures for federal lands, developed lands, and nonfederal rural lands in the region. Developed lands (urban and transportation uses) increased by 123,813 acres or 5.2 percent, most of which was in Washington and Oregon.

Public concern over urbanization of resource lands has resulted in state legislation to protect these lands in all three states. In 1975, Oregon adopted land-use laws severely restricting the conversion of farm and forest lands. Urban-growth boundaries have been established around incorporated cities, while resource zones are administered for resource-related uses. Washington enacted a growth-management act in 1991, which requires counties experiencing growth pressures to designate urban-growth areas and to protect resource lands. While Idaho does not have similar statewide requirements, several fast-growth counties have developed land-planning programs.

LAND UNDER FEDERAL MANAGEMENT

- Bureau of Land Management
- O and C Lands
- Forest Service
- National Park Service
- Fish and Wildlife Service
- Department of Defense
- Nuclear Regulatory Commission

MILES 100
KILOMETERS 100 200

Table 9. Prime farmland by land cover/use, 1982 and 1987

	CROP	PASTURE	RANGE	FOREST	MINOR	TOTALS
PACIFIC NORTHWEST						
1982	5,795,600	888,400	98,300	477,900	137,300	7,397,400
1987	5,696,500	980,200	85,600	477,300	165,900	7,404,600
Change	-1.7%	+10.3%	-12.8%	-0.1%	+20.7%	+0.1%
OREGON						
1982	1,340,500	308,600	44,700	144,000	39,100	1,876,900
1987	1,285,600	365,200	41,400	142,500	39,000	1,873,700
Change	-4.1%	+18.3%	-7.4%	-1.0%	-0.3%	-0.2%
WASHINGTON						
1982	1,418,500	343,100	27,600	330,200	70,000	2,189,400
1987	1,379,900	374,800	22,300	329,300	82,000	2,188,300
Change	-2.7%	+9.2%	-19.2%	-0.3%	+17.1%	-0.1%
IDAHO						
1982	3,036,600	236,700	25,900	3,700	28,200	3,331,100
1987	3,031,000	240,200	21,000	5,500	44,900	3,342,600
Change	-0.2%	+1.5%	-18.9%	+48.6%	+59.2%	+3.0%

SOURCE: Summary Report, *1987 National Resources Inventory*, Statistical Bulletin 790, USDA Soil Conservation Service, 1989.

Table 10. Land use change, 1982-87.

	FEDERAL LANDS	DEVELOPED LANDS	RURAL NONFEDERAL LANDS
PACIFIC NORTHWEST			
1982	77,966,500	2,381,664	75,730,200
1987	77,965,000	2,505,477	75,511,800
Change	-0.002%	+5.2%	-0.3%
OREGON			
1982	32,057,300	901,600	28,343,300
1987	32,304,900	940,600	27,977,200
Change	+0.8%	+4.3%	-1.3%
WASHINGTON			
1982	12,450,100	1,479,600	28,488,200
1987	12,470,500	1,564,400	28,383,000
Change	+0.2%	+5.7%	-0.4%
IDAHO			
1982	33,459,100	464	18,898,700
1987	33,189,600	477	19,151,600
Change	-0.8%	+2.7%	+1.3%

SOURCE: Summary Report *1987 National Resources Inventory*, Statistical Bulletin 790, USDA Soil Conservation Service, 1989.

Table 11. Land ownership by federal agencies in acres[a]

	OREGON	WASHINGTON	IDAHO
Department of Agriculture			
Forest Service	15,616,397.6	8,902,434.9	21,244,494.1
O & C Lands[b]	492,399.0	—	—
Other agencies	14,607.8	394.0	32,462.8
Department of Commerce	9.3	123.5	—
Department of Energy	4,889.5	370,872.1	572,442.8
Environmental Protection Agency	20.9	17.5	—
General Services Administration	377.5	372.0	175.2
Department of Health, Education & Welfare	1.4	—	0.5
Department of the Interior			
Bureau of Indian Affairs	401.7	102.7	32,816.5
Bureau of Land Management	13,572,654.8	310,674.5	11,906,668.9
O & C Lands[b]	2,151,318.0	—	—
Bureau of Mines	43.8	21.0	—
Bureau of Reclamation	66,308.0	100,818.0	283,391.6
Fish & Wildlife Service	479,062.8	128,713.5	44,218.3
National Park Service	168,993.6	1,811,070.5	97,153.2
Department of Justice	—	4,456.0	4.1
Department of Labor	800.7	—	—
Department of Transportation	1,066.4	1,067.0	624.3
U.S. Postal Service	71.3	140.1	9.8
Veterans Administration	613.8	255.6	67.3
Department of Defense	176,267.1	472,574.0	67,382.2
Total	32,251,744.0	12,104,326.1	34,281,911.6

SOURCES: [a] *Public Land Statistics*, Bureau of Land Management, 1984. This was the last date in which non-BLM ownership was published. [b] *Public Land Statistics*, Volume 175, Bureau of Land Management, 1991. NOTE: Figures may vary from Census, other sources, and other tables in this *Atlas* due to differences in definitions and data-gathering methods.

Land Ownership

Land ownership in the region is dominated by two federal agencies, the U.S. Department of Agriculture Forest Service and the U.S. Department of Interior Bureau of Land Management, although land is also administered by a variety of other federal agencies (see map on page 34 and the table above). Federal lands are primarily managed for timber production and grazing, followed by recreation, fish and wildlife habitat, and mineral and energy rights leasing. In addition, the BLM and the Forest Service in Oregon administer Oregon and California Railroad grant lands that reverted to federal management. Fifty percent of the revenues from these lands are shared with counties.

State governments own 2.7 percent of the land base in Oregon, 8.5 percent in Washington, and 4.6 percent in Idaho. The land-management agency in Oregon is the Division of State Lands, in Washington the Department of Natural Resources, and in Idaho the Department of Lands. Each of these agencies is directed by a land board made up of elected officials, including the governor of the state. These state lands were acquired by federal grants when each state entered the Union. Oregon has disposed of approximately 60 percent of its lands, while Washington and Idaho have disposed of only 27 percent and 30 percent, respectively.

LAND CAPABILITY CLASSES

SUITED FOR CULTIVATION
Good Cultivable Land
—Class II
Moderately Good Cultivable Land
—Class III
Fairly Good Land
—Class IV

UNSUITED FOR CULTIVATION
Moderately Well Suited For Grazing or Forestry
—Class VI
Fairly Well Suited For Grazing or Forestry
—Class VII
Not Suited For Grazing or Forestry
—Class VIII

Individual areas of class I and V
are too small to show on this generalized map.

MILES
0   100

0   100   200
KILOMETERS

Lands under state ownership are managed for timber production, grazing leases, mineral and energy rights leasing, and recreation. While state land agencies manage public lands for maximum long-term economic gain, the multiple-use concept must also be accommodated. Like the federal public-land managers, state land-management agencies have come under increasing pressure from groups concerned with how and for whom public lands should be managed.

In the private sector, well over 75 percent of farmland is owned by families as proprietary farms or family corporations. Nonfamily incorporated farms tend to be larger than proprietary farms but account for only about 5 percent of the agricultural land base. Foreign ownership, while increasing in recent years, includes less than one-half of one percent of farmland in the Pacific Northwest.

Land Capability

Land capability is a primary determinant of resource land use, while geographic and economic factors are more important for urban land use. The map above shows the general distribution of Soil Conservation Service land capability classes in the Pacific Northwest. This classification system grew out of a concern for the protection and enhancement of the nation's soil resources and groups soils according to erosion potential and limitations on use. This classification is not based on economic productivity. However, because they require less care, lands in the highest categories (I-IV) of land capability often are the most productive. Deep, well-drained, nearly level, loamy soils are likely to have low erosion potential and high economic productivity.

Four broad categories of limitations are considered: erosion and runoff, excess water, root zone limitations, and climatic limitations. Integrating these limitations, eight land capability classes are recognized which are summarized with their major characteristics in Table 12. Lands in classes I to IV are regarded as suitable for cultivation, while those in classes of V and greater have limited use and are generally not suited for cultivation.

37

Table 12. Summary of land characteristics in Soil Conservation Service land-capability classes

	CLASS I	CLASS II	CLASS III	CLASS IV	CLASS V	CLASS VI	CLASS VII	CLASS VIII
Limitations for crops	Few	Some	Severe	Very severe	Impractical	Unsuited	Unsuited	Preclude
Required conservation	None	Moderate	Special	Very careful	NA	NA	NA	NA
Range improvements	NA[a]	NA	NA	NA	NA	Practical	Impractical	Impractical
Physical limitations								
Slope	Nearly level	Gentle	Moderate	Moderate/ steep	Nearly level	Steep	Very steep	Very steep
Erosion potential	Low	Moderate	High	Severe	Limited	Severe	Severe	Severe
Past erosion	None	Moderate	Severe	Severe	Slight	Severe	Severe	Severe
Hazard of overflow	None	Occasional	Frequent	Frequent	Frequent	Excessive	NA	NA
Soil depth	Deep	Moderate	Shallow	Shallow	Variable	Shallow	Shallow	Shallow
Soil structure	Good	Unfavorable	Moderate salinity	Severe salinity	Usually poor	Salinity	Salts	Salinity
Drainage	Good	Correctable	Wetness	Wet soils	Poor	Poor	Wet soils	Wet soils
Climatic limitations	None	Slight	Moderate	Moderate/ adverse	Short season	Severe	Unfavorable	Severe
Moisture capability	Good	Fair	Low	Low	NA	Low	Low	Low
Stones	None	Few	Few	Few	Possible	Present	Severe	Severe

In the Pacific Northwest, there are relatively few areas with class I and class II lands; indeed, the areas of class I land are so small that they have been generalized together with class II land on the map. The Willamette, Yakima, Middle Snake, and Grande Ronde valleys have the most land in these top classes. Most of the Pacific Northwest is class VI land, unsuitable for cultivation but used for pasture, range, and forestry. The area of class V lands is small and is included as part of the class VI mapping unit.

In the capability class system, soils are grouped at three levels: class, subclass, and unit. Soil surveys, which classify and map soils at the series level, relate this finer level of classification to land capability and management.

While soil quality, to a large extent, determines potential resource use, ownership is often the deciding factor in formulating resource policies. Federal agencies, state governments, and the private sector each have objectives that may well differ, as may local city and county policies. The federal land-management agencies, primarily the Bureau of Land Management and Forest Service, are required to develop and administer strategic plans to accommodate the full range of land-use demands under their jurisdiction. The states of Oregon and Washington have enacted statewide requirements for land-use plans by local governments and state agencies to ensure that new growth conforms to state land and water-conservation policies. Local governments in all three states have undertaken land-use planning programs.

Clearly, the patterns and trends of land-use change reflect market demands and public policies, both of which are reflections of social goals. The geographic factors of climate, soils, topography, and water provide the framework for land use potential; society's economic and environmental needs will determine actual use.

Landforms and Geology

CHARLES L. ROSENFELD

The Pacific Northwest is comprised of five physiographic provinces, which in turn are subdivided into one or more terranes as shown on the map on page 41. The following is a brief description of the major physiographic features of each province.

Pacific Border Province

The Pacific Border Province includes the Klamath-Siskiyou terrane, Coast Range, Olympic Mountains, and Willamette-Puget Lowlands.

The Klamath Mountains section is defined on a partially geologic and partially topographic basis. The steep topography, dense vegetation, and structural complexity have produced a confusing geologic record. Metamorphic recrystallization masks much of the deposition history of the ancient sedimentary and volcanic strata of the region. This section has been folded, uplifted a few thousand feet, and dissected by erosion. Topographically, these mountains merge with the younger Coast Range to the north and with the southern end of the Cascade Range.

The Coast Range of Oregon and Washington consists of moderately folded marine tuffaceous sandstones and shales together with basaltic volcanic rocks and related intrusives. These also have been uplifted 1,000-2,000 feet or more, and then eroded by streams to form rounded mountains of moderate relief. Resistant igneous rocks account for certain summits and for several capes projecting seaward. Sea terraces, sand dunes, and other shore features occupy narrow strips along the coast. Drowned valleys provide many harbors and the drowned lower course of the Columbia River offers a route through the Coast Range.

The Olympic Mountains consist of a mass of folded and metamorphosed rocks eroded into sharp, steep-sided ridges standing 4,000-8,000 feet above sea level. The highest peaks bear perpetual snowbanks and several small glaciers. The mountains were severely glaciated during the ice age.

The Willamette and Cowlitz Lowlands are primarily stream valleys eroded to low elevations in belts of relatively nonresistant tilted or folded

LANDFORM REGIONS
of the
PACIFIC NORTHWEST

I. Pacific Border
  a. Klamath - Siskiyou Mtns.
  b. Coast Range
  c. Olympic Mtns.
  d. Willamette - Puget Lowland
II. Cascade Mtns.
III. Columbia Intermontane
  a. Columbia Basin
  b. Central Mtns.
  c. High Lava Plains
IV. Rocky Mtns.
  a. Northern Rockies
  b. Middle Rockies
V. Basin and Range

Tertiary rocks (see map of geology on page 45). Resistant rocks locally form hills and watergaps. Both valleys contain alluvial terraces. The Puget Lowland, eroded by streams and Pleistocene glaciers, is a partially drowned system of valleys. Bordering Puget Sound are hummocky plains of till and fairly smooth sheets of glaciofluvial gravel.

The Cascade Mountains

The Cascade Mountains of Oregon and the southern half of Washington are a broad upwarp composed of (1) underlying layers of early Tertiary tuffs, breccias, lavas, and mudflows, exposed in the Columbia River Gorge and other deep valleys; (2) a thick middle section of Tertiary basalts that form the deeply eroded Western Cascades; and (3) an upper section of Tertiary and Quaternary andesites and basalts that form the less dissected High Cascades lava platform, which is generally 15-25 miles wide and 4,000-6,000 feet high along the crest of the range. Crowning the range are a number of well-known snow-capped volcanic peaks in various stages of dissection—Mt. Rainier, Mt. St. Helens, Mt. Adams, Mt. Hood, Mt. Jefferson, Three Sisters, Mt. McLoughlin, and others. Crater Lake occupies a caldera which resulted from the eruptive collapse

of the summit of Mt. Mazama about 6,600 years ago.

The northern half of the Cascade Range of Washington is a dissected upland underlain mainly by upper Paleozoic sediments that have been folded, metamorphosed, and intruded by granites with ridges rising to elevations of 6,000-8,000 feet. Above them rise several volcanic cones (Mt. Baker and Glacier Peak). The northern Cascades were extensively glaciated, and the mountains now harbor many small glaciers.

Columbia Intermontane Province

The Columbia Intermontane Province, often inappropriately called the Columbia Plateau, includes the Columbia Basin, Central Mountains, Harney High Lava Plains, Malheur-Owyhee Upland, and Snake River Lava Plain.

The Columbia Basin is an irregular structural and topographic basin underlain by Tertiary basalt flows that have been depressed below sea level in the Pasco area and upwarped on the flanks of the surrounding mountains. Fluvial, lacustrine, eolian, and glacial sediments overlie much of the basalt, and locally form terraces or other subordinate physiographic features.

MAJOR TECTONIC FEATURES

PLATE TECTONIC RELATIONSHIPS
IN THE PACIFIC NORTHWEST

The portion in north central Oregon is partly a plateau incised by canyons and partly a low plain of sand and gravel. The portion in south central Washington is comprised of a series of anticlinal ridges (partly faulted) and synclinal valleys. The outstanding features include Horse Heaven Hills, Yakima Valley, Saddle Mountain, Kittitas Valley, and the Wenatchee Mountains-Frenchman Hill. The Columbia and Yakima rivers cross several of these ridges forming watergaps. Most of the remainder is a plateau with steeply incised stream valleys. Noteworthy are the Waterville Plateau, Quincy Basin (alluvium filled), Palouse Hills (loess covered), and Tristate Upland (on the southeast). The northern edge of the plateau was glaciated and the channeled scablands reflect the drainage ways of ice age floods. The Grand Coulee is the most spectacular of these channels.

The Blue Mountains comprise a complex group of folded and faulted uplifts, including the Seven Devils, Wallowa, Elkhorn, Greenhorn, Aldrich, and Ochoco mountains. They rise 2,000-5,000 feet above their surroundings and reach elevations of 6,000-10,000 feet. They include various rocks of differing resistance to erosion. Because of orographic rainfall, the mountains are well dissected. The higher portions, especially the Wallowa Mountains,

GLACIAL AND PERIGLACIAL FEATURES

Wisconsin Continental Glaciation
Wisconsin Alpine Glaciation
Glacial Outwash
Pleistocene Lakes
Wisconsin Loess Deposits >32 Feet
Existing Glaciers

were glaciated. Alluvium-filled fault troughs occur within the mountains, as at La Grande, Oregon.

The Harney High Lava Plains are situated between the Central Mountains, the Basin and Range area, the Cascade Mountains, and the Malheur-Owyhee Upland. They are mainly a flattish tract of recent lavas, ranging in elevation generally from about 4,000-5,000 feet. The surface is lower near the Deschutes River canyon, the only major stream in the area. Volcanoes are abundant in the western portion. Chief among them is Newberry Volcano (Paulina Mountain), with its breached caldera. Hundreds of faults, mostly of small throw, are present; they become more pronounced southward toward the Basin and Range Province.

The Malheur-Owyhee Upland occupies parts of southeastern Oregon and southwestern Idaho. It is a partly dissected, warped plateau, mostly 4,000-8,000 feet high and underlain mainly by Cenozoic lava flows, tuffs, and lakebeds. Most of the area is poorly mapped and little studied. The Owyhee River and its tributaries drain much of the area in deeply incised canyons.

The Snake River Lava Plain is an arcuate downwarp 30-60 miles wide and about 400 miles long. It descends gently from an elevation of about 6,000 feet above sea level at its east end to about 2,200 feet on the west. The eastern part is a more or less silt-covered recent lava plain, almost featureless except for low lava domes and occasional cinder cones. Very young lavas occur at Craters of the Moon, Hell's Half Acre, and elsewhere. The western part of the plain is underlain by lakebeds and alluvium as well as lava, and is partly dissected to terraces, box canyons, and open valleys.

Rocky Mountains Province

The Northern Rocky Mountains Province includes parts of northeastern Washington, northern and central Idaho, and western Montana. It is characterized by high mountain ridges and deep intermontane valleys eroded from rocks of moderately complex structure. Where the rocks have been folded and faulted, the ridges are aligned as in the Selkirk ranges. Some valleys (e.g., Bitterroot and Purcell) are 10-20 miles wide and favor settlement and transportation. The mountains of central Idaho, developed by erosion of massive granite rocks (the Idaho batholith), are irregular and resist exploration and settlement.

GEOLOGY

SEDIMENTARY ROCKS

QUATERNARY
Recent and Pleistocene

UPPER TERTIARY
Pliocene and Miocene including Recent
and Pleistocene

LOWER TERTIARY
Oligocene, Eocene, and Paleocene

CRETACEOUS
In parts of Rocky Mountains includes
Jurassic and Triassic

JURASSIC AND TRIASSIC

UPPER PALEOZOIC
Permian, Pennsylvania, and Mississippian, parts
of Rocky Mountains - middle and lower Paleozoic

MIDDLE PALEOZOIC
Devonian and Silurian

LOWER PALEOZOIC
Ordovician and Cambrian

YOUNGER PRECAMBRIAN

OLDER PRECAMBRIAN
Metamorphic and igneous rocks

VOLCANIC ROCKS

QUATERNARY AND TERTIARY
Includes small areas of intrusive rocks

INTRUSIVE ROCKS

**LOWER TERTIARY AND
MESOZOIC** – Chiefly granitic rocks

45

Most of the province drains into the Columbia River and its tributaries, although the eastern part outside the Pacific Northwest drains into the headwaters of the Missouri River system. Although much of this section is well dissected, Pleistocene glaciation has produced some of North America's most spectacular mountain scenery.

A part of the Middle Rocky Mountains section extends into southeastern Idaho, where northerly to northwesterly trending mountain ridges and valleys have eroded from folded, thrust-faulted, or tilted rocks. The valleys are about 6,000 feet above sea level, and the ridges reach 2,000-4,000 feet higher. Block faulting, characteristics of the Basin and Range Province, extends into this area also; therefore, the boundary is somewhat arbitrary.

Basin and Range Province

The northern edge of the Great Basin section of the Basin and Range Province extends into south central Oregon and into southern Idaho. The part in Idaho consists of a series of tilted fault blocks and parallel stream valleys developed in a region of folded rocks. By contrast, the part in Oregon is a high lava plain interrupted by fault block mountains and by fault troughs. Representative of the high-standing blocks are Steens Mountain, Hart Mountain, Abert Rim, and Winter Ridge. Typical fault troughs are Alvord Basin, Warner Valley, and

the basins of Abert, Summer, Goose, and Klamath lakes. The western part of this province is covered by the ash and pumice of the Mt. Mazama and Mt. Newberry eruptions, which greatly alter the appearance, drainage, and vegetation of the area. The presence of so many young faults attests to the recency of tectonic activity in the region, as do the numerous hot springs and geothermal areas.

Tectonic Setting of the Pacific Northwest

The geologic deformation of the earth's crust has undergone radical re-examination in light of discoveries linking such movement with sea-floor spreading and continental drift, which have been combined to form a body of theory called plate tectonics. Submarine volcanic activity produces new sea-floor material, forcing older oceanic crust to spread laterally away from the activity. In some cases, the sea floor is thrust beneath the margins of a continent, back into the mantle of the earth. This process is called subduction. At present many earth scientists believe such a process is active in the Pacific Northwest; however, it appears to be a complex and rather special case.

The diagram of plate tectonic relationships on page 43 illustrates the concept of subduction as applied to this region. The movement of the oceanic Gorda Plate has been indicated by seismic and paleomagnetic evidence, providing the source of tectonic stress and material which results in the continued volcanic activity of the Cascades and the moderate seismic activity of the region. The 1980 eruption of Mount St. Helens generated considerable scientific inquiry into the mechanisms of Cascade volcanism and its relation to plate tectonics. The creation of the Cascades Volcanoes Observatory and the regional seismic network promise to yield new insights into the tectonic origins of the region.

Glacial Features

The complexity of the landscape history of the Pacific Northwest is well illustrated by the sequence and variety of landforms related to the Pleistocene ice ages. Lobes of ice pushed southward from the Cordilleran ice in western Canada, forcing their way along river valleys and lowland areas. Although we have identified several periods of glaciation during the Pleistocene, the complexity of glacial activity within the region has masked any simple sequence. For example, the large lobes were part of a continental ice sheet of great thickness which advanced by pressure flow, whereas the local glaciers in the mountains contained much less ice and moved down their valleys by gravity. The mechanics and volume of these different glacial systems indicate that they responded differently to changes in climate and their respective advances were not necessarily synchronous.

Glacial features also include all the modifications brought about by glacial meltwater and associated climatic changes. These effects include glacially diverted rivers, large inland lakes, and the effects of frozen ground upon the landscape. Among the most dramatic effects were the sequence of mammoth floods which formed the Channeled Scablands of eastern Washington. Glacial Lake Missoula formed when the Clark Fork of the Columbia River was dammed by a Cordilleran ice lobe. When the lobe began to melt, the ice dam burst, releasing up to 50 cubic miles of water which rushed westward over the Columbia Plateau near Spokane. As the floods raged over the plateau, the water ripped off the soil cover and cut channels into the basalt bedrock.

Other features include the shorelines of lakes that were greatly expanded during the wetter, cooler glacial periods of the Pleistocene. Some of these lakes have dried up completely, while others, like Summer Lake and Goose Lake in Oregon, remain as small remnants of their former extent.

Climate

PHILIP L. JACKSON

Climatic diversity is the hallmark of the Pacific Northwest. The several climates found in the region reflect geographic circumstances that, in human terms, provide a unique mosaic of varied living environments. The climatic characteristics of the region favorably support a broad spectrum of human activities, including forest resource use, crop and animal agriculture, and a wide variety of outdoor recreation activities. Climatic moderation is said to be characteristic of the Pacific Northwest, but extremes are here too. While the region is relatively free of violent weather phenomena, there are sufficient local occurrences of windstorms, ice storms, blizzards, floods, and droughts to keep the subject of weather and climate high on the list of conversational topics.

Throughout the Pacific Northwest, distinctive seasonal changes in temperature and precipitation occur, due in part to geographic circumstances that include a west coast position astride the mid-latitude cyclonic storm belt, oceanic and continental influences, and the effect of surface form and elevation. Dominance of one or more factors produces subregional climatic differences. In combination, these features translate into a distinctive climatic regime characterized by relatively dry, warm summers and cooler, wetter winters. This winter seasonality of precipitation is the unifying factor in a region of climatic diversity.

Climatic diversity in the Pacific Northwest is largely attributable to the Cascade Mountain chain, which creates a major east-west moisture divide and shields the higher elevation interior from the moderating temperatures of the Pacific Ocean. Sharp vertical temperature and precipitation gradients are also induced by the Olympics, the Blue Mountains, and the Rocky Mountain complexes of Idaho. In general, there are more rainy days and mean annual precipitation totals are higher west of the Cascades. Annual temperature ranges are low and freeze-free periods are generally long, especially in those locations influenced by marine air. To the east, in the rain shadow of the Cascades, precipitation totals are low, there is greater seasonal temperature range, and a greater variability in the length of the freeze-free period.

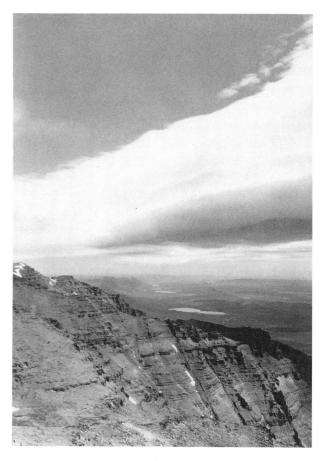

Climate Elements

Because the Pacific Northwest is situated roughly halfway between the equator and the north pole, at latitude 42° to 49° north, days in summer are long and insolation is more direct, producing higher average temperatures than during winter months. Atmospheric circulation and the seasonal temperature lag of ocean waters have a moderating influence and serve to make winter temperatures milder and summer temperatures cooler west of the Cascades.

Landforms play a major role in directing the movement of surface air; both marine and continental air masses are influenced by terrain barriers. The moderating influence of marine air penetrates some distance inland through river valleys and terrain gaps in the Coast Range, extending nearly 130 miles inland through the unique water gap feature of the Columbia Gorge. The Cascades, however, form an effective barrier to marine air, and contrasts between winter and summer temperatures are most apparent east of the mountains, as illustrated by the relative length of the freeze-free season. Above freezing temperatures persist from 240 to 300 days from north to south along the coastal margin and the western lowlands. East of the Cascades, however, except for the Columbia River borderlands and the Snake River Plain, the freeze-free season is generally less than 120 days, and it is less than 30 days in the Cascades and the Rocky Mountains of Idaho.

Atmospheric circulation varies from summer to winter, producing important temperature and precipitation variations throughout the region. Summer wind flow is generally from the northwest, the result of high-pressure domination in the northeastern Pacific. Cooler, drier air flow from the north Pacific contributes to mild summer temperatures west of the Cascades. With clear skies and long hours of sunshine, eastern areas have higher summer temperatures, a result of rapid landmass heating. The generally higher elevations to the east moderate summer extremes, but low-elevation stations along the Columbia and Snake rivers often experience some of the highest summer temperatures in the region.

Winter precipitation in the Pacific Northwest is associated with cyclonic storms embedded in the eastward atmospheric flow across the Pacific. In the late fall and winter, warm, moisture-laden air travels northeasterly across the Pacific, paralleling the pressure gradient between the subtropical high- and the north Pacific low-pressure systems. This generally southwest air flow meets contrastingly cooler and drier air, creating frontal zones that move through the Pacific Northwest. Vast cloud sheets form as air is drawn into low-pressure cyclonic disturbances and is forced to rise up over frontal surfaces. As the moisture-laden air cools, clouds form and precipitation results. During December, January, and February, precipitation is widespread and incessant throughout much of the Pacific Northwest, but totals are greater on the west side of the mountain barriers that force air moving inland from the Pacific to rise and cool. Rain falls abundantly on the Coast Range and lower slopes of the Olympics and Cascades. At higher elevations, winter snowfall generally exceeds 300 inches. In parts of the Cascades, as much as 1,000 inches has been recorded. Typically, windward (western slope) locations are comparatively wetter, with drier conditions at leeward (eastern slope) locations. Air descending the leeward slopes inhibits the precipitation process, because air warms as it descends, a condition that contributes to aridity. Some distance to the east of the Cascades, annual amounts of precipitation increase on the southwestern flanks of the mountains of northeast Oregon, southeast Washington, and southwestern and northern Idaho.

July and August are the driest months over most of the Pacific Northwest, but because of the contrast between total amounts of precipitation, western stations show a more dramatic seasonal regime than do the stations to the east. Some stations in Idaho show a spring precipitation peak caused by mountain ranges that produce atmospheric instability and convective thunderstorm precipitation.

GENERALIZED PRESSURE AND WINDS

Climatic Regions

Climatic diversity in the Pacific Northwest is strongly influenced by two factors: distance from the Pacific Ocean and physiographic relief. Five broad regional climates result and are described below. Climographs have been prepared to assist in the visualization of the specific regions described. Stations selected are representative of the region, but it should always be kept in mind that climatic statistics from nearby stations may differ considerably due to the influence of local terrain features. Maps of climatic elements are necessarily generalized to depict broad regional patterns.

The Coast Region. A mild, wet marine climate extends along a narrow coastal strip and into the river valleys of the Coast Range. The freeze-free season varies from 300 days at Brookings, Oregon, to 240 days at Tatoosh, Washington, though stations more than 30 miles inland show a reduction of a month in the freeze-free period.

Summer temperatures peak in August, with maximums rarely exceeding 70°F, although Astoria, Oregon, has recorded 100°F temperatures. Average temperatures are in the range of 55° to 59°F but,

while winters are mild on the coast, they are also raw, windy, wet, and cloudy. Summer coolness and reduced sunshine are related to the frequency of fog in the coastal zone; sunshine duration is only about one-half of that possible. Cape Disappointment, Washington, just north of the mouth of the Columbia River, has the distinction of being the foggiest place on the U. S. Pacific Coast, averaging 2,552 hours a year.

Evergreen forest growth is highly favored in the coastal mountains where rain falls over 200 days of the year, and annual totals may exceed 125 inches. Average precipitation ranges from 60-80 inches in the south to 80-100 inches in the north. Summer is relatively drier than winter with, on the average, only about 10 percent of the total annual precipitation occurring during June, July, and August.

The windward slope of the Coast Range receives the most rain at elevations from 500 to 2,000 feet due to orographic lifting. Snow is not uncommon at higher elevations during winter. The Olympic Mountains of Washington contain peaks ranging from 4,000 to 8,000 feet above sea level and cause east-moving cyclonic storms to deposit copious

PREVAILING SURFACE WIND DIRECTION AND SPEED

—January—

amounts of rain and over 100 inches of snow during the winter months. Summer precipitation amounts are also higher in the Olympics due to orographic lifting and convective disturbances.

The Western Lowlands. The Western Lowlands, extending from the Rogue Valley in the south to the Willamette Valley and Puget Sound Lowlands in the north, have dry, sunny summers and moist, mild winters. The north-south orientation of the Coast Range produces a lee effect and consequently slightly larger annual temperature ranges, with higher maximums and lower minimums. In the southern valleys, hot summer days in excess of 90°F are not unusual, whereas daytime average temperatures are more moderate to the north. The average July maximum for Portland, Oregon, is 78°F and for Seattle, Washington, is 75°F. Since precipitation is primarily a winter season phenomenon, summer daytime humidity averages 50 percent or less, a delightful situation, favorable to human comfort. Cool nights are also more likely in summer, with average July minimums from 50° to 55°F. Dry, hot winds occasionally invade the lowlands, funneling through the Columbia Gorge from the

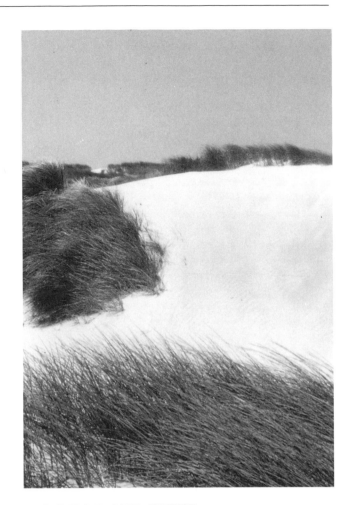

PREVAILING SURFACE WIND DIRECTION AND SPEED

—July—

SNOWFALL

Mean annual inches

DAYS WITH DENSE FOG

Mean annual
number of days

ANNUAL PRECIPITATION

Mean number
of inches

DAYS WITH PRECIPITATION

Mean annual number
.01″ or more

WINTER PRECIPITATION

Mean number of inches
—December, January,
February

SUMMER PRECIPITATION

Mean number of inche
—June, July, August

east. On these occasions, clear, hot, and dry conditions may last for several days, greatly increasing irrigation requirements, electricity demand, and forest fire hazard.

Dry spells may last 30-60 days in the summer, especially during July and August, but the dry summer merges into the rainy season in mid-October. Winter is mild, cloudy, and moist. Cloud cover reduces the possible sunshine to 25-30 percent, and low-intensity, gentle rains last an average of 16-18 days in each month during December and January. The highest monthly precipitation is in December, usually from six to nine inches. To the south, the Rogue Valley is shielded from marine influences by the Siskiyou Mountains and receives only about one-half the monthly totals of the northern lowlands. Throughout this region, some winters may pass without snowfall, but it is not uncommon for winter snows to total 10 inches. Total annual precipitation ranges from 35 to 45 inches, a relatively small amount considering the large number of rainy days.

The Cascades. Sharp temperature and precipitation gradients are induced by the Cascade Range. The high mountains to some extent create their own microclimates that correspond with changes in elevation, slope, and aspect. With the exception of the Columbia Gorge, the high average elevation and orientation of the range creates an effective orographic barrier, resulting in a major east-west moisture divide. Winter precipitation is dominant as in the other climatic regions of the Pacific Northwest. The Cascades receive copious amounts of rain on the western slopes, but it is the annual snowfall

that sets the region apart. Total annual precipitation ranges from 70 to over 100 inches, with the highest amounts normally falling in the northern Cascades of Washington. Paradise Ranger Station on Mt. Rainier holds North America's seasonal snowfall record with a total of 1,122 inches. Snowfall is heaviest at elevations from 5,000 to 7,000 feet, with winter totals of 200-600 inches and ground accumulations of up to 25 feet. Crater Lake in Oregon receives, on average, over 100 inches each month during December, January, and February. Year-round snow fields and glaciers are found on the highest peaks. In other areas, snow fields may last from April to the end of July. Winter temperatures are distinctly colder at higher elevations, but the Pacific slopes of the Cascades have mean minimum winter temperatures above 30°F. The average January temperature at Snoqualmie Pass, Washington (3,020 feet), is 27°F. The higher eastern slopes have less snow accumulation, but there is a greater abundance of sunshine, enhancing winter recreational activities.

Summer is brief in the higher Cascades; in some areas the length of the freeze-free season is less than 30 days. The northern Cascades have a higher frequency of summer storms than do the more southerly mountains. Still, only about 8 percent of the total annual precipitation falls during the summer. Temperature maximums are generally from the 70s to 80s during the day but may drop to freezing at night due to the clear and relatively dry atmosphere found at higher elevations.

FREQUENCY OF DRY YEARS

Percent of years with less than 15" of precipitation

FREEZE-FREE PERIOD

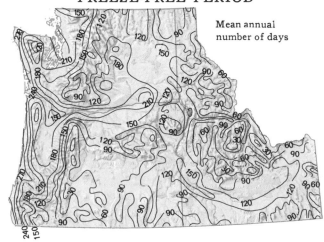

Mean annual number of days

The Intermontane Region. The distinctive climatic characteristics of the intermontane region are low precipitation totals, large temperature ranges between summer and winter, and fewer cloudy days than to the west. This is a very large region, extending from the Columbia Basin in the north through the High Lava Plains to the fault-block Basin and Range to the south. Average annual precipitation totals over the area range from 10 to 20 inches, with up to 30 inches falling in elevated locations. In general, precipitation amounts increase in response to elevation increases: Pendleton, Oregon, for example, averages only 11-14 inches of precipitation, while Moscow, Idaho, in the elevated Palouse Hills, averages 22 inches. Boise, Idaho, at about the same elevation as Moscow but 250 miles to the southeast, averages only 12 inches of annual precipitation.

The Blue Mountains of northeastern Oregon receive only one-third to one-half the precipitation that falls in the Cascades. Fall, winter, and spring precipitation totals here are nearly the same. Convective thunderstorms in spring contribute 1-2 inches of rain per month, an important climatic feature for dryland grain farming. The cool nights and dry sunny days of July and August provide ideal conditions for ripening wheat in the Palouse and the Snake River Plain and foster the growth of quality orchard crops in Oregon's Hood River and Washington's Yakima and Wenatchee valleys.

During the winter, precipitation is generally in the form of snow, ranging from 10 to 30 inches, depending on elevation and exposure. Snow tends to remain on the ground for some time due to colder winter temperatures than are experienced in the western part of the region. Except for areas along the Columbia and Snake rivers, characteristic continental temperature ranges are experienced. July daytime temperatures in the 80s and 90s are common, dropping to the mid-50s at night. January mean temperatures average 20° to 30°F, but in some locations daytime temperatures may not rise above 0°F. As cold, dry air masses flow into the region from the Rocky Mountains, temperatures may drop to -20° to -30°F. During the winter, strong winds flow across the plateau in response to pressure system movements. Soils of the Palouse and Columbia borderlands are particularly susceptible to severe wind erosion at this time of year if left unprotected.

LAST KILLING FROST OF SPRING

Mean date

FIRST KILLING FROST IN FALL

Mean date

JANUARY MAXIMUM TEMPERATURE

Mean degrees
Fahrenheit

JULY MAXIMUM TEMPERATURE

Mean degrees
Fahrenheit

JANUARY MINIMUM TEMPERATURE

Mean degrees
Fahrenheit

JULY MINIMUM TEMPERATURE

Mean degrees
Fahrenheit

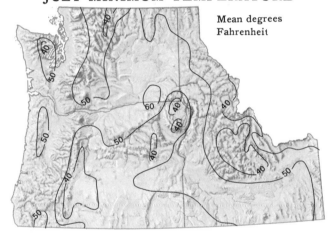

JANUARY SUNSHINE

Mean total hours

JULY SUNSHINE

Mean total hours

Northeastern Mountains and Valleys. Continental influences dominate the highlands of northeastern Oregon and central Idaho. Within this region, the considerable elevation differences are responsible for strikingly different mountain and valley climates. Over the region, an average annual temperature range of 50°F or more is common. January temperatures average 19° to 21°F, and temperatures below 0° F are not uncommon, with -40° to -50°F reported. Precipitation in winter is almost entirely snow, which falls 70-80 days a year. The higher mountains, such as the Wallowas, Bitterroots, and Selkirks, capture large amounts of moisture from winter cyclonic storms, but at moderate elevations snowfall totals are only 40-80 inches.

The clear days of summer are punctuated by thunderstorms. These local storms are short in duration but serve to cool down temperatures and contribute significantly to the 10-20 inches of precipitation at most valley stations. Summer is relatively short at the higher elevations but, in the valleys, the freeze-free period is sufficient for forage and some small grain production. Temperatures may rise into the 80s on July days and drop into the low 50s at night at moderate elevations.

VARIATIONS IN TEMPERATURE AND PRECIPITATION

*30 year average precipitation (1961-1990)

Vegetation

ROBERT E. FRENKEL

The vegetation of the Pacific Northwest exhibits a complex pattern reflecting diversity in climate, soils, relief, incidence of fire, biotic interaction, and history. Recent impacts on pristine vegetation by logging, agriculture, grazing, industrial development, and urbanization have greatly altered the natural pattern. Although it is possible to map this altered pattern and create a map of actual vegetation, the map on page 60 shows the natural plant cover as it might appear if the effects of logging, agriculture, and urban-industrial use were not present.

Major vegetation differences, especially those determined by regional climate, are reflected by three vegetation provinces—Forest, Shrub-Steppe, and Alpine—embracing fifteen vegetation zones or zone complexes. As used here, a vegetation zone is the area within which maturely developed soils support a specific climatic climax vegetation. It is a broad area of relatively uniform regional climate and typical regional topography within which one plant association is capable of becoming dominant under prevalent climatic conditions over a long period of time. In practice, alteration of plant cover has been profound. As a result, the potentially dominant species characteristic of the mapped vegetation zones may not currently prevail.

Numerous plant communities exist within a given vegetation zone. When fully described by their species composition and structure, these plant communities are called plant associations. The classification and description of these localized plant associations and related habitat types has been well developed in the Pacific Northwest under the leadership of the U.S. Forest Service research scientists.

Despite much research, the vegetation of the region is imperfectly known. A general review of the plant cover of Oregon and Washington was conducted by Franklin and Dyrness (1988). Other major works introducing the interested individual to broad aspects of Pacific Northwest vegetation include a detailed study of steppe vegetation (Daubenmire 1970), a description of the forest vegetation of eastern Washington and northern Idaho (Daubenmire and Daubenmire 1968), and many comprehensive technical reports for Oregon and Washington issued as "Regional Guides" by the U.S. Forest Service, Pacific Northwest Region 6, Portland, Oregon, such as the report by Henderson et al. (1989). For Idaho, comparable studies are published as "General Technical Reports" by the U.S. Forest Service at the Intermountain Research Station, Ogden, Utah, such as the report by Steel et al. (1981).

Species Range and Ecotype

A quite different concept than that of vegetation zones concerns the distribution of individual plant species within the region of their occurrence is termed a species' range. An organism does not occupy all the area within its range owing to differences in soil, topography, and local climate. Plant species often consist of a series of races, genetically adapted to localized ecological conditions, called ecotypes. The maps on page 59 show the ranges of eight prominent tree species and some major ecotypes in the Pacific Northwest.

Ecoregions

Regional variations in climate, vegetation, soil, and landforms in the Pacific Northwest are integrated into a single map of ecoregions. An outgrowth of regional planning at the federal level, ecoregion mapping helps with (1) planning where broad management problems must be considered; (2) organizing and retrieving resource inventory data; and (3) interpreting and analyzing these data. This system has been useful in assessments required under the Resources Planning Act and the National Forest Management Act and for various regional and national studies conducted by the U.S. Environmental Protection Agency, and in the National Wetlands Inventory conducted by the U.S. Fish and Wildlife Service.

Although combining different kinds of physical and biological data into a single system of regionalization is not new, the ecoregion map developed by R. G. Bailey (1976 and 1978) establishes a hierarchical system based on independent data bases. Since broad similarity in zonal heat and moisture availability is the major

Continued on page 63

PONDEROSA PINE

Pinus ponderosa
Laws.

SHORE PINE/LODGEPOLE PINE

Pinus contorta var.

latifolia Engelm.
murrayana (Grev. & Balf.)
Engelm.
contorta Dougl.

QUAKING ASPEN

Populus tremuloides
Michx.

OREGON WHITE OAK

Quercus garryana
Dougl.

ENGELMANN SPRUCE

Picea engelmanii
Parry

WESTERN JUNIPER

Juniperus occidentalis
Hook.

WESTERN HEMLOCK

Tsuga heterophylla
(Raf.) Sarg.

DOUGLAS-FIR

Pseudotsuga menziesii var.

glauca (Beissn.) Franco
menziesii (Mirb.) Franco

VEGETATION ZONES

(legend on following page)

Western Juniper Zone. This open woodland dominated by western juniper (*Juniperus occidentalis*) is the northern counterpart of the Pinyon-Juniper type of the Great Basin. Shrub-steppe dominated by big sagebrush (*Artemisia tridentata*) and Idaho fescue typically comprises the understory of this zone. Throughout the arid regions of interior Oregon, juniper woodland characterizes rimrock habitat where local moisture supplies permit establishment of this xerophytic tree.

Shrub-Steppe Province

Steppe Zone Complex. Grassland without shrubs mantles areas of north-central Oregon and the Palouse of southeastern Washington and adjacent Idaho. Among the various communities within this grassland is the *Agropyron-Festuca* type characterized by bluebunch wheatgrass (*Agropyron spicatum*) and Idaho fescue. In moister situations, Sandberg's bluegrass (*Poa sandbergii*) and Idaho fescue are prominent together with many forbs and shrubby common snowberry. The steppe type is intermediate between ponderosa pine forest and more xeric shrub-steppe, and the communities of the Steppe Zone Complex form understory unions in these adjacent vegetation types.

Big Sagebrush Zone. The most widespread vegetation zone in the Pacific Northwest extends from Canada to Nevada and from the Cascades to the Rockies. Dominated by big sagebrush, the zone intermingles with juniper woodland in central Oregon and supports nonintensive grazing. Plant communities have been identified based on understory grasses, shrub cover, soils, and slope. Two prominent communities are *Artemisia tridentata/ Festuca idahoensis* and *Artemisia tridentata/Agropyron spicatum* associations. Low sagebrush (*Artemisia arbuscula*) frequently replaces big sagebrush in eastern Oregon on shallow stony soils. Other prominent shrubs include several species of sagebrush and rabbit brush (*Chrysothamnus* spp.). Commonly referred to as "high desert," the shrub-steppe in this zone consists of nondesert species and exhibits a shrub-grass structure which is distinct from true desert.

Desert Shrub Zone Complex. Occupying pockets within the Big Sagebrush Zone, the Desert Shrub Zone Complex is the most xeric of the region. Frequently the type occupies playas where saline conditions prevail, but also occurs in the rainshadow of several mountain ranges in southeastern Oregon and southern Idaho. Important shrubs, most of which are halophytic, include shadscale (*Atriplex confertifolia*), salt sage (*A. nuttalli*), greasewood (*Sarcobatus vermiculatus*), and spring hopsage (*Grayia spinosa*). Grasses and forbs are occasionally found in this open vegetation.

Alpine Province

Alpine Zone Complex. Found near and above the tree line, this zone complex is narrowly represented in the Cascades and more extensively in the Rocky Mountains. Mainly comprising herbaceous plants and low shrubs, these zones contain a few trees displaying krummholz form and occupying protected habitats. Alpine heath communities of the subalpine park land extend into the alpine zones, and glaciers, permanent snow fields, and extensive areas of talus and rock cover much of the area.

Forest Province

Sitka Spruce Zone. Confined to the coast, this coniferous zone extends from Alaska to southwestern Oregon and has been extensively altered by logging and fire. Sitka spruce (*Picea sitchensis*) characterizes the zone although in many places western hemlock (*Tsuga heterophylla*) and Douglas-fir (*Pseudotsuga menziesii*) dominate. Red alder (*Alnus rubra*) often forms patches in disturbed areas and riparian situations, while western redcedar (*Thuja plicata*) characterizes swampy habitats. Besides stabilized dune communities in which shore pine (*Pinus contorta*) is a prominent successional species, there are salt marsh communities in estuaries and communities associated with shifting dunes. The Sitka Spruce Zone grades into the Western Hemlock Zone to which it is closely related.

Western Hemlock Zone, mantling both the Coast Range and western slopes of the Cascades, this zone is one of the most extensive in the region, stretching from British Columbia to California. Although named for the shade-tolerant western hemlock characterizing the persistent vegetation, the dominant tree is often the seral Douglas-fir. Extensive logging has occurred throughout the area. Communities within this zone have been studied in detail and have been related to site characteristics. Some important species are western redcedar in moist sites and, in the south, ponderosa pine (*Pinus ponderosa*) and incense cedar (*Calocedrus decurrens*). In disturbed moist sites, red alder and bigleaf maple (*Acer macrophyllum*) are common. Western hemlock gives way to Douglas-fir in drier sites and Pacific silver fir (*Abies amabilis*) at higher elevations.

Cascade Subalpine Forest Zone Complex. A group of zones marked by heavy snow flanks the Cascades and Olympics and extends into British Columbia. This group includes the Pacific Silver Fir Zone marked by *Abies amabilis*. At higher elevations, silver fir gives way to a more stunted forest of mountain hemlock (*Tsuga mertensiana*) and subalpine fir (*Abies lasiocarpa*) and forms a parklike pattern of open meadow and forest stringers. In areas of volcanic ash or areas recently disturbed by fire, even-aged stands of lodgepole pine (*Pinus contorta* var. *murrayana*) prevail. In southern Oregon, the zones bear close relationship to the California red fir forest.

Grand Fir and Douglas-fir Zones. Mesic coniferous forests occur in interior areas and exhibit a broad distribution. Often both grand fir (*Abies grandis*) and Douglas-fir occur in mixed stands, although Douglas-fir tends to be more prevalent in Idaho. Other trees of importance, in order of increasing moisture tolerance, are ponderosa pine, western larch (*Larix occidentalis*), and lodgepole pine; the latter two species are fire-responsive pioneers. In northern Idaho, Pacific yew, western redcedar and western hemlock are prominent. Oregon boxwood (*Pachystima myrsinites*) and common snowberry (*Symphoricarpos albus*) dominate two prevalent understory communities.

Ponderosa Pine Zone. In a broad belt below the Grand Fir and Douglas-fir zones is an open coniferous forest dominated by *Pinus ponderosa.* Understory vegetation varies from shrubby mats of bitterbrush (*Purshia tridentata*) and snowbrush (*Ceanothus velutinus*) in central Oregon to meadows of Idaho fescue (*Festuca idahoensis*) further to the east. This zone has been severely altered by timber harvest.

Western Redcedar Zone. At moderate altitudes in moist locales in the northwestern portion of the region, this zone occurs between the more xeric Grand Fir and Douglas-fir zones and the spruce-fir type. Dominant trees include western redcedar, western hemlock, and western white pine (*Pinus monticola*), but grand fir and western larch are found in drier sites. Understory unions in this zone are often similar to those of the Grand Fir and Douglas-fir zones.

Engelmann Spruce and Subalpine Fir Zones. Confined to higher elevations to the east, this type is the counterpart of the Cascade Subalpine Forest. Varying from dense to open parklike stands of subalpine fir and Engelmann spruce (*Picea engelmannii*), the zone has occasional intrusions of subalpine larch (*Larix lyallii*) and whitebark pine (*Pinus albicaulis*) at higher elevations and Douglas-fir at lower elevations.

Mixed Needleleaf-Broadleaf Forest Zone Complex. A highly intricate set of zones closely related to plant communities in California, this mixed evergreen forest straddles the Siskiyou Mountains in southwestern Oregon. Edaphic, fire history, and climatic contrasts lead to sharp breaks in plant cover. Douglas-fir dominates the upper canopy, but various sclerophyllous trees and shrubs are found in the understory including tanoak (*Lithocarpus densiflorus*), canyon live oak (*Quercus chrysolepis*), Pacific madrone (*Arbutus menziesii*), and golden chinquapin (*Castanopsis chrysophylla*). Serpentine soil bears a distinctive flora and sparse vegetation, and other dry rocky areas support sclerophyllous broadleaf chaparral.

Rogue-Umpqua Forest-Shrub Zone Complex. Occupying valleys in the rainshadow of the Siskiyou Mountains is a vegetation mosaic exhibiting many xeric characteristics. Woodlands are dominated by Oregon white oak (*Quercus garryana*), with California black oak (*Q. kelloggii*) on mesic sites. Pacific madrone, ponderosa pine, sugar pine (*Pinus lambertiana*), and incense cedar distinguish this zone from Willamette Valley forest. On shallow soils, south slopes, and recently burned areas, sclerophyllous shrub communities are found with narrow-leaved buckbrush (*Ceanothus cuneatus*) and white-leaved manzanita (*Arctostaphylos viscida*).

Willamette Forest-Prairie Zone Complex. Confined to bottomland and adjacent slopes of the Willamette Valley is a mosaic of forest, woodland, open savanna, and prairie. Prairie and oak savanna at the time of first settlement was maintained by aboriginal burning. Woodlands dominated by Oregon white oak have since been invaded by Douglas-fir and grand fir, with bigleaf maple important on north-facing slopes. Grasslands maintained by grazing include many introduced species and occupy drier sites. Lacing this mosaic of forest and prairie are bands of riparian woodland in which Oregon ash (*Fraxinus latifolia*), black poplar (*Populus trichocarpa*), and willow (*Salix* spp.) are prominent.

WETLANDS 1991

Areas predominately wetland

Area typified by a high density of small wetlands intermixed with uplands

Rivers or streams which are predominately wetland

Miles

Kilometers

0   100   200

control on physical systems, the Pacific Northwest is first divided into two domains, the Humid Temperate Domain and the Dry Domain. Each domain includes several divisions based on more specific macroclimatic criteria at the level of broad climatic types, e.g., Warm Continental Climate Division. At the third level, each division is divided into several provinces reflecting bioclimatic and soil criteria as generally expressed at the level of soil order and vegetation formation, e.g., Douglas-fir Forest Province.

This hierarchical system of regionalization may be refined at lower levels; for example, provinces are subdivided into sections reflecting potential natural vegetation types, and sections are broken down into districts based on land surface form. Ultimately, the system is capable of defining a site, a more-or-less homogeneous unit of land with respect to local climate, landform, soil, and vegetation for which a management prescription can be effectively prepared (Bailey 1982).

A very similar system has been refined by Omernik and Gallant (1986) in which ecoregions in the Pacific Northwest are synthesized from independent regional data sets describing (1) land surface form, (2) potential natural vegetation, (3) land use, and (4) soils.

Wetlands

Wetlands are those transitional lands between terrestrial and aquatic environments in which water saturation is the dominant factor governing soil development and plant and animal communities. Seasonal wetlands are only saturated for short periods of time during the growing season; other areas such as marshes and many swamps are saturated, or even inundated, throughout the year. In the Pacific Northwest wetlands constitute a very small proportion of the total land area, less than 1.5 percent.

Once considered waste places, many wetlands have been drained, filled, or otherwise destroyed. Nationally, the United States has lost approximately 50 percent of its wetland resources (Tiner 1984, Dahl et al. 1991, Frayer et al. 1983). In the Pacific Northwest losses are about 39 percent, most of which were caused by historical draining of interior freshwater wetlands for farming. Idaho has lost 56 percent of its wetlands, Oregon 38 percent, and Washington 31 percent (Dahl 1990). Coastal wetlands, the majority of which are salt marshes, constitute probably less than 5 percent of the total wetland acreage. Conversion of coastal wetlands has nonetheless been profound, with losses varying from 30 to 90 percent per estuary.

ECOREGIONS

Coast Range

Puget Lowland

Willamette Valley

Cascades

Sierra Nevada

Eastern Cascades Slopes
And Foothills

Columbia Basin

Blue Mountains

Snake River Basin/
High Desert

Northern Basin And Range

Northern Rockies

Middle Rockies

Wyoming Basin

Wasatch And Uinta
Mountains

In the early 1970s, the multiple values of wetlands began to be recognized. These resources provide critical habitat for wildlife, help purify polluted water, reduce flooding, and provide important areas for recreation, education and research. Today, many practices that damage wetlands are regulated as required under federal and state legislation, yet still the region continues to lose wetlands, particularly by the conversion of wetlands to urban and commercial uses.

The U.S. Fish and Wildlife Service is in the process of inventorying the wetlands of the nation. The National Wetlands Inventory is based on the interpretation of aerial photographs, and identified wetlands are classified and mapped at the scale of U.S. Geological Survey quadrangles. The inventory is complete for Oregon and Washington and is in progress for Idaho. The small-scale map of Pacific Northwest wetlands on page 62 is based on the national map of Wetland Resources of the United States (Dahl 1991). In part, mapped wetlands represent aggregated data from the National Wetlands Inventory and the judgement of staff in the regional offices of the U.S. Fish and Wildlife Service. Mapped are (1) areas that are predominantly wetland and (2) areas within which there is a high density of small wetlands. Deepwater habitats are excluded from the map.

References

Bailey, R.G. 1976. *Ecoregions of the United States.* U.S.D.A. For. Serv. Intermtn. Reg., Ogden, Utah.

Bailey, R.G. 1978. *Description of the Ecoregions of the United States.* U.S.D.A. For. Serv. Intermtn. Reg., Ogden, Utah.

Bailey, R.G. 1982. "Classification systems for habitat and ecosystems," p.16-26 in *Research on Fish and Wildlife Habitat.* U.S. Env. Protect. Agcy. EPA 600/8-82-022.

Cronquist, A., et al. 1972. *Intermountain Flora, Vascular Plants of the Intermountain West, U.S.A.,* Vol. 1. Hafner Publ. Co., New York.

Dahl, T.E. 1990. *Wetland Losses in the United States 1780s to 1980s.* U.S. Dept. Int., Fish & Wild. Serv., Washington, D.C.

Dahl, T.E. 1991. *Wetland Resources of the United States.* (Map at 1:3,168,000). U.S. Dept. Int., Fish & Wild. Serv., National Wetlands Inventory, St. Petersburg, FL.

Dahl, T.E. et al. 1991. *Status and Trends of Wetlands in the Conterminous United States, mid-1970s to mid-1980s.* U.S. Dept. Int., Fish & Wild. Serv., Washington, D.C.

Daubenmire, R. 1970. *Steppe Vegetation of Washington.* Wash. Agric. Exp. Sta. Tech. Bull. 62.

Daubenmire, R. and J.B. Daubenmire. 1968. *Forest Vegetation of Eastern Washington and Northern Idaho.* Wash. Agric. Exp. Sta. Tech. Bull. 60.

Franklin, J.F. and C.T. Dyrness. 1973. *Natural Vegetation of Oregon and Washington.* U.S.D.A. For. Serv. Pac. Northw. For. and Range Exp. Sta. Gen. Tech. Rep. PNW-8. Reprinted by Oregon State University Press, 1988.

Frayer, W.E. et al. 1983. *Status and Trends of Wetlands and Deepwater Habitats in the Conterminous United States, 1950s to 1970s.* U.S. Dept. Int., Fish & Wild. Serv., Washington, D.C.

Henderson, J.A., D.H. Peter, R.D. Lesher, and D.C. Shaw. 1989. *Forested Plant Associations of Olympic National Forest.* U.S.D.A. For. Serv. Pac. Northw. Reg. R6 Ecol. Tech. Pap. 001-88.

Kuchler, A.W. 1964. *Potential Natural Vegetation of the Conterminous United States.* Amer. Geog. Soc. Spec. Publ. No. 36.

Little, E.L., Jr. 1971. *Atlas of United States Trees. Vol. 1. Conifers and Important Hardwoods.* U.S.D.A. For. Serv. Miscel. Publ. No. 1146.

Omernik, J.M. and A.L. Gallant. 1986. *Ecoregions of the Pacific Northwest.* U.S. Env. Protect. Agcy., Res. and Devel. Rep., EPA/600/3-86/033.

Steele, R., R.D. Pfister, R.A. Ryker, and J.A. Kittams. 1981. *Forest Habitat Types of Central Idaho.* U.S.D.A. For. Serv. Intermtn. For. and Range Exp. Sta., Gen. Tech. Rep. INT-114.

Tiner, R.W. Jr. 1984. *Wetlands of the United States: Current Status and Recent Trends.* U.S. Dept. Int., Fish & Wild. Serv., Washington, D.C.

Soils

JULIA A. JONES

Differences among soils result from the interaction of several major soil-forming factors: 1) geology—the parent material from which the soil developed; 2) the climate during soils development, especially soil temperature and moisture regimes; 3) the nature of the organic materials in the soil, reflecting the influence of the biota, particularly vegetation; 4) the relief, reflecting local physiography; and 5) the time over which the soil developed.

Soil Taxonomy

Soils may be differentiated and classified in many ways; the two major approaches in recent years have been by soil genesis or development (inferential classification) and by diagnostic soils properties (taxonomy). The taxonomy classification system presented here depends largely on soil properties that can be observed in the field or laboratory. It is commonly referred to as the Soil Taxonomy system and has been adopted by the U.S.D.A. Soil Conservation Service. Table 13 facilitates comparison between the two systems.

Soil orders. Of the ten soil orders which have worldwide distribution, seven, comprising a total of twelve dominant suborders, are shown on the map on pages 68-69. Soil orders are the highest taxonomic category and are generalized by common properties, including horizon development and pattern, color, soil moisture, and degree of oxidation. Hence, the distinguishing characteristics selected for the orders tend to give a broad climatic grouping of soils. Soil orders have the suffix *-sol*. The formative element of the order name is usually descriptive, e.g., *Aridisols* are soils developed in areas with little moisture.

Suborders. Each order is subdivided into suborders primarily on the basis of characteristics which produce classes with the greatest genetic homogeneity. These characteristics include moisture regime, temperature, mineralogy, color, texture, and horizon properties. Altogether, 47 suborders have been identified; the twelve dominant suborders in the Pacific Northwest are shown on the map. Suborder nomenclature employs a prefix for that characteristic which is important in defining the suborders and a suffix derived from the appropriate order name, e.g., *Argids* are soils in the Aridisol order with argillic or clay horizons.

Great groups. The great group level attempts to consider the soil assemblage (similarity of diagnostic horizons), together with similarity of soil moisture and temperature regimes. It is the highest category evaluating the whole soil. The Soil Conservation Service recognizes 203 great groups,

---

Table 13. Soil orders in the soil taxonomy compared with examples of great soil groups in the 1938 genetic system

FORMATIVE ELEMENT OF SOIL TAXONOMY	DERIVATION OF FORMATIVE ELEMENT	EXAMPLES OF GREAT SOIL GROUPS IN THE 1938 GENETIC SYSTEM
Alfisols	Nonsense syllable from "pedalfer"	Gray-Brown Podzolic soils, Noncalcic Brown soils, & Planosols
Aridisols	Latin *aridus*, "dry"	Desert, Sierozem, Solonchak, Brown soils & Reddish Brown soils
Entisols	Nonsense syllable from "recent"	Azonal soils
Histisols	Greek *histos*, "tissues"	Bog soils
Inceptisols	Latin *inceptum*, "beginning"	Sol Brun Acide, Ando, Brown Forest & Jumic Grey soils
Mollisols	Latin *mollis*, "soft"	Chernozem, Chestnut, Brunizem & Brown Forest soils
Oxisols	French *oxide*, "oxide"	Laterite soils & Latosols
Spodosols	Greek *spodos*, "wood ash"	Podzols & Brown Podzolic soils
Ultisols	Latin *ultimus*, "last"	Red-Yellow Podzolic soils & Reddish-Brown Lateritic soils
Vertisols	Latin *verto*, "to turn"	Grumosols

SOURCE: Soil Conservation Service, *Soil Classification, A Comprehensive System*, 1960.

SOIL SURVEY STATUS
-1992-

Published

In Progress

Miles

Kilometers

and these are named by affixing a prefix of one or more formative elements to the suborder name. Therefore a great group will have a name of three or more syllables ending in the suborder name, e.g., Dur*argid* for an indurate, clay-layered Aridisol.

Families and series. Soil families are differentiated on the basis of properties important for utilization, especially for plant growth; soil series comprise a collection of soil individuals with essentially uniform differentiating characteristics. Soil series are given place names suggesting the fusion of the hierarchical soil taxonomy outlined above with real soils observed as soil individuals. Soil series are mapped and described in considerable detail and provide the resource manager with important information. It should be noted, however, that mapped soil series represent dominant groupings of soil individuals, while the actual region mapped will almost certainly include a minority of other soil individuals.

Type and phase. The comprehensive soil taxonomy also identifies soil type, which represents a lower category based on texture of the plow layer, and soil phase, of which texture is just one significant property distinguishing a variety of soil species.

The U.S.D.A. Soil Taxonomy has undergone several important modifications since this atlas was first published but, since these modifications have not been incorporated in revisions to soil surveys, they are not reflected in the map of soil orders. The two most notable modifications, which are likely to affect the mapping of soils in the Pacific Northwest in two important ways, are: 1) the addition of a kandic subsurface horizon and the kandi- and knaphli- great groups, and 2) the addition of a new soil order, Andisols.

A kandic horizon is similar to an argillic horizon except that it contains low-activity clays and high amounts of exchangeable aluminum, reflecting long periods of intense weathering. Because extreme weathering of clay may occur in some portions of the Coast Range and the foothills of the Cascades, it is conceivable that some soils previously classified as Haplohumults in these areas might now have the designation Kandihumults or Knaphlohumults.

Continued on page 70

SOIL ORDERS AND SUB-ORDERS

(legend below and on following page)

MILES

KILOMETERS

Inceptisols

Inceptisols are soils with weakly differentiated horizons exhibiting some alteration of the parent material, but still containing weatherable materials. The B horizon typically has little clay accumulation. In the Pacific Northwest, these soils generally occur under cool summer climate where parent materials are of late of post-Pleistocene origin and do not show translocation of clay. The order is present in the Puget Lowland, Coast Range, Cascades, and Idaho mountains. Two suborders are shown:

Umbrepts are soils with surface horizons darkened by high contents of organic matter, having crystalline clay minerals, with relatively high capacity to hold exchangeable cations but with acidic reaction, and are freely drained. They develop in areas of high winter precipitation and moderate winter temperatures in the Coast Range, Oregon Cascades, and Puget Lowland where coniferous forest is the prevailing vegetation.

1   *Cryumbrepts*—in cold regions.

2   *Haplumbrepts*—in temperate to warm regions.

Andepts are soils with high contents of volcanic ash and are therefore of low bulk density. They are of recent development, occurring in mountainous areas in Idaho and in the North Cascades under cool summer conditions.

3   *Cryandepts*—in cold regions.

Ultisols

Strong weathering and leaching and a warm (mean annual temperature 46°F), moist (40-120 inches mean annual precipitation), and a summer-dry climate help produce Ultisols. These soils have a clay-rich horizon low in bases. Ultisols develop in a variety of parent materials and usually exhibit considerable stability. This order is found in the low hilly regions between the Cascades and Coast Range, where they generally support coniferous forest growth, have good drainage, and display increasing acidity and decreasing base saturation with depth. Vegetative nutrient cycling is a key factor in the formation of these soils. Many are reddish. Two suborders are distinguished:

Humults are highly organic Ultisols developing under moist, cool to cold winters, and warm to hot dry summers. Humults show good drainage and are mostly dark colored. They develop on steep slopes, are easily eroded, and are found in southwestern Oregon and the foothills of the Cascades and Coast Range.

4   *Haplohumults*—with subsurface horizon of clay and/or weatherable minerals; in temperate climates.

Xerults are freely drained Ultisols in areas of Mediterranean climate with little organic material in the upper horizons and are seldom saturated with water. They are confined to the hilly regions in the middle portions of the Rogue and Umpqua drainages and support a mixed coniferous-broad-leaved evergreen vegetation with xeric elements.

5   *Haploxerults*—with a surface clay-rich horizon either having weatherable minerals or a decreasing clay content with depth, or both.

Mollisols

Soils that have dark-colored, friable, organic-rich surface horizons and which are high in bases, occurring in areas having a cold subhumid and semiarid climate. Mollisols are widespread in the region, especially in areas of steppe and shrub-steppe vegetation. These soils may have clay-enriched horizons, calcic horizons, sodium-rich horizons, or indurate horizons. Most soils are well drained, but wet soils may have soluble salts or high exchangeable sodium or both. Three suborders are shown:

Aquolls are Mollisols that are seasonally wet with a thick, nearly black surface horizon and gray subsurface horizon. In south-central Oregon in the Warner Valley and Klamath Lake area, horizons have been altered, but no accumulation of calcium or clay has taken place.

 Haplaquolls—with horizons in which some materials have been altered or removed, but still may contain some calcium carbonate or gypsum.

Xerolls are Mollisols in winter-moist, summer-dry climates. Such soils are continually dry for long periods of time. With irrigation and when adequate natural soil moisture is available, these soils are important for grain and forage. These are the prevailing soils in the steppe and shrub-steppe areas of the region.

 Argixerolls—with subsurface clay horizon, either thin or brownish.

Haploxerolls—with subsurface horizon high in bases, but with little clay, calcium carbonate, or gypsum.

Borolls are Mollisols of cool and cold regions exhibiting black surface horizons. In the Pacific Northwest they are confined to the extreme eastern portion of Idaho.

 Argiborolls—with subsurface clay horizon, in cool regions.

Aridisols

As suggested by the name, this order occurs in dry areas where the soils are never moist for periods of more than three consecutive months. The soils are low in organic content and the horizons are light in color and have a soft consistency when dry. These soils are found in the rainshadow area of the Cascades and in extensive areas in southern Idaho. Two suborders are shown:

Orthids are Aridisols that display accumulations of calcium carbonate and other salts but do not have clay accumulations in horizons. Such soils are found in scattered localities in the drier areas of the Pacific Northwest.

Calciorthids—with a horizon containing much calcium carbonate or gypsum.

Camborthids—with horizons from which some materials have been removed or altered, but still contain calcium carbonate or gypsum.

Argids are Aridisols distinguished by a horizon in which clay has accumulated. These are mostly found in the Snake River Plain to the south of Boise.

Haplargids—with loamy horizon of clay, without sodium (alkali) accumulation, but may have calcium accumulation below the argillic horizon.

Natrargids—with a clay accumulation horizon and alkali (sodium) accumulation.

Entisols

Soils in this order exhibit little or no horizon development. In the Pacific Northwest these soils develop in sandy parent material and are of very recent origin on gently sloping terrain. They continue to receive parent material. They occur east of the Cascade Range. One suborder is shown on the map:

Psamments are Entisols with loamy fine sand to coarser sand texture developing in areas of shifting to stabilized sand dunes. Sand origin is largely fluvial but with local redeposition by wind.

 Torripsamments—moist for less than three consecutive months and developing under cool to warm soil temperatures promoting soluble salt accumulation.

Xeropsamments—freely drained soils developing from weatherable materials under moist-winter, dry-summer climates.

Alfisols

Soils in this order are differentiated by clay-enriched horizons, moderate organic matter accumulation, and a gray to brown color. They are usually leached and are acidic occurring where at least three months of growing season are cool and moist. Three areas are dominated by Alfisols: the hilly region north of Portland; the area northeast of Moscow; and the mountains near the eastern boundary of Idaho. Two suborders are shown:

Udalfs are Alfisols with a mesic or warm temperature regime and are almost always moist despite periods of summer dryness. These soils are brownish or reddish. The area north of Portland in which Udalfs prevail has a complex of other soils as well. The Udalf area in Idaho occurs in steep mountainous terrain.

Hapludalfs—with subsurface clay horizon below a thin eluvial horizon. These are good farming soils.

Boralfs are found in cool and cold regions and may be water-saturated in winter. A bleached eluvial horizon often grades into a horizon containing clay or alkali. They occur in the mountains of eastern Idaho.

Cryoboralfs—in cold regions; with sandy upper layers, grayish color, and subsurface clay horizon.

Vertisols

Relegated to this order are clayey soils that have wide, deep cracks which form during the dry season. They occur in areas with marked dry-wet periods. One suborder is present:

Xererts are Vertisols that have wide, deep cracks that open and close once a year, remaining open for more than two months in summer and closing for more than two months in winter. In the Pacific Northwest, one area in the vicinity of Medford is characterized by this suborder.

Chromoxererts—with a brownish surface horizon.

More importantly, most of the soils mapped as Cryandepts and perhaps other soil great groups in the Pacific Northwest may well be reclassified in the new order Andisols. Andisols are soils which have andic soil properties throughout a depth of 14 inches or more in subhorizons which may be buried but are within 24 inches of the soil surface. Andic soil properties are low bulk density, high aluminum and iron oxide content, and high phosphate retention, characteristic of volcanic ash and the weathering products of other volcanic materials. Since many of the soils of the Cascades, Coast Range, and mountains of Idaho are dominated by volcanic materials, many soils in these areas may eventually be remapped as Andisols.

Soil Survey Status

The map on page 67 shows the status of soil surveys in the Pacific Northwest as of 1992. Soil surveys for agricultural, engineering, and planning purposes are made cooperatively by federal and state government personnel, usually with the U.S.D.A. Soil Conservation Service in charge and the agricultural experiment stations attached to land-grant universities as chief contributors. Other agencies, including Bureau of Land Management, Bureau of Indian Affairs, Bureau of Reclamation (irrigation suitability studies), Forest Service, and state forest departments, may enter into cooperative agreements. This joint effort, initiated in 1899, is referred to as the National Cooperative Soil Survey.

Modern soil surveys are extensive documents describing the geography of the region's soils, normally on a county basis, initiated on a priority basis depending on the presence of productive agricultural lands. Soil maps on a scale of 1:20,000 based on air photos and soils series descriptions are qualified by pedological notes. The surveys include sections on use and management of soils for a variety of purposes.

Water Resources

KEITH W. MUCKLESTON

The Pacific Northwest, considered as a whole, appears to be richly endowed with water. The volume of runoff from the region exceeds that of any other major water resources region in the conterminous United States, surpassing most regions manyfold. In terms of per capita runoff, the relative position of the region is even more favorable. The utility of the resource is diminished, however, by marked variations in spatial and temporal patterns of supply.

Supply

The most significant source of fresh water within the Pacific Northwest is the Columbia River system. Rising in the Rocky Mountains of the United States and Canada, this system provides drainage for approximately 75 percent of the region and accounts for about 55 percent of the total runoff.

When runoff from Canada is included, the Columbia system discharges approximately 65 percent of the total.

East of the Cascade Range, the Columbia Basin is divided into seven sub-basins (see map below). Much of the land is subhumid to arid, and traversed by rivers that originate in various mountain ranges lying both within and to the north and northeast of the region. The Rocky Mountains are the source of much of the flow.

Three additional sub-basins east of the Cascade Range are not part of the Columbia system. A number of streams in Oregon with internal drainage are designated as the Oregon Closed Basin, and portions of the Klamath and Bear rivers also drain small parts of the region. The Klamath rises in Oregon, flows through northern California, and discharges into the Pacific Ocean. Waters of the

DRAINAGE BASINS AND SUB-BASINS

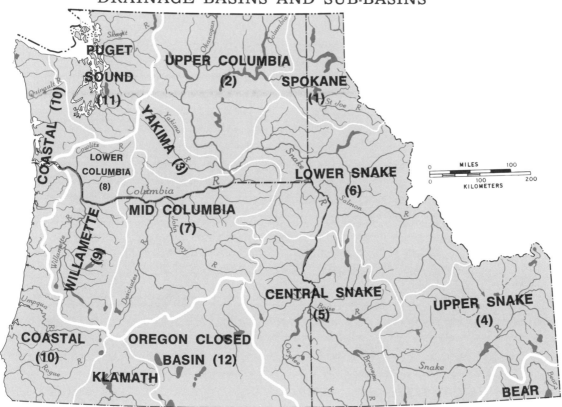

Bear River rise in Utah and Wyoming before crossing southeastern Idaho, and finally discharge into Utah's Great Salt Lake.

Of the four humid sub-basins west of the Cascade Range, two—the Willamette and Lower Columbia—are part of the Columbia River system, while the streams of the Coastal and Puget Sound sub-basins discharge into waters of the Pacific Ocean.

The relative discharge of some regional rivers is shown in Table 14. The runoff value for an area is derived by subtracting evapotranspiration and deep percolation from the amount of precipitation received. The values on the map below refer to the mean annual depths in inches of water entering streams and rivers as surface flow from locations along the various isolines. The depths of runoff from areas between the isolines may be inferred.

The Pacific Northwest may be divided into two subregions based on runoff characteristics. West of the Cascade Mountains, runoff is generally high, reflecting relatively heavy precipitation and

Table 14. Discharge of selected rivers in the Pacific Northwest

RIVER	MILLIONS OF ACRE-FEET/YR
Columbia	180.1
Columbia (at The Dalles)	133.7
Snake	36.8
Willamette	23.8
Rogue	11.3
Skagit	10.3

moderate levels of evapotranspiration. Indeed, the yield of runoff west of the Cascades is unrivaled in the conterminous United States. Yields of more than 80 inches are common in the Coast and Cascade ranges, while some of the windward slopes of the Olympic Mountains contribute more than 160 inches. Streams west of the Cascades produce about two-thirds of the total runoff from the Pacific Northwest although they drain less than one-fourth of the region.

SURFACE RUNOFF

Runoff In
Mean Annual Inches

By contrast, the much larger subregion east of the Cascade Range generates markedly lower levels of runoff, contributing less than 10 inches per square mile, and most of the surface waters originate in relatively small mountainous areas. The position of mountains can be identified on the map by locating areas of relatively high runoff (20 inches or more). For example, the Blue Mountains in northeastern Oregon and southeastern Washington, the Wallowa Mountains in northeastern Oregon, and the Bitterroot and Coeur d'Alene mountains along the northeastern border of Idaho stand out as islands of relatively high runoff.

The map on this page indicates that about one-half of the Pacific Northwest is underlain by aquifers with moderate to large potential yields of groundwater. The potential value of this source is great because it generally coincides with areas of heavy water use. At present, aquifers in the Snake River Plain account for most of the groundwater use in the region, although extensive withdrawals are also made in some parts of the Puget Sound and Willamette sub-basins.

The map on page 74 illustrates that the patterns of temporal distribution of surface runoff vary considerably within the region. The hydrographs show average monthly discharges as a percentage of the

MAJOR AQUIFERS

MAJOR AQUIFERS

Alluvial And Sedimentary Deposits

Volcanic Rocks

Alluvial, Sedimentary, And Volcanic Rocks

yearly average. If the runoff remained constant throughout the year, 8.33 percent would be discharged each month.

Until recent decades the temporal patterns of runoff largely reflected natural phenomena within a river basin including: the mean elevation of the drainage basin; its location in either marine or continental subregions of the Pacific Northwest; the type and extent of natural vegetation within the drainage basin; and the structure of aquifer units underlying the basin. Although the combined effects of natural phenomena remain dominant in most river basins within the region, anthropogenic influences have become more important in some basins during recent decades of increasingly intensive water use. Principal anthropogenic influences include stream flow depletions from extensive irrigation withdrawals and the construction and operation of large dams and storage reservoirs, the major purpose of which is to reduce temporal variations of runoff.

Columbia River. The hydrograph of the Columbia River at The Dalles, Oregon, reflects average discharge conditions for a 35-year period from 1930-65. It shows that a disproportionately high percentage of discharge takes place during the late spring and early summer. This pattern results because most of the precipitation above The Dalles falls on the various ranges of the Rocky Mountains stretching from northwestern Wyoming through Idaho and western Montana and far into British Columbia. Although most of this precipitation takes place in the late autumn and winter, it is retained in the mountainous headwater areas of the Columbia in the form of snow and ice, being released months later as melt water.

Since the late 1960s this hydrograph has been somewhat modified by the provision of large volumes of upstream storage. Thus the mean flows of May, June, and July, although still noticeably higher than those of other months, are reduced while, conversely, the mean discharge levels in the late fall and winter are increased by the release of stored water.

Salmon River. The hydrograph for the Salmon River illustrates the mean monthly discharge for a 55-year period of record from 1910-65. In this case the combined discharge of May and June constitutes approximately one-half of the yearly total. The July discharge as a percentage of the total is somewhat less than that of the Columbia River because the more southerly location of the Salmon drainage basin results in an earlier period of maximum runoff. Very little storage or irrigation development in the Salmon River Basin means that the monthly pattern of discharge in the 1990s remains essentially as shown.

Snake River. The hydrograph of the Snake River at Milner, Idaho, reflects the headwater conditions in the Middle Rockies as well as anthropogenic modifications. The relatively heavy spring runoff is characteristic of a snowmelt regime, but occurs earlier than those in the Salmon and Columbia river drainages because of a more southerly location. Heavy irrigation use above Milner further reduces the already modest summer flows.

Deschutes River. The unusually moderate temporal variation of runoff in the Deschutes Basin reflects the fact that much of it is underlain with porous basalts. These basaltic and andesitic volcanic rocks of Quaternary and late Tertiary age absorb potentially high runoff and later release it when discharge would otherwise fall to much lower levels. Provision of storage and irrigation development have not notably altered the hydrograph at its confluence with the Columbia, but significant modifications are present in some other reaches of the system.

Willamette River. The temporal flow regime of the Willamette River is representative of many rivers west of the Cascades in both Washington and Oregon. Runoff reflects the temporal distribution of precipitation because relatively little is retained as ice and snow. The Willamette hydrograph is compiled from a 55-year period of record (1909-66) and the temporal distribution of present flows has been modified somewhat by the completion of many flood-control reservoirs since the end of World War II. While the high mean flows of the winter months have remained practically unchanged and those of March and April have been reduced somewhat, the low mean flows of July, August, and September have been increased appreciably.

Skagit River. This hydrograph is atypical of rivers west of the Cascades. Relatively higher mean flows occur in June and July because much of the runoff originates at high elevations in the North Cascades of Washington and British Columbia. Since completion of Ross Dam by Seattle City Light in 1949, considerable reservoir storage space reduces summer high flows while increasing flows during the winter when energy demands are highest.

Water Use

Water uses may be divided into two major categories: offstream uses which divert water out of its channel before use, and instream uses which utilize water within stream banks.

Offstream uses include rural domestic use, stock watering, irrigation, public water supply (municipal, commercial, and light industrial), self-supplied industrial, and thermoelectric cooling. The map on page 77 illustrates the spatial variation of the four most important offstream uses.

Irrigation is clearly the dominant offstream use in the Pacific Northwest, accounting for about ten times the combined volumes of water withdrawn by public supply, industry, and thermoelectric power plants. In nine of the fourteen sub-basins for which data are shown, irrigation withdrawals represent more than 80 percent of the total. In the Upper Snake sub-basin alone, agricultural withdrawals are several times those by all public suppliers and industries in the Pacific Northwest. Irrigation withdrawals are even significant in some of the relatively humid sub-basins west of the Cascades where population and water-using industries are concentrated. Here normally dry summers require supplemental irrigation for many types of crops. In the Willamette and Coastal sub-basins irrigation withdrawals account for approximately 28 and 62 percent respectively of total withdrawals.

Withdrawals by public suppliers are relatively significant in the populous Puget Sound and Willamette sub-basins, accounting for about 84 and 42 percent of the total, respectively.

Self-supplied industrial withdrawals in the Lower Columbia sub-basin comprise approximately 80 percent of the total. The distribution of industrial withdrawals reflects in large measure the location of the pulp and paper industry, which is concentrated in the Lower Columbia, Puget Sound, and Coastal sub-basins. Food processing is usually the most significant industrial use of water east of the Cascades, but primary metals are significant in the Clark Fork—Kootenai—Spokane and Mid-Columbia sub-basins. Unlike many other major water resources regions in the United States, withdrawals for cooling thermoelectric plants are relatively unimportant. In the Hanford area, however, thermonuclear power plants withdraw an appreciable volume of surface water for cooling.

Instream uses comprise the other major division of water use and include generation of hydroelectric energy, navigation, fish and wildlife habitat, waste carriage and assimilation, recreation, preservation of wild and scenic rivers, and aesthetic appreciation. Unlike other regions of the western United States, water utilization in the Pacific Northwest is characterized by heavy dependence on instream uses, especially for the generation of hydroelectric energy. The Pacific Northwest is the nation's leading producer of hydropower, in the early 1990s utilizing an average 1,250 billion gallons per day for that purpose. This volume is several times larger than the total runoff of the region because the same water is used repeatedly at successive dams and powerhouses along several large rivers. For example, in the U.S. the mainstem of the Columbia River includes eleven large dams with hydroelectric generating facilities. For more detail on hydroelectric generation see the following chapter on energy resources.

Navigation is another major instream use. Large expenditures by the federal government have been made to enhance inland water navigation on the Columbia System. From the Bonneville Locks at river mile 145 to the Port of Lewiston in Idaho, a chain of eight reservoirs stretches 320 miles, which not only allows slack water navigational conditions for inland water carriers but also guarantees a navigation channel of 15 feet depth. Navigation locks at the eight dams lift barge tows from 8 feet above mean sea level at the Bonneville lock to 738 feet on the reservoir reaching Lewiston, Idaho. The eight dams are equipped with large single lift locks, the dimensions of which are 86 by 675 feet. If congressional action extends commercial navigation up the Columbia to Wenatchee, the existing Public Utility District dams will be retrofitted with navigation locks matching those on the Columbia-Snake system. Such an extension does not, however, appear probable for environmental and economic reasons.

Early concerns to promote navigation have altered hydrologic conditions even though navigation is no longer significant on some rivers. The situation on the Willamette is a case in point. Although there is no longer commercial navigation on the river above Willamette Falls, releases of water from flood-control reservoirs continue to be made in accordance with a 1938 Act which directs that releases be adequate to maintain a flow of 6,000 cubic feet/second for navigation at Salem. During the normal low water months of July-September these releases coincidentally contribute significantly to improved water quality in the Willamette.

SURFACE WATER WITHDRAWALS

WITHDRAWALS
Acre Feet/Day

25,000
10,000
5000
2500
1000
500

Thermoelectric Cooling — Agricultural

Industrial/ Mining — Public Supply

numbers refer to sub-basins

Another significant flow use is the maintenance of fish and wildlife habitat. Water resource developments in the region have affected aquatic life markedly. Although enhancement of habitat sometimes results, the consequences have more frequently been negative. Inadequate consideration of biological factors during project design and/or operation have resulted in severe losses. Animal communities, especially fur bearers, have in general been negatively impacted by the development of water resources. On the other hand, one very large irrigation project (the Columbia Basin Project) has greatly enhanced the habitat for migratory waterfowl by creating many lakes and extensive marshes in a semiarid area.

Valuable anadromous fisheries (salmon and steelhead) have been adversely affected by the development of water resources. This is particularly evident in the Columbia-Snake system. The once bountiful natural runs that were thought to be inexhaustible have declined sharply and some have even disappeared. Remaining runs are the focus of controversy among competing interests: between sports, commercial, and Indian fishers; between the states of the Pacific Northwest; and, more recently, between the U.S. and other countries.

Hatchery programs have mitigated some of the losses. Indeed, hatchery fish now far outnumber wild stocks. Hatchery programs are less successful above the confluence of the Columbia and Snake rivers, however, because of the cumulative effects of losses at dams below the hatcheries. Over the last several years some runs of anadromous salmonids have been listed under the Endangered Species Act and approximately 40,000 miles of streams and rivers reserved for anadromous fish habitat. If anadromous fisheries are to be substantially increased over the present low levels, some reduction in the future output of hydropower, irrigated agriculture, and perhaps other water-related goods and services probably will be necessary.

Another instream use of water is by recreationists. Many outdoor recreational activities are water oriented. The region has a disproportionately large per capita supply of surface waters suitable for outdoor recreation and all types of recreational uses of water in the Pacific Northwest have grown rapidly over the last four decades.

The Pacific Northwest has a disproportionately large number of rivers designated under the Wild and Scenic Rivers Act. As shown in the chapter covering recreation, many of the wild and scenic rivers are in rugged and remote parts of the region—locations ideal for upstream storage. Implementation of the Wild and Scenic Rivers Program requires tradeoffs. Superior aesthetic/leisure-time experiences, white-water recreation, and scientific benefits are gained at the expense of such traditional benefits as slack-water recreation, hydroelectric generation, and provision of upstream storage. For example, over twenty million acre-feet of storage is foregone at major potential storage sites in existing and study river areas.

One of the principal instream uses of water is to carry away, dilute, and assimilate wastes. When the ratio of wastes to the volume of receiving waters is small, assimilation of organic wastes and adequate dilution of many other waste products takes place. In such instances, water quality is not seriously impaired, and this was the case in the early settlement period of the region. During the twentieth century, however, the rapid growth of population and economic productivity in the Pacific Northwest have caused the volume and variety of wastes deposited in the region's waters to increase markedly. This has overtaxed the capacity of some of the receiving waters to assimilate and/or dilute wastes. The result is poor water quality (pollution) in some of the region's surface waters. In some tributaries of the Columbia-Snake system east of the Cascades, heavy irrigation withdrawals and consumptive use also reduce the assimilative capacity of the streams.

Improved treatment by industries—especially in chemical recovery—has been chiefly responsible for decreased levels of biochemical oxygen demand in the region, thus freeing up oxygen for fish and other aquatic life. However, there is an apparent widespread increase in the presence of organic and inorganic toxins from non-point sources of pollution, including over 20 million acre-feet of irrigation return flows. In addition, water quality problems exist downstream from densely populated areas, including excessive counts of coliform bacteria and low levels of dissolved oxygen. Although the region has few problems associated with siltation, erosion of the loess-mantled Palouse Hills creates undesirable levels of turbidity and turbine scour at some of the generating plans on the lower Snake River.

Thermal pollution is considered a serious problem in some river reaches because anadromous salmonids have a low tolerance to temperatures exceeding 68°F. Such temperatures are occasionally encountered, for example, in reaches of the lower Snake River and in the Yakima sub-basin.

Despite considerable flood storage, levee construction, and channel improvements, much riverine land remains susceptible to inundation. Unregulated flows on some tributaries of the Columbia and in the Puget Sound and Coastal sub-basins contribute to continued losses. Another contributing factor is the continued conversion of flood-prone lands to more intensive uses. This is particularly significant in the Puget Sound sub-basin.

Transboundary Water Management

Transboundary water management in the Pacific Northwest is significant because rivers cross jurisdictional boundaries at many points in the region, potentially carrying negative and/or positive attributes with them. Actions by water managers upstream may significantly alter the quantity, quality, and/or timing of runoff in the rivers of a downstream jurisdiction. Conversely, water management downstream may affect those upstream through creation of impoundments that encroach into the upstream area or by limiting access of migratory fish or barge traffic to upstream areas. Water-related externalities such as these may involve both national and subnational jurisdictions in the region.

International water management. The Columbia River system is shared by seven U.S. states and the Canadian province of British Columbia. The Columbia's drainage area in Canada comprises 15.4 percent of the total watershed but contributes 30.6 percent of the total runoff. British Columbia contributes about as much runoff to the Columbia-Snake system as the combined input from Idaho, Montana, Wyoming, Nevada, and Utah.

Cooperation between the U.S. and Canada results from a treaty finalized in 1964, under the terms of which the U.S. and Canada agree to the principle of sharing downstream benefits. Canada provides storage capacity and in return receives one-half of the value of the resulting benefits accruing to the U.S. In 1964, Canada received a lump-sum payment of $254 million as its share of

Dams

Existing or under construction

(Army Corps of Engineers
(Bureau of Reclamation
(Non-Federal public
(Non-Federal private
(Other

Natural lake with
storage control

Columbia drainage
boundary

**TRANSBOUNDARY
WATER MANAGEMENT**

anticipated increased hydroelectric generation in the U.S. over a 30-year period. In addition, the U.S. paid Canada $64 million for 60 years of reduced flood damages which will result from Canadian storage.

The U.S. and Canada both benefit from the cooperative development of the Columbia River system. Cooperative development has markedly increased hydroelectric output, while also decreasing flood damage in both countries. This was achieved for the most part through provision of large storage reservoirs in Canada which reduce high flows from snow melt in the late spring and early summer and in-

crease flows during the October to March period when the regional demand for electrical energy is high. The graph of the Columbia River's annual flow cycle before additions of large increments of upstream storage is shown on page 74.

In the early 1990s negotiations were underway over details of sharing future hydroelectric benefits on the Columbia. Both Canadian storage and contribution to total runoff are very important to hydroelectric output in the Pacific Northwest. Most of the region's total hydroelectric generating capacity is installed on the mainstem of the Columbia River at eleven dams from Grand Coulee to Bonneville Dam (see map of electric generating facilities on page 82). On this 725-mile reach of the Columbia, 19,000 Mw of generating capacity have been installed, much of it since the treaty to take advantage of increased flows from storage releases during the autumn and winter seasons. Canada contributes significantly to the total volume of water flowing in this major power-producing reach of the Columbia River: approximately three-quarters of the flow at Grand Coulee and two-fifths of the total river flow at Bonneville Dam.

Cooperative development of the Columbia River also creates important flood damage reduction benefits in both countries. The major benefits in the U.S. are in the Portland-Vancouver area. Here total storage in the system—much of it in Canada—is projected to reduce record flood flows by 45 percent. In Canada, the principal flood damage reduction benefits are along a major tributary, the Kootenay (Kootenai in the U.S.), which rises in Canada and then swings through Montana and Idaho before flowing back into Canada. The 1964 treaty allowed the U.S. to build Libby Dam on the Kootenai River in Montana, which provides flood control and hydropower benefits downstream in Canada. The dam also backs water across the U.S.-Canadian border and many miles into British Columbia, which Canada agreed to allow under the terms of the treaty. It is noteworthy that Libby Dam also provides flood crest reduction benefits on the U.S. side of the border, as well as increasing hydropower output in the autumn-winter period at downstream power plants in Canada and the Pacific Northwest.

The Ross Dam agreement is another example of innovative cooperation. Seattle City Light wanted to increase the output of hydroelectric generation at its Ross Dam facility by increasing the height of the structure. But doing this would have caused the existing reservoir to encroach onto Canadian territory, which was strongly resisted by British Columbia. A solution was reached when the provincial utility, BC Hydro, agreed to supply Seattle City Light with the electrical energy that increasing the height of the dam would have provided. This energy is supplied in return for payment to BC Hydro of the funds Seattle would have expended on increasing the height of the dam.

The United States and Canada have made commendable progress on cooperative transboundary water management, but challenges remain. For example, how will water quality be maintained on the U.S. reach of the North Fork Flathead River after a large Canadian open-pit mine located upstream in that watershed goes into operation? Maintenance of good water quality is critical for U.S. interests because the North Fork Flathead River is part of the National Wild and Scenic River System.

Intraregional water management. There is also need for increased transboundary water management within the Pacific Northwest. Idaho, Montana, Utah, and Wyoming are usually considered to be the upstream states while Washington and Oregon are downstream. Water management in one part of the region can have repercussions on water users in others. For example, if new large-scale irrigation developments are undertaken in Idaho's Snake River Plain, the quantity of water available for hydropower is diminished in the downstream states of Washington and Oregon. Conversely, salmon harvest in reaches of the Columbia system in Washington and Oregon adversely affect fishing interests in Idaho.

Relative to international agreements on transboundary management issues, little has been done within the region. Over the last several decades, sporadic attempts by states in the Pacific Northwest to allocate waters of the Columbia-Snake system between them have been unsuccessful. Only piecemeal progress has been made: Idaho and Wyoming have concluded an interstate compact on division of the Snake River while Oregon and California have done the same for the Klamath River. Much progress remains to be made if present transboundary water management issues are to be resolved.

Energy Resources and Distribution

STEVEN R. KALE & B. ALEXANDER SIFFORD III

During the early 1980s, growth in the demand for energy in the Pacific Northwest slowed considerably from the 1970s. By the late 1980s and into the early 1990s, economic recovery and in-migration contributed to moderate to moderately high rates of growth in regional energy demand and consumption. Increasing demands for energy are leading to renewed concerns about future supplies and trade-offs between resource development and environmental impacts.

Hydroelectricity

Hydroelectricity accounts for nearly half the energy consumed in the Pacific Northwest, and for about 90 percent of the electricity generated. While just over 3 percent of the nation's population lives in the region, 40 to 50 percent of the national consumption of hydroelectricity occurs here.

Much of the region's hydroelectricity comes from generating facilities at Columbia River Basin dams built by the U.S. Bureau of Reclamation, the Army Corps of Engineers, and others (see map on page 82). Of the eleven dams and generating facilities on the main stem of the Columbia, the largest is Grand Coulee in northeastern Washington. Generating capacity at Grand Coulee is

Continued on page 84

ELECTRICITY GENERATION
-1991-

Coal · Other · Hydro

PACIFIC NORTHWEST ELECTRICITY EXPORTS AND IMPORTS
1970 - 1990

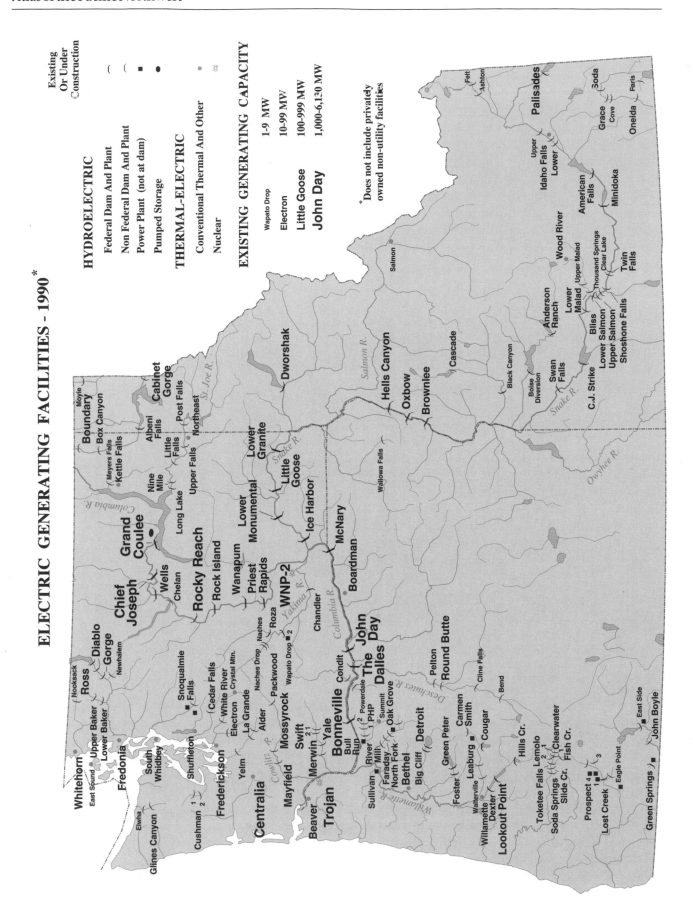

ELECTRIC GENERATING FACILITIES - 1990 *

HYDROELECTRIC

Federal Dam And Plant

Non Federal Dam And Plant

Power Plant (not at dam)

Pumped Storage

THERMAL-ELECTRIC

Conventional Thermal And Other

Nuclear

Existing Or Under Construction

EXISTING GENERATING CAPACITY

Wapato Drop   1-9 MW

Electron   10-99 MW

Little Goose   100-999 MW

John Day   1,000-6,120 MW

*Does not include privately owned non-utility facilities

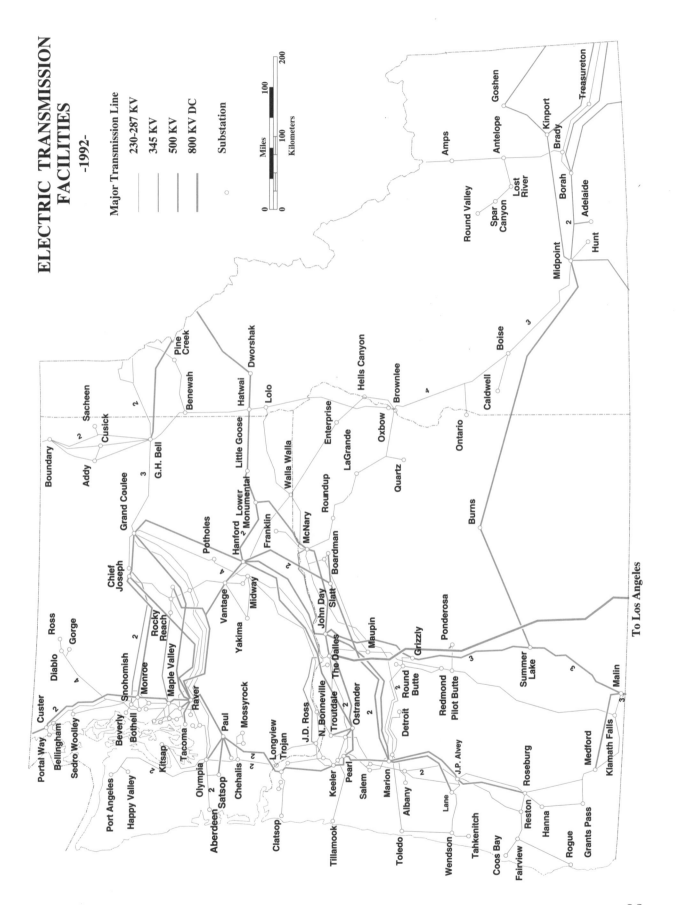

ELECTRIC TRANSMISSION FACILITIES
-1992-

Major Transmission Line
230-287 KV
345 KV
500 KV
800 KV DC

Substation

about 6,500 megawatts, which exceeds the total capacity in fifteen states and is over five times as much as at the Washington Nuclear Plant-2 near Hanford, Washington. Hydro facilities also are located on streams outside the Columbia River system in western Oregon, western Washington, and southeastern Idaho.

Electricity generated at federal system dams is marketed by the Bonneville Power Administration (BPA), a subagency of the U.S. Department of Energy. The BPA wholesales electricity to utility districts and cooperatives, investor-owned utilities, and selected industrial customers, the largest of which are companies in the aluminum industry.

Consumption of hydroelectricity varies considerably from year to year. When production exceeds needs, as it did during much of the 1970s and 1980s, the region is a net exporter of electricity, nearly all from hydro plants. During the late 1980s, however, the region was a net importer of electricity, most of which was derived from non-hydro sources.

Transmission lines move electricity to destinations within and outside the region. The

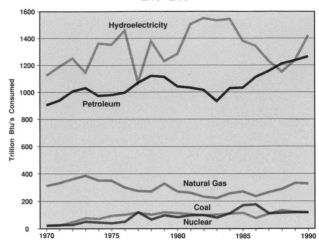

PACIFIC NORTHWEST ANNUAL ENERGY CONSUMPTION
1970 - 1990

Note: Negative values for "other" represent exports of electricity from the region. Positive values represent imports.

PIPELINES AND REFINERIES - 1990

transmission line network is most developed between generating facilities and major population centers (see map on page 83). Currently, the Pacific Northwest and Pacific Southwest exchange electricity seasonally: the Pacific Northwest exports power in summer and imports it in winter. Transmission lines also import electricity from Montana, North Dakota, Wyoming, and Canada.

Most, if not all, of the region's sites for large hydroelectric facilities have been developed. Any future additions to hydroelectric capacity likely will occur through increased efficiency, since the development of new small-scale hydro systems is restricted by concerns about protection of habitat for fish and wildlife. About 44,000 miles of streams in the Pacific Northwest are now protected from future hydroelectric development. Stringent criteria are in place to protect fish and wildlife habitat in and near streams still available for development.

Agreements between the U.S. and Canada determine costs and coordination of hydroelectric development in the entire Columbia River Basin. Expiration of these agreements could lead to substantial changes in the availability of hydroelectricity from Canada. Under one agreement that expires in 1998 about 500 megawatts of Canadian hydroelectricity is sold annually to the U.S. Another agreement expiring in 2003 stipulates how the Columbia River hydropower system will be coordinated between the two countries.

Petroleum

During most of the 1970s and 1980s, petroleum was second to hydro, accounting for about 40 percent of the Pacific Northwest's energy consumption. The transportation sector uses about 75 percent of the region's consumption of petroleum; another 20 percent is attributable to the industrial sector.

No petroleum is produced in the Pacific Northwest. Regional crude oil supplies are obtained via the Trans-Mountain Pipeline from Canada, and ocean tankers, primarily from Alaska but also from other sources, such as Indonesia and the Middle East. Refineries in Anacortes, Ferndale, and Tacoma, Washington, process the crude oil into gasoline and other products. The region also imports finished petroleum products from Montana and Wyoming by tanker and pipeline, and from Utah by pipeline. Finished products are transported away from pipelines primarily by barges and trucks.

It has been estimated that 50 to 60 million barrels of petroleum might be recoverable from deposits off Pacific Northwest coasts, though none has yet been found. In part due to opposition from various regional groups, former president George Bush in 1990 banned new off-shore oil leasing until the year 2000.

Natural gas

Natural gas accounts for about 10 percent of the Pacific Northwest's energy consumption, with just under 50 percent used by the industrial sector, and 20 percent each by the residential and commercial sectors.

Northwest Pipeline Corporation serves all regional investor-owned utilities. Pacific Gas Transmission Company, which primarily serves customers in California, also provides natural gas to the Pacific Northwest. Most of the region's natural gas comes from Canada and the San Juan Basin in Colorado. Nearly all new gas supplies come from Canada.

Northwest Natural Gas Co. produces about 3 percent of Oregon's natural gas needs from a field northwest of Portland near the small community of Mist. Production is declining, and empty reservoirs are now being used for natural gas storage.

Natural gas also is produced at sewage-treatment plants and former landfill sites. Natural gas from biomass is termed biogas, which is more dilute than natural gas and typically must be processed before it can be used. Most cities over 40,000 population have sewage-treatment plants that use biogas for heating or generating electricity.

Biogas facilities at landfill sites include Northwest Natural Gas Company's biogas recovery project at the Rossman Landfill near Oregon City, Oregon, and the Emerald People's Utility District Short Mountain Project near Eugene, Oregon. The Rossman Landfill project began operating in 1984. The facility collects and processes gas on-site, and uses it in adjacent county shops for heating. Until 1990, Rossman's gas was cleaned and fed directly into the pipeline grid. Peak gas production was the equivalent of about 3,700 homes. The Short Mountain landfill gas project began operating in 1992. Gas is converted to electricity on-site and then delivered to the equivalent of between seven and eight hundred homes.

Deregulation of natural gas prices and higher electicity costs have led many consumers in the Pacific Northwest to switch to natural gas. Several of the region's electrical utilities have advocated fuel switching due to the high costs of obtaining additional supplies of electricity.

The Bonneville Power Administration and several utilities are planning to develop gas-fired power plants to meet future electricity needs. Development of such facilities is controversial because using gas to generate electricity is less efficient than using it directly for heating. Concerns remain about future supplies of gas, leading to recommendations to design natural gas-fired plants to operate on other fuels, such as fuel oil or coal, if natural gas becomes too expensive or unavailable.

Natural gas-fired plants also produce steam for industrial processing and generating electricity. This application is termed cogeneration. Most current cogeneration capacity in the Pacific Northwest is located at pulp and paper mills.

Coal

Coal provides 3 to 4 percent of the Pacific Northwest's energy. About 86 percent of the region's consumption of coal is used to generate electricity; another 12 percent is used in the industrial sector.

PacifiCorp operates a 1310-megawatt coal-fired facility near Centralia, Washington. This facility is fueled by nearby deposits extracted from an open-pit mine. Portland General Electric operates a 530-megawatt coal-fired plant near Boardman, Oregon; coal for this plant is shipped by rail from Wyoming. The Pacific Northwest also imports electricity from coal-fired facilities outside the region, primarily in Montana and Wyoming.

Nuclear energy

From the mid-1970s to the early 1990s, nuclear fuels accounted for 3 to 4 percent of the Pacific Northwest's energy consumption. Nuclear generation of electricity began in 1984 at the 1100-megawatt Washington Nuclear Plant-2 at the Hanford Nuclear Reservation near Richland, Washington, one of five nuclear facilities started in the 1970s by the Washington Public Power Supply System. Due to enormously high cost overruns and the regional oversupply of electricity, construction of four facilities was terminated in the 1980s. Two of these facilities (WNP-4 and WNP-5) were cancelled. Two others (WNP-1 and WNP-3) are 65 to 75 percent complete and as of 1993 are being held in "preservation status" pending decisions about future energy needs, costs, safety, and other considerations.

From 1976 to late 1992, Portland General Electric operated the 1100-megawatt Trojan Nuclear Plant near Rainier, Oregon. Trojan faced considerable opposition in the 1980s and early 1990s, including several ballot measures calling for its closure. In January 1993, PGE decided to close Trojan permanently due to the high costs of replacing defective generators and the availability of replacement power.

A third nuclear power plant, the N-Reactor at the Hanford Nuclear Reservation, was operated by the U.S. Department of Energy to produce plutonium and steam for the 800-megawatt Hanford Generating Project. The N-Reactor was placed in standby condition in 1988 following a two-year shutdown.

PACIFIC NORTHWEST ELECTRICITY CONSERVATION AND EFFICIENCY IMPROVEMENT GOALS FOR THE YEAR 2000

(1500 Megawatt Total Goal)

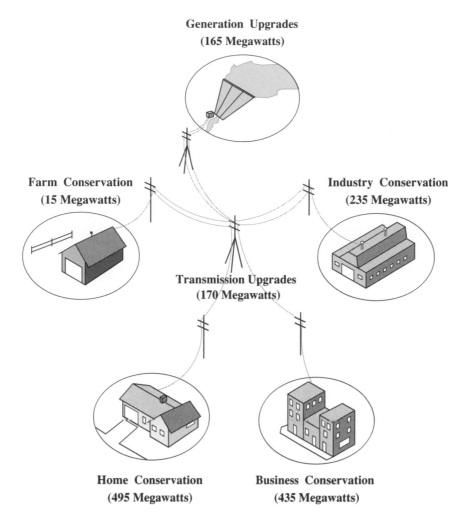

Generation Upgrades
(165 Megawatts)

Farm Conservation
(15 Megawatts)

Industry Conservation
(235 Megawatts)

Transmission Upgrades
(170 Megawatts)

Home Conservation
(495 Megawatts)

Business Conservation
(435 Megawatts)

Conservation

Conservation is an energy resource because it reduces the need to obtain new energy supplies. It is a major contributor to the Pacific Northwest's energy needs. Conservation is often defined as increased efficiency in using energy. In response to the oil embargos of the 1970s, government and utilities developed programs to encourage conservation. The biggest push for conservation in the Pacific Northwest began when the U.S. Congress passed the Pacific Northwest Power Planning and Conservation Act of 1980. The act created the Northwest Power Planning Council, which is charged with adopting a 20-year electrical power plan for the region (Idaho, Oregon, Washington, and western Montana), and with developing a pro-

gram to mitigate and enhance fish and wildlife affected by hydroelectric development in the Columbia River Basin.

Since 1980, the council has developed four editions of the power plan, the most recent of which was in 1991. The 1991 plan examines the region's electricity needs to the year 2010, and identifies specific strategies for meeting them through the year 2000. The plan identifies conservation as the cheapest way to meet the region's needs for electricity. Through the year 2000, the plan calls for the acquisition of about 1,500 average megawatts of savings, the equivalent of the combined needs of the cities of Seattle and Portland. This additional "conservation power plant" would be obtained by conserving electricity in residences, commercial

SOLAR POWER RESOURCE

Mean Annual
Hours of
Sunshine

ANNUAL AVERAGE WIND POWER

Mean Wind Speed
(at 33 Ft.)

1	<9.8 mph
2	9.9-11.5
3	11.6-12.5
4	12.6-13.4
5	13.5-14.3
6	14.4-15.7

GEOTHERMAL RESOURCES AND FACILITIES

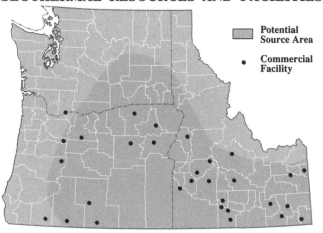

Potential
Source Area

• Commercial
Facility

buildings, industrial processes, and irrigated farming practices.

Savings sought in the 1991 plan would add to the estimated 550 average megawatts of conservation savings obtained from utility and state programs implemented during the 1980s. Additionally, existing building codes and appliance efficiency standards are expected to result in another 1,300 average megawatts of savings by the year 2010. Implementing the Power Planning Council's recommendations with existing conservation programs could result in more than 4,500 megawatts of savings by the year 2010.

Renewable energy sources

Hydroelectricity, biomass, solar, and wind are the main types of renewable sources used for energy in the Pacific Northwest. Geothermal energy also is available in the region and, if developed in small increments, is renewable. As noted earlier, hydroelectricity accounts for about half of the region's energy consumption.

Except for hydroelectricity and geothermally generated electricity, the federal government collects few data at the state level for renewable energy consumption or production. Thus it is impossible to determine how the contribution of biomass, solar, wind energy, and direct-use geothermal compares to the contribution of nonrenewable sources. Much of the following discussion is based on regionally generated information.

Biomass supplies about 10 percent of the demand for energy in the Pacific Northwest. Industrial mill-residue use and residential wood burning each account for about half of the biomass consumed. The wood products industry has long burned wood residues to provide steam for drying lumber, plywood, and other products. Most of the region's pulp mills supplement wood fuel with oil or natural gas to produce steam for industrial use. Regional generating capacity from biomass cogeneration plants is estimated to be about 660 megawatts.

Forty to fifty percent of the region's households contain wood-burning appliances, and just over 13 percent used wood as the primary heating fuel in 1990. Estimates indicate that residential wood burning displaces the equivalent of about 1,000 average megawatts of electric power in the Pacific Northwest.

In 1983, Oregon became the first state in the nation to pass a law requiring wood stoves to meet emissions limits for particulates. A similar law was passed in Washington in 1987. Subsequent state and federal legislation further identifies measures intended to improve air quality in non-attainment areas for particulates. Additionally, utilities and other groups have programs to replace older wood stoves with weatherization and either new clean-burning stoves or other types of heating systems.

Garbage and sewage are used for heating or generating electricity at several locations in the Pacific Northwest. As noted in the discussion of natural gas, landfills in Eugene and Oregon City, Oregon, supply biogas for heating and electricity, and most larger cities use biogas from sewage. Garbage also is burned in incinerators to generate electricity. The largest solid-waste incinerator in the region is at Spokane, Washington, where an 800-ton-per-day (tpd) plant has a generating capacity of 22 megawatts. Other solid-waste incinerators include a 550-tpd plant with a capacity of 11 megawatts near Brooks, Oregon; a 100-tpd plant with a capacity of 1 megawatt at Bellingham, Washington; a 180-tpd plant with a capacity of 2 megawatts in Skagit County, Washington; and a 50-megawatt plant that burns garbage, wood waste, and coal in Tacoma, Washington.

Other types of biomass fuels used in the Pacific Northwest include agricultural residues and ethanol. Agricultural residues have received increased attention in recent years as grass seed growers in the Willamette Valley and elsewhere seek ways to use straw for fuel or other products rather than burning it in the field.

Ethanol is mixed with gasoline to create an oxygenated fuel which is being sold in gasoline stations in urban areas where standards for carbon monoxide emissions are not being met. Three large ethanol plants in Washington produce over 10 million gallons annually.

Solar energy. Active and passive space and water heating are the main uses for solar energy in the Pacific Northwest. The amount of solar radiation east of the Cascade Mountains is almost as much as is available in the southwestern U.S. The contribution of solar to the region's energy needs, however, is greater west of the Cascades where most of the region's population resides. In 1990, shipments of solar collectors to the Pacific Northwest totalled about 81,000 square feet, less than 1 percent of the nation's total.

The installation of solar collectors nationally dropped dramatically with the expiration of federal solar tax credits at the end of 1985. The decline was less dramatic in Oregon, which has energy tax credit programs for solar and other types of renewable energy. Tax credit records indicate that over 14,000 solar systems have been installed in Oregon. Information from energy analysts in Idaho and Washington suggest that a total of about 35,000 solar systems have been installed in the region.

About three dozen cities and counties in the Pacific Northwest have implemented solar access ordinances to insure that access to sunlight is protected from shading by vegetation or buildings. Field investigations have shown that protection from shading and proper orientation of houses can result in energy savings of 10 to 20 percent without the installation of solar equipment. The potential for additional electricity savings from solar access protection in the Pacific Northwest has been estimated at 5 to 34 average megawatts.

Sunlight also can be converted to electricity via photovoltaic collectors, solar thermal facilities based on concentrating collectors, and salt ponds. Several small-scale photovoltaic collectors are located at demonstration facilities and remote locations throughout the Pacific Northwest. No solar-thermal power plants or salt ponds are presently in the region.

Whiskey Run Wind Farm

Wind potential is greatest in the Columbia River Gorge, along the coast, and in certain mountainous parts of the region. Considerable potential for wind energy exists in the Pacific Northwest. About 2,200 megawatts of capacity and 435 average megawatts of generation are estimated at sites in the three states. In 1992, several regional utilities announced their intent to erect 140 wind turbines by 1996 in the Rattlesnake Hills about 20 miles north of Richland, Washington. When fully operational, these turbines would produce 50 megawatts, enough electricity to serve about 9,400 homes.

The Whiskey Run Wind Farm near Bandon, Oregon, began operation with 25 wind turbines in 1983, and is the region's first and only commercial wind farm. Less-than-expected winds, machine failures, corrosion, and poor siting contributed to disappointing performance, though the operation has yielded valuable information for future coastal wind energy applications.

Geothermal resources. Known and potential geothermal resources underlie much of the region. Geothermal's direct use applications in the region include heating buildings, swimming pools, hot tubs, and baths at commercial resorts, heating and cooling water to raise plants and fish, and heating and cooling facilities for industrial purposes, such as mushroom production at the Oregon Trail Mushroom Company in Vale, Oregon. Additionally, buildings in a few locations are meeting their heating and cooling needs with heat exchangers using water from low-temperature geothermal wells.

The first large-scale use of geothermal energy in the region began with construction of the Warm Springs Heating District in Boise, Idaho, in the 1890s. In Klamath Falls, Oregon, over four hundred homes, businesses, schools, and other buildings use geothermal heat. During the early 1980s, experiments to generate electricity using geothermal water began at Raft River, Idaho. After disappointing results, the efforts were discontinued.

To help meet future needs for electricity, the Northwest Power Planning Council is calling for the development of three pilot geothermal projects. These would be located at Newberry Volcano about 35 miles south of Bend, Oregon; Vale, Oregon; and Glass Mountain in northeastern California, about 25 miles south of the Oregon border. Resource availability and cost, environmental risks, and land-use conflicts are among the issues that will be addressed in the demonstration projects.

Energy analysts believe that geothermal has considerable potential for generating electricity. Recent estimates indicate that several thousand megawatts potentially may be available at the region's most promising geothermal sites. The potential may be greatest in Oregon where the geological setting is similar to those underlying over fifty commercial geothermal plants in California, Nevada, and Utah.

Future consumption and supply of energy

Among the most important forces determining the future supply and consumption of energy in the region are population and economic growth, and fish and wildlife concerns. Growth is resulting in pressure to use more fossil fuels, primarily natural gas. Rapid growth could lead to renewed pressure for nuclear, coal, or coal-gasification facilities; such development would be highly controversial due to concerns about costs and environmental impacts.

Increased emphasis on conservation is likely. Geothermal and wind energy will be emphasized more in the 1990s, and over the long term could make a significant contribution to the region's energy needs.

Non-utility companies will increase their share of the region's energy production, most noticeably for electricity. Much of the power from independent producers will be sold to large utilities or the Bonneville Power Administration.

Concerns about wildlife and fish, especially salmon and steelhead, will continue to receive much attention. More water for salmon runs could mean less water for hydroelectricity. Reduced availability of hydroelectricity could result in higher prices for electricity. Adverse economic consequences for industrial, agricultural, and other interests could occur as past mistakes are addressed.

In recent years, global warming has become an increasingly important issue. A warmer climate in the Pacific Northwest likely would lead to less water for hydroelectricity and other uses. Greater usage of fossil fuels could accelerate the build-up of carbon dioxide and other gases that appear to cause the greenhouse effect and global warming. The success of regional, national, and international efforts to slow global warming undoubtedly will affect the long-run energy future of the region.

References

Bain, Don. *Wind Resources*. Staff Issue Paper 89-40. Portland: Northwest Power Planning Council, October 16, 1989.

Bonneville Power Administration. *1992 Conservation Resources Supply Document*. Portland, March 1992.

Chockie, A.D., D.E. Eakin, and J.C. King. *Assessment of Electric Power Conservation and Supply Resources in the Pacific Northwest*. Volume 5. *Biomass*. Richland, WA: Battelle Pacific Northwest Laboratories, 1982.

Edison Electric Institute. *Statistical Yearbook of the Electric Utility Industry 1991*. Washington, D.C., October 1992.

Elliot, D.L., and W.R. Barchet. *Wind Energy Resource Atlas*. Volume 1. *The Northwest Region*. PNL-3195 WERA-1. Richland, WA: Battelle Pacific Northwest Laboratories, 1980.

Geyer, John., L.M. Kellerman, and R.G. Bloomquist. *Geothermal Resources*. Staff Issue Paper 89-36. Portland: Northwest Power Planning Council, October 16, 1989.

Kale, Steven R. "Solar Access Protection in the Pacific Northwest," *Northwest Environmental Journal* 5, no. 2 (1989):241-69.

Kerstetter, James. *Assessment of Biomass Resources for Electric Generation in the Pacific Northwest*. Staff Issue Paper 89-41. Portland: Northwest Power Planning Council, October 16, 1989.

"Natural Gas in the Pacific Northwest: Regulation and Economics," *Pacific Northwest Executive* 4, no. 2 (1988): 9-15.

Northwest Power Planning Council. *Nuclear Resources*. Staff Issue Paper 89-43. Portland, November 3, 1989.

———. *1991 Northwest Conservation and Electric Power Plan*. Portland, April 1991.

Oregon Department of Energy. *Fourth Biennial Energy Plan*. Salem, January 1991.

"The Oil Industry in the Pacific Northwest," *Pacific Northwest Executive* 4, no. 2 (1988): 14-16.

Tonn, Bruce, and Dennis White. "Residential Wood Use Trends in the Pacific Northwest," *Energy and Systems Policy* 11, no. 3 (1987): 231-50.

U.S. Bureau of the Census. *1990 Census of Population and Housing*. Summary Tape File 3A. Washington, D.C., 1992.

U.S. Department of Energy. "Electric Power Plants in the Pacific Northwest and Adjacent Areas." Map. Portland: Bonneville Power Administration, November 1991.

———. *Inventory of Power Plants in the United States 1990*. DOE/EIA-0095(90). Washington, D.C., October 1991.

———. *Solar Collector Manufacturing Activity 1990*. DOE/EIA-0174(90). Washington, D.C., February 1992.

———. *State Energy Data Report, Consumption Estimates, 1960-1990*. DOE/EIA-0214(90). Washington, D.C., May 1992.

U.S. Department of the Interior. *The National Atlas of the United States of America*. Washington, D.C., 1970.

Agriculture

PHILIP L. JACKSON

Agriculture in the Pacific Northwest is diverse, reflecting differences in climate, topography, soils, and water supply. This broad natural resource base combined with agricultural technology has sustained a strong, varied, and adaptable agricultural economy. Agriculture in the region includes wheat and dry pea production in the Palouse, cattle and sheep grazing in the open spaces of eastern Oregon and southern Idaho, production of vegetables and grass seed in the Willamette Valley, and dairying in the Puget Lowland and in Oregon's coastal zone. High-value specialty crops such as berries, vegetables, grapes, Christmas trees, and nursery stock are grown on relatively small tracts, while cattle and sheep are grazed and forage crops are grown on extensive acreages.

Approximately 29 percent of the land area of the Pacific Northwest is in farms. For the most recent agriculture census period, 1978 through 1987, trends indicate modest decreases in the number of farms, acreage in farms, cropland in farms, and irrigated land. During this decade, the number of farms declined by 9,135, or about 9 percent. Total acreage in farms declined by nearly 2.5 million acres, approximately 4.8 percent. However, less than 1 percent decrease in farm cropland was observed. The number of irrigated acres decreased by 723,766 between the 1978 census and the 1987 census. This is a reduction of approximately 10 percent from the regional historical record of 6,995,412 acres in 1978;

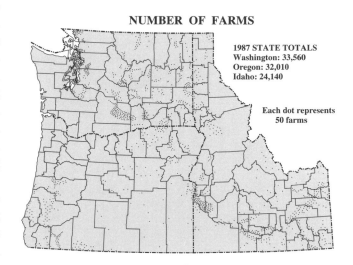

NUMBER OF FARMS

1987 STATE TOTALS
Washington: 33,560
Oregon: 32,010
Idaho: 24,140

Each dot represents
50 farms

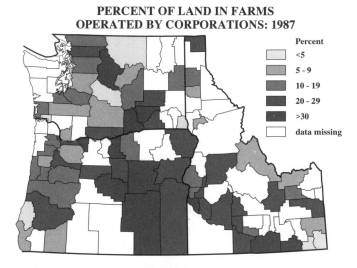

**PERCENT OF LAND IN FARMS
OPERATED BY CORPORATIONS: 1987**

Percent
<5
5 - 9
10 - 19
20 - 29
>30
data missing

Table 15. Land in farms and farmland use in Idaho, 1974-87

	1974	1978		1987	
	acres	acres	% change	acres	% change
Land in farms	14,274,258	14,869,911	+4.2	13,931,875	-7.1
Total cropland	6,247,750	6,631,994	+6.2	6,742,285	+2.1
Harvested	4,531,164	4,877,569	+7.7	4,349,122	-12.4
Pasture	873,607	765,918	-12.3	816,308	+6.3
Other	842,934	988,507	+17.3	1,576,855	+37.3
Woodland	818,549	891,162	+8.9	1,153,837	+23.2
Other land	7,208,004	7,346,755	+1.9	6,035,753	-22.1
Irrigated land	2,859,047	3,508,254	+22.7	3,219,192	-9.2

SOURCE: 1987 Census of Agriculture

CROPLANDS

■ Irrigated
▨ Non-Irrigated

AVERAGE FARM SIZE

☐ 0 - 200
▨ 201 - 400
▨ 401 - 750
▨ 751 - 1300
■ 1301 - 2000
■ 2001 - 6000

In Acres

VALUE OF FARMLAND PER ACRE

Value In Dollars

☐ 0 - 300
▨ 301 - 700
▨ 701 - 1200
■ 1201 - 2100
■ 2101 - 3100
■ 3001 - 7500

however, the relative proportion of irrigated land as a percentage of land in farms did not change appreciably.

Some valuable farmland has been replaced by residential, commercial, and other uses in urban fringe areas, especially in the Seattle and Portland metropolitan areas. However, these modest downturns in farm acreages may also reflect short-term market or production cost factors as well as federal Crop Reduction Program policies.

The value of farmland increased from 1978 to 1987, but values are somewhat lower than recorded in the interim 1982 census. The overall value of farm land and buildings also increased from 1978 to 1987, with more farms enumerated in the $100,000-$200,000 range. Washington and Oregon recorded about a 10 percent increase in the number of farms valued at over one million dollars. For Idaho, there was a slight decline in the number of the highest valued farms.

Table 16. Land in farms and farmland use in Washington, 1974-87

	1974	1978		1987	
	acres	acres	% change	acres	% change
Land in farms	16,661,902	17,002,288	+2.0	16,155,568	-6.2
Total cropland	7,945,063	8,410,749	+5.9	8,168,454	-3.1
Harvested	4,946,306	5,073,078	+2.6	4,597,476	-10.1
Pasture	688,343	614,240	-10.8	578,864	-6.4
Other	2,310,414	2,723,431	+17.9	2,992,114	+9.3
Woodland	2,733,151	2,683,874	-1.8	2,541,513	-6.2
Other land	5,983,688	5,907,665	-1.3	5,405,601	-9.0
Irrigated land	1,309,018	1,681,268	+13.8	1,518,684	-11.2

SOURCE: 1987 Census of Agriculture

Table 17. Land in farms and farmland use in Oregon, 1974-87

	1974	1978		1987	
	acres	acres	% change	acres	% change
Land in farms	18,241,445	18,414,484	+1.0	17,809,165	-3.3
Total cropland	5,074,988	5,427,487	+3.4	5,236,393	-0.3
Harvested	3,213,399	3,280,005	+2.1	2,832,663	-13.7
Pasture	815,197	814,484	-0.1	858,429	+5.4
Other	1,046,392	1,152,998	+10.2	1,545,301	+34.0
Woodland	1,730,245	1,786,919	+3.3	1,636,531	-8.4
Other land	11,436,212	11,380,078	-0.5	10,936,241	-3.9
Irrigated land	1,561,438	1,920,318	+23.0	1,648,205	-14.2

SOURCE: 1987 Census of Agriculture

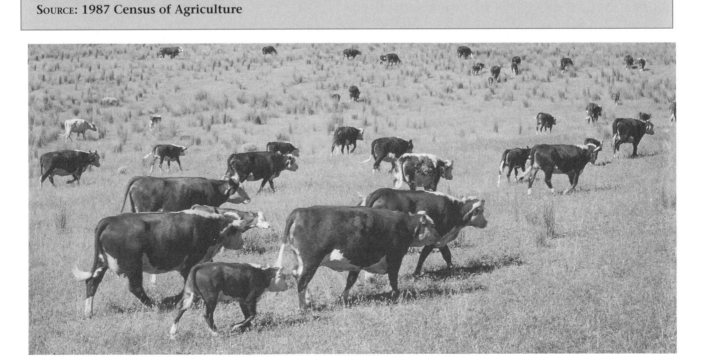

Farm sales total over seven billion dollars a year, nearly 40 percent more than in 1978, and less than 3 percent of all the farms in the Pacific Northwest produce well over half of the region's total sales. The maps on pages 93-97 indicate the distribution of farms in the Pacific Northwest and the regional variation of average farm size and value per acre.

Livestock grazing remains the most extensive agricultural land use in the Pacific Northwest, and cattle and calves are the source of the highest annual agricultural revenue. Grazing utilizes 55 percent of total private farmlands on 26.5 million acres. Stock ranches for cattle and sheep production are generally of large size, over 500 acres, with ranches over 10,000 acres in size fairly common in eastern Oregon, southeastern Idaho, and north-central Washington where acreage requirements are high—often between 25 and 70 acres per animal unit. Ranches are often situated near federal forest or rangeland which is often leased for seasonal grazing; 46.7 million acres of federal land are leased in this way.

Cropland represents 42 percent of total farmland in the Pacific Northwest. Nearly 50 percent of both Washington and Idaho farmland is classed as cropland, along with 29 percent for Oregon. Nearly 30 percent of cropland is irrigated, using surface water diversion or pumped groundwater. Expansion of cropland acreages through irrigation has occurred since the 1950s and has stabilized at approximately 20.2 million acres. Future cropland development is largely dependent on the potential for irrigation.

Wheat, barley, and hay account for 8.76 million acres of cropland, nearly 44 percent of the total harvested. By value, however, fruits, nuts, and berries have replaced wheat as the leading crop commodity in the Pacific Northwest. Over fifty additional crops are grown in significant quantities in the region, and several are important in national totals. Hops, dry peas, peppermint, grass seeds, apples, winter pears, sweet cherries, bush berries, filbert or hazelnuts, and potatoes are but a few of the crops of special note. A growing consumer preference for fine table wines has encouraged the planting of varietal grape vineyards in Oregon and Washington, and production continues to increase.

IRRIGATED LAND AS A PERCENT OF LAND IN FARMS: 1987

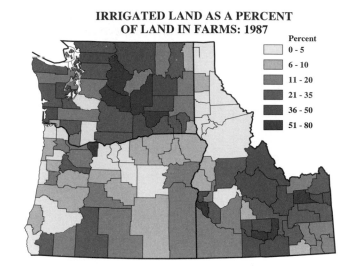

Percent
- 0 - 5
- 6 - 10
- 11 - 20
- 21 - 35
- 36 - 50
- 51 - 80

VALUE OF AGRICULTURAL PRODUCTS SOLD: 1987

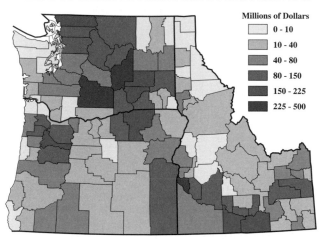

Millions of Dollars
- 0 - 10
- 10 - 40
- 40 - 80
- 80 - 150
- 150 - 225
- 225 - 500

Table 18. Pacific Northwest farms by value of land and buildings

	OR	WA	ID
$39,999 and under	4,103	3,817	3,712
$40,000 to $99,999	9,105	7,599	5,888
$100,000 to $149,999	4,899	4,702	3,136
$150,000 to $199,999	3,205	3,340	2,095
$200,000 to $499,999	6,564	8,366	5,204
$500,000 to $999,999	2,353	3,388	2,441
$1,000,000 and over	1,788	2,351	1,663

SOURCE: 1987 Census of Agriculture

AVERAGE VALUE PER FARM OF AGRICULTURAL PRODUCTS SOLD: 1987

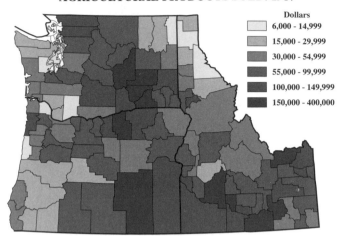

Dollars
- 6,000 - 14,999
- 15,000 - 29,999
- 30,000 - 54,999
- 55,000 - 99,999
- 100,000 - 149,999
- 150,000 - 400,000

LAND IN FARMS

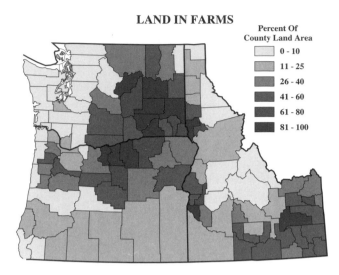

Percent Of County Land Area
- 0 - 10
- 11 - 25
- 26 - 40
- 41 - 60
- 61 - 80
- 81 - 100

AVERAGE VALUE PER ACRE OF AGRICULTURAL PRODUCTS SOLD: 1987

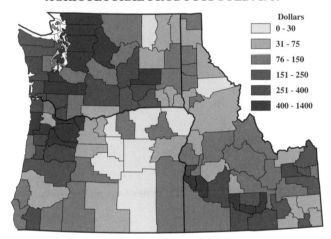

Dollars
- 0 - 30
- 31 - 75
- 76 - 150
- 151 - 250
- 251 - 400
- 400 - 1400

PERCENT CHANGE IN NUMBER OF FARMS: 1982-1987

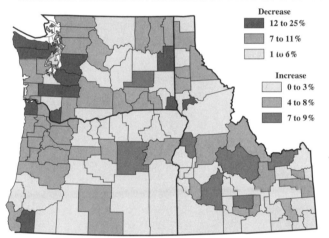

Decrease
- 12 to 25 %
- 7 to 11 %
- 1 to 6 %

Increase
- 0 to 3 %
- 4 to 8 %
- 7 to 9 %

Table 19. Value of farm sales in Pacific Northwest states, 1974-87

	1974	1978			1987		
	NUMBER OF FARMS	NUMBER OF FARMS	% OF FARMS	% OF SALES	NUMBER OF FARMS	% OF FARMS	% OF SALES
$100,000 and over	9,163	10,969	11.1	72.4	14,238	15.8	83.6
$40,000 to $99,999	11,305	12,680	12.8	16.1	10,215	11.4	9.6
$20,000 to $39,999	9,688	9,569	9.7	5.5	7,791	8.7	3.2
$10,000 to $19,999	9,103	9,647	9.8	2.7	8,418	9.5	1.7
$9,999 and under	39,870	55,759	56.4	3.1	49,052	54.6	1.9
Totals	79,629	98,624	100.0	100.0	89,714	100.0	100.0

Orchard crops. The Pacific Northwest has earned an international reputation for high-quality orchard crops. Major centers of orchard acreages include the Wenatchee, Yakima, and Okanogan valleys of Washington, The Dalles, Hood River, Rogue, and Willamette valleys of Oregon, and the Payette area in the Emmet Valley of Idaho.

Filbert or hazelnut orchards are found almost exclusively in Oregon, in the northern Willamette Valley. The number of farms has declined, but hazelnut acreage has expanded by more than 15 percent representing over 600,000 additional trees. Grape vineyard acreages have grown by about 13 percent since 1982, but production has nearly doubled to 71.5 million pounds in 1987. Washington remains the chief producer of grapes, but vineyard acreage has doubled in both Oregon and Idaho.

Washington's Yakima Valley has highly favored growing conditions for fruits, nuts, hops, and grapes. Heavy production of high-quality produce for the fresh fruit export market is made possible by hot, dry, clear summer days, cool nights, and ample irrigation water. The Okanogan district also produces apples, pears, and cherries. Best orchard sites are located along river and lake-shore terraces to reduce frost hazard by promoting late spring blooming. Production of apples, pears, and cherries is also favored in The Dalles and Hood River Valley, where spring dormancy is extended, summer days are hot and dry, and nights are cool. The Rogue Valley of southern Oregon is primarily a pear-growing area. Moderate winters and hot, dry summers favor ripening of many pear varieties. The winter pear is a nationally important specialty crop, and Bartlett pears are summer harvested and shipped throughout the United States as well.

The Willamette Valley of Oregon represents one of the largest concentrations of diversified cropland in the Pacific Northwest. Production includes orchard crops, vegetables for the fresh, frozen, and canned markets, grains, hay, berries, livestock, poultry, and many specialty crops. Seed crops have become increasingly important high-value commodities. In recent years, grass seeds have achieved national importance, with rye, fescue, and orchard grass seeds leading production. Nearly 250 million pounds of ryegrass seed alone is harvested annually on 195,000 acres to make the Willamette Valley the "grass seed capital" of the world. Wet winters and poorly drained soils initially promoted grass seed production as an alternative crop, but today grass seed crops earn over $134 million a year. Field-burning practices with associated air

Table 20. Value of commodity groups, 1987 (in $1,000)

	OREGON	WASHINGTON	IDAHO
Grains	174,093	440,013	407,776
Field seeds, hay, forage	192,762	130,953	120,329
Vegetables, sweet corn & melons	126,188	128,755	39,169
Fuits, nuts & berries	181,678	601,383	21,748
Poultry & poultry products	73,579	125,777	14,314
Dairy products	179,169	444,441	241,252
Cattle & calves	431,728	612,125	828,875
Sheep, lambs & wool	37,448	4,519	24,104
Hogs & pigs	14,277	10,301	11,901
Other livestock & livestock products	22,556	33,845	51,703
Nursery & greenhouse products	203,615	119,315	24,819

pollution have caused a public outcry and threatened the industry. However, innovative research into alternatives to extensive burning and the marketing of straw residue appear to have resolved the worst of the safety and environmental issues.

The Snake River Plain of Idaho and eastern Oregon is known chiefly for potato production. "Famous Potatoes," Idaho's license plate motto, announces the pride that state takes in the economically important crop. Centers of production are the Idaho Falls, Twin Falls, and Boise-Payette districts. However, potatoes are not the only crops grown in this agriculturally rich region: dry onions, alfalfa, melons, vegetables, and forage crops are also of importance. Groundwater and surface water from the Snake River irrigation projects remain key to continued production.

The maps which follow show the distribution patterns of the region's principal crops and livestock by county.

WHEAT

1987 STATE TOTALS
Washington: 2,160,640
Idaho: 1,239,480
Oregon: 838,850

Each dot represents
1000 acres

BARLEY FOR GRAIN

1987 STATE TOTALS
Idaho: 833,230
Washington: 609,130
Oregon: 186,500

Each dot represents
1000 acres

FIELD CORN FOR ALL PURPOSES

1987 STATE TOTALS
Washington: 125,550
Idaho: 103,100
Oregon: 39,690

Each dot represents
500 acres

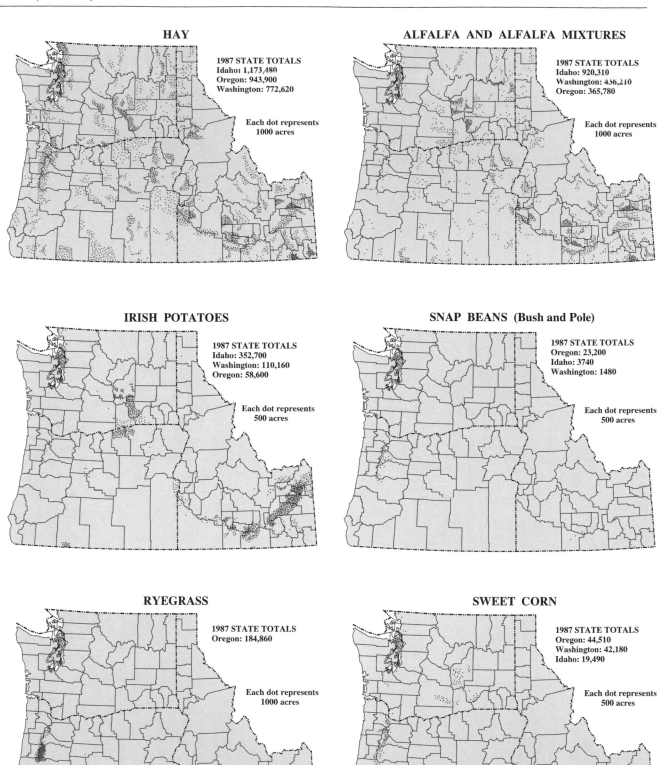

HAY

1987 STATE TOTALS
Idaho: 1,173,480
Oregon: 943,900
Washington: 772,620

Each dot represents
1000 acres

ALFALFA AND ALFALFA MIXTURES

1987 STATE TOTALS
Idaho: 920,310
Washington: 436,210
Oregon: 365,780

Each dot represents
1000 acres

IRISH POTATOES

1987 STATE TOTALS
Idaho: 352,700
Washington: 110,160
Oregon: 58,600

Each dot represents
500 acres

SNAP BEANS (Bush and Pole)

1987 STATE TOTALS
Oregon: 23,200
Idaho: 3740
Washington: 1480

Each dot represents
500 acres

RYEGRASS

1987 STATE TOTALS
Oregon: 184,860

Each dot represents
1000 acres

SWEET CORN

1987 STATE TOTALS
Oregon: 44,510
Washington: 42,180
Idaho: 19,490

Each dot represents
500 acres

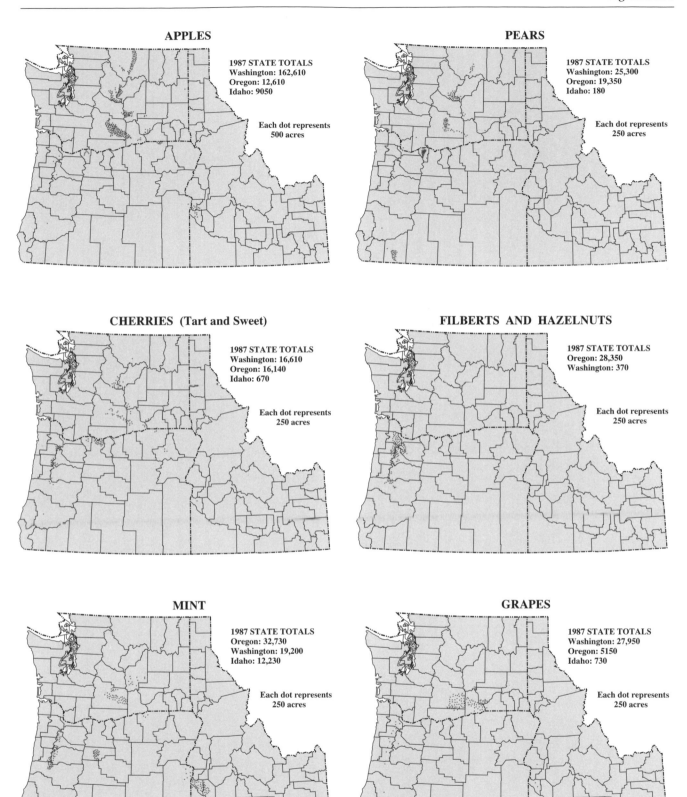

APPLES

1987 STATE TOTALS
Washington: 162,610
Oregon: 12,610
Idaho: 9050

Each dot represents
500 acres

PEARS

1987 STATE TOTALS
Washington: 25,300
Oregon: 19,350
Idaho: 180

Each dot represents
250 acres

CHERRIES (Tart and Sweet)

1987 STATE TOTALS
Washington: 16,610
Oregon: 16,140
Idaho: 670

Each dot represents
250 acres

FILBERTS AND HAZELNUTS

1987 STATE TOTALS
Oregon: 28,350
Washington: 370

Each dot represents
250 acres

MINT

1987 STATE TOTALS
Oregon: 32,730
Washington: 19,200
Idaho: 12,230

Each dot represents
250 acres

GRAPES

1987 STATE TOTALS
Washington: 27,950
Oregon: 5150
Idaho: 730

Each dot represents
250 acres

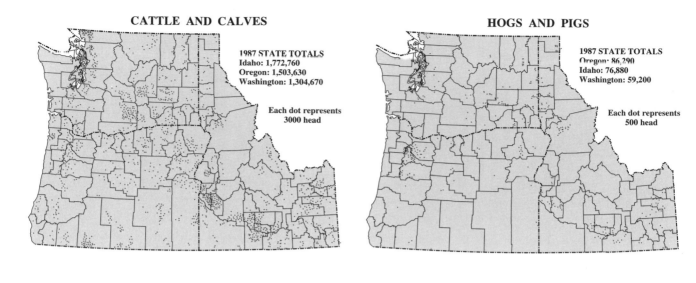

CATTLE AND CALVES

1987 STATE TOTALS
Idaho: 1,772,760
Oregon: 1,503,630
Washington: 1,304,670

Each dot represents
3000 head

HOGS AND PIGS

1987 STATE TOTALS
Oregon: 86,290
Idaho: 76,880
Washington: 59,200

Each dot represents
500 head

SHEEP AND LAMBS

1987 STATE TOTALS
Oregon: 470,290
Idaho: 316,110
Washington: 80,180

Each dot represents
1000 head

MILK COWS

1987 STATE TOTALS
Washington: 220,840
Idaho: 157,670
Oregon: 95,330

Each dot represents
500 head

Commercial Timberland Resources

J. GRANVILLE JENSEN

The Pacific Northwest is generously endowed with forest lands, including some of the world's best tree-growing areas. Especially west of the Cascade Mountains, ample moisture, mild temperatures, soils, and topography combine to favor quality forest growth. In total, 46 percent of the three-state area supports some degree of forest cover and three-fourths of the forest land is productive enough to be classified as commercial timberland.

Commercial timberlands considered in this chapter are forest lands that are naturally capable of growing at least 20 cubic feet of wood per acre per year and are not reserved or restricted from commercial harvests, such as in parks, wilderness areas, wildlife habitat, or scenic preserves. Commercial timberlands in the three-state Pacific Northwest account for one-third of the total land area of the region, but for only 11 percent of the total U.S. timberland (Table 21). Annual harvest of timber in the Pacific Northwest supports a major basic segment of the basic industrial economy, providing employment in timber-related industries for at least 500,000 persons (see Manufacturing and Industries chapter).

Timberland Ownership

Ownership of commercial timberland has significant consequences for forest management, timber harvest, and the regional economy. Forest industry ownerships are generally concentrated in the region's more productive forest lands and are managed for timber production to support their own processing mills. In contrast, public ownerships commonly include lands of lower productivity and areas restricted from timber harvest in favor of other societal benefits.

All forests, whether public or private and including commercial timberlands, provide a wide range of societal benefits, such as aesthetic values, erosion control, wildlife habitat, and outdoor recreation. Consequently, it is appropriate that some areas of public forest resource be withdrawn from commercial harvest and preserved for other benefits. The difficult question and problem is how much should be preserved and where.

For the Pacific Northwest, the dominating reality is that 60 percent of the region's timberlands are in public ownership. Over half of the three-state timberland area is under federal ownership and control, mostly through the Forest Service with 46 percent and the Bureau of Land Management with 5 percent. In major contrast, the much larger U. S. Southern Forest area is overwhelmingly in private ownership with only 8 percent in federal ownerships plus another 2 percent in local public ownerships.

Private timberland ownerships in the Pacific Northwest are evenly divided between forest industry ownerships and other private plus farm ownerships with about 20 percent each. Considering only the Douglas-fir subregion west of the Cascade Mountain crest, forest industry ownerships are higher (31 percent), reflecting the concentration of most productive classes of timberland in that area as well as locations of timber-processing centers. In significant contrast, 90 percent of timberland in the American South is in private ownership, notably farm and other.

TIMBERLAND OWNERSHIP
PACIFIC NORTHWEST IN THE NATIONAL CONTEXT
1987 Base

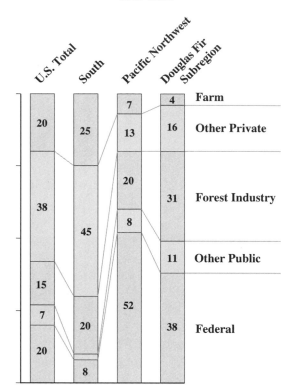

GENERALIZED COMMERCIAL FOREST TYPES

Hemlock-Sitka Spruce
Douglas Fir
Firs-Englemann Spruce
Ponderosa Pine
White Pine
Lodgepole Pine
Larch

Major Forest Types

Two forest types dominate the forest lands of western Washington and Oregon. The Douglas-fir type (*Pseudotsuga menziesii*) is by far the most important and most extensive, occupying nearly two-thirds of all forest lands westward from the Cascade Mountain slopes and lending its name to the Douglas-fir subregion. Pure stands occur, but commonly Douglas-fir is intermixed with western hemlock (*Tsuga heterophylla*) and western red cedar (*Thuja plicata*). Douglas-fir, being relatively intolerant of shade, does not regenerate well under forest cover so that sustained yield management prefers patch clear-cutting or shelterwood harvest systems followed by artificial restocking. A western hemlock-Sitka spruce forest type (*Tsuga heterophylla-Picea sitchensis*) occupies the very humid, temperate coastal zone extending from the western Olympic Mountain area southward into Oregon, accounting for about 15 percent of the subregion's timberland (see map on facing page and Table 22).

In the Douglas-fir subregion, hardwood types, notably Oregon white oak (*Quercus garryanna*) and red alder (*Alnus rubra*), occupy as much as 15 percent of the timberlands. Although there is a developing hardwood industry, Pacific Northwest hardwood stands are under used, accounting for only about 4 percent of the subregion's annual timber harvest.

The major forest type in the drier, more severe climate areas of eastern Oregon, eastern Washington, and Idaho is the pine subregion. Here, forest cover is more varied and occupies only more humid lands, especially the eastern slopes of the Cascades, the Blue and Wallowa mountains of Oregon, the Okanogan area of northeastern Washington, and the Rocky Mountain areas of Idaho. Ponderosa pine (*Pinus ponderosa*) stands occupy 25 percent of timberlands east of the Cascades. Lodgepole pine (*Pinus contorta*) stands occupy about 14 percent. Stands of a Douglas-fir variant scattered throughout the pine subregion occupy as much as one-fourth of timberlands.

Forest Land Productivity

Forest scientists evaluate forest land quality according to natural capability to grow wood volume based on factors of soils, moisture, temperature, and topography. Five classes of productivity are identified. The lowest, capable of producing less than 20 cubic feet per acre per year, is considered to be non-commercial forest land. The highest class includes land naturally capable of growing more than 120 cubic feet of wood volume per acre per year. Thirty percent of Pacific Northwest commercial timberland is estimated to be in the highest class of natural productivity. In contrast, for the total U. S., only 11 percent is in the highest class and for the large southern forest region, only 12 percent (see graph of timberland productivity on facing page).

The Douglas-fir subregion of the Pacific Northwest is outstanding in its capability to grow

---

Table 21. Area of timberlands by ownerships

	ALL LAND AREA	TOTAL TIMBER LAND	NATIONAL FORESTS	BLM	OTHER FEDERAL	STATE	OTHER PUBLIC	INDIAN	FOREST INDUSTRY	OTHER PRIVATE	FARM
PNW total	156,721	53,468	24,716	2,899	183	3,888	378	1,729	10,900	5,172	3,603
Washington	42,483	16,849	4,859	37	130	2,025	225	1,376	4,588	2,773	836
Oregon	61,546	22,085	10,152	2,304	6	827	102	315	5,114	1,935	1,330
Idaho	52,692	14,534	9,705	558	47	1,036	51	38	1,198	464	1,437
South	534,395	195,384	11,767	11	4,122	2,919	747	117	38,231	88,761	48,709
United States	2,257,618	483,319	85,223	5,800	5,890	26,705	7,017	5,628	70,605	179,361	97,000
PNW 1952 data	—	60,416	27,937	3,029	129	3,759	488	2,836	10,000	6,050	6,189

NOTES: In thousands of acres, 1987 base.
SOURCE: Karen L. Waddell, Daniel D. Oswald, and Douglas D. Powell, "Forest Statistics of the United States, 1987," Tables 1 and 2. U.S. Department of Agriculture Forest Service, Pacific Northwest Research Station, Research Bulletin PNW-RB-168, 1989.

Table 22. Area of major forest types on timberlands with 20 cubic feet per acre per year or more productivity

	TOTAL	DOUGLAS-FIR	HEMLOCK-SITKA SPRUCE	LODGE-POLE PINE	FIR-SPRUCE	PONDER-OSA PINE	OTHER SOFT-WOODS	HARD WOODS	NON-STOCKED
Douglas-fir subregion (OR, WA)	23,140	14,009	3,254	46	1,294	282	128	3,678	449
Ponderosa pine subregion (OR, WA)	15,791	3,716	659	1,845	2,762	5,680	782	92	255
Idaho	13,962	4,142	——	2,175	——	1,392	5,087	408	758
Pacific Northwest (total)	52,893	21,867	3,913	4,066	4,056	7,354	5,997	4,178	1,462

NOTES: In thousands of acres. Oregon and Washington data 1987 base, Idaho data 1981 base. Idaho data not fully comparable with Oregon-Washington data for forest type inventory.
SOURCES: Karen L. Waddell, Daniel D. Oswald, and Douglas S. Powell, "Forest Statistics of the United States, 1987," Table 5, United States Department of Agriculture Forest Service, Pacific Northwest Research Station, Research Bulletin PNW-RB-168, 1989.
Robert E. Benson, Alan W. Green, and Duane D. VanHooser, "Idaho's Forest Resources," Table 10, U.S. Department of Agriculture Forest Service, Intermountain Research Station, Resource Bulletin INT-39, 1987.

TIMBERLAND PRODUCTIVITY

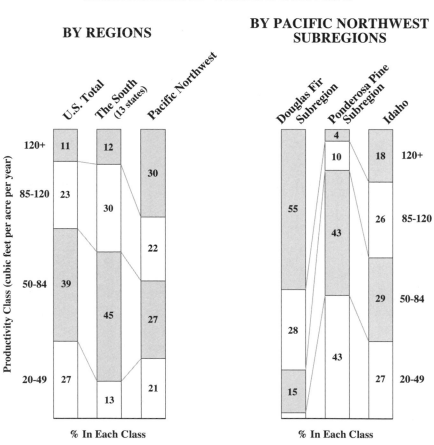

BY REGIONS

BY PACIFIC NORTHWEST SUBREGIONS

wood volume, with 83 percent of the timberlands in the top two classes (55 percent in the highest class and 28 percent in the second highest class). In contrast, the South has only 42 percent in the two highest productivity classes, and the national total is only 34 percent. East of the Cascades, timberlands are mostly in the lower two classes of potential productivity.

Forest land productivity by ownerships in the Pacific Northwest reveals the reality that private ownerships, especially forest industry ownerships, are concentrated on the most productive lands. Over half (55 percent) of forest industry timberlands are in the highest productivity class. In contrast, Forest Service lands in the Pacific Northwest include only 8 percent in the most productive class. The high percentage (36 percent) for other public timberlands in the highest productivity class is mostly Bureau of Land Management ownerships in western Oregon (see graph on this page).

In reality, much timberland never attains its natural productivity level, mainly because of understocking with desirable trees. Certainly, for the future of the Pacific Northwest, the forest industries, and the regional economy, there is need for continued and expanded forest management for sustained yields and for fiscal realities that foster optimum restocking of harvested timberlands.

PACIFIC NORTHWEST
FORESTLAND PRODUCTIVITY BY OWNERSHIPS
1987 base (Idaho 1981)

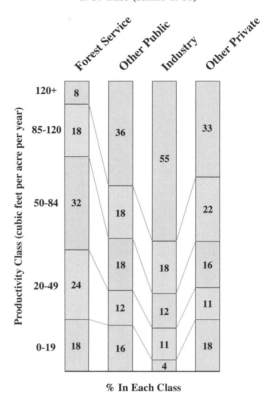

% In Each Class

Table 23. Timber harvest by forest ownerships and by Pacific Northwest states

	OR	WA	ID	PNW TOTAL
Private	3,282	3,893	738	7,913
National forests	2,971	1,153	697	4,821
BLM	901	3	18	922
State	224	771	169	1,164
BIA	113	241	14	368
Other public	33	36	---	69
Total	7,524	6,097	1,636	15,257

NOTES: In million board feet-Scribner Scale, average 1980s decade.
SOURCE: Debra D. Warren, "Production, Price, Employment and Trade in Northwest Forest Industries, First Quarter, 1991," Tables 15 and 16, U.S. Department of Agriculture Forest Service, Pacific Northwest Research Station, Resource Bulletin PNW-RB-188, 1991.

PACIFIC NORTHWEST
TIMBERLAND-GROWING STOCK-HARVEST
By Ownerships - 1986 Base

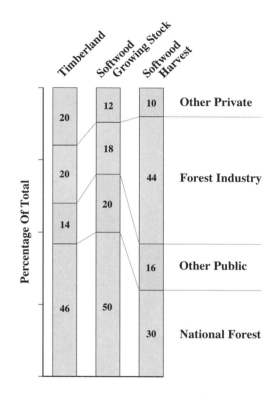

Growing Stock and Timber Harvest

Pacific Northwest timber harvest, providing about 30 percent of the national total softwood harvest and 2 percent of the hardwood harvest, continues to be a major basic support of the Pacific Northwest economy and important in the national context for quality timber. In contrast, it is notable that the 13-state southern forest region accounts for 50 percent of the nation's softwood harvest and for 55 percent of the hardwood harvest, but from a timberland area two and one-half times that of the three-state Pacific Northwest (Tables 23 and 24).

Pacific Northwest timber harvest is dominated by Douglas-fir, which accounts for at least half of the total harvest from western Oregon and Washington, but only for about one-fourth of the harvest from the Ponderosa pine subregion of eastern Oregon-Washington and Idaho.

In the Pacific Northwest, significant differences are notable in ownership relationships between timberlands, growing stock volume, and annual timber harvest (see graph on this page). Public ownerships, with 60 percent of the timberlands, control 70 percent of the softwood growing stock resource, but account for only 46 percent of the annual harvest. In major contrast, forest industry ownerships, accounting for only 20 percent of the timberlands and with only 18 percent of the growing stock, account for 44 percent of the annual harvest.

In the future, it is likely that public lands will contribute even less to timber harvest as additional public timberlands ownerships are restricted or removed from harvest. Decreases in area of private nonindustrial and farm timberlands resulting from expanding urbanization, highway construction, and conversion to other nonforest land uses are also likely to result in lesser timber harvests. Note the loss of 7 million acres of timberland during 1952-87 shown in Table 21.

Most timber harvested is transported as logs out of the actual forest area to processing mills located at sites favored with a combination of level land, access to water supply, labor pool, and provisions of rail and highway facilities for shipment of products. Sophisticated log-loading and specialized road haulage equipment characterizes the basic timber harvesting industry (see the Manufacturing and Industries chapter).

TIMBER HARVEST BY COUNTY - 1990

Million Board Feet

■	Over 800
■	400 - 800
■	100 - 399
■	20 - 99
■	1 - 19
■	0.01 - 0.9
□	No Harvest

Table 24. Softwood growing stock harvest by subregions and ownerships, 1986

	WASHINGTON-OREGON		IDAHO	PNW TOTAL
	DOUGLAS-FIR SUBREGION	PONDEROSA PINE SUBREGION		
National forests	538,491	387,174	136,821	1,062,486
Other public	418,841	102,155	32,324	553,320
Forest industry	1,221,525	179,102	121,659	1,522,286
Farm & other private	203,422	70,314	76,403	350,139
Totals	2,382,279	738,745	367,207	3,488,231
United States total	11,367,172			
South total (13 states)	5,741,025			
Southeast	2,835,520			
South central	2,905,505			

NOTES: In thousands of cubic feet.
SOURCES: Karen L. Waddell, Daniel D. Oswald, and Douglas S. Powell, "Forest Statistics of the United States, 1987," Table 29, U.S. Department of Agriculture Forest Service, Pacific Northwest Research Station, Research Bulletin PNW-RB-168, 1989. Robert E. Benson, Alan W. Green, and Duane D. VanHooser, "Idaho Forest Resources," Table 42, U.S. Department of Agriculture Forest Service, Intermountain Research Station, Resource Bulletin INT-39, 1987.

Direct income from timber harvest is important for most Pacific Northwest counties. Southwest Oregon, including Douglas and Lane counties, each of which recorded close to a billion board feet harvest in 1990, is clearly outstanding. Other significant harvest areas include northwest coastal Washington, Cascade slope areas, Blue and Wallowa mountain areas of Oregon, the Rocky Mountain timberlands of Idaho, and the Okanogan hills of Washington. Counties with only minor timber harvest include the mainly nonforested areas of the Columbia Basin and Palouse hills of Washington, the semi-arid nonforested sage brush areas of southeastern Oregon, and the urban agricultural Snake River Plain of Idaho.

For the Pacific Northwest during the decades of the 1990s, some reduction in area of commercial timberland resource is almost certain, as population increases, forests are converted to various urban uses, and additional areas are reserved or restricted from timber harvest. Nevertheless, the commercial forest resources of the Pacific Northwest under sustained management will continue to provide quality timber for national requirements and basic support for a major sector of the Pacific Northwest economy.

Ocean Resources

JAMES W. GOOD

The ocean off the Pacific Northwest coast is rich in natural resources. Abundant salmon, crab, shrimp, groundfish, and other species contribute to important commercial fisheries that provide high-quality protein for domestic consumption and export. Ocean sport fishers vie for many of the same species. Offshore deposits of minerals and oil and gas resources are as yet largely unexploited. Maritime commerce is a dominant industry in the region. Large and small ships and barges transport oil, other bulk cargo, containers, agricultural products, and logs to and from Pacific Northwest ports, linking the Northwest through trade with many nations on the Pacific rim and beyond.

Human use of marine resources is not without its environmental and economic costs. Domestic and industrial pollution threaten coastal and deepwater habitats and marine life, periodic oil spills foul beaches, marine mammals, and seabirds,

and the viability of the fishing industry is threatened by both over-harvest of fisheries and other land-based activities.

This chapter describes ocean resources in the Pacific Northwest and how these resources are used and managed for public and private benefit. The growing number of conflicts in marine resource use are also described, as are attempts to resolve them.

Living on the "Ring of Fire"

Located on the Pacific Rim's "ring of fire," the Northwest is a tectonically active region. Not far offshore is the Juan de Fuca-Gorda Ridge mid-ocean spreading center complex which forms the boundary between the small Juan de Fuca plate and the massive Pacific plate to the west (see map below). Even closer to shore is yet another plate boundary, the Cascadia Subduction Zone (CSZ).

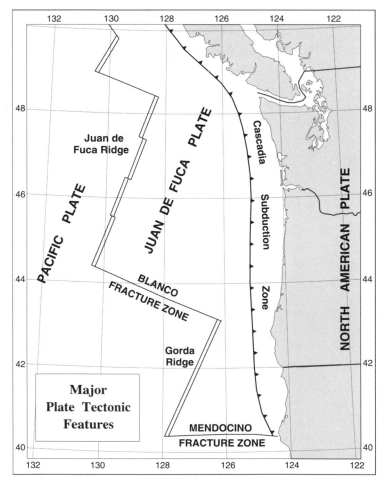

The CSZ is the junction between the westward-moving North American continental plate and the eastward-moving Juan de Fuca oceanic plate. At the CSZ boundary, the oceanic plate dives under the continental plate. While there have been no earthquakes along this giant fault since European settlement, recent evidence suggests that it is seismically active, yielding very large (magnitude 8-9+) earthquakes approximately every three to four hundred years. The implications of this discovery are just beginning to be understood.

The continental margin is composed of sedimentary and volcanic rocks covered with mud and sand. Its major structural features landward of the CSZ are the continental shelf and slope.

The continental shelf underlies shallow coastal waters out to about 650 feet in depth and ranges in width from about 12 nautical miles (nm) at Cape Blanco to nearly 50 nm off Grays Harbor. Numerous nearshore rocks and islands host large populations of breeding seabirds and marine mammals. Prominent submarine banks occur near the outer edge of the shelf and are important habitats for many forms of marine life.

At the edge of the shelf, the continental slope plunges more than a mile to the seafloor. The slope is dissected by seven steep submarine canyons, such as the prominent Astoria Canyon at the mouth of the Columbia River. These canyons serve as channels for movement of sediments across the slope into the deep ocean abyss.

Sand and mud cover most of the continental margin, although there are significant rock outcroppings. Movement of these sediments is greatest close to shore where they are transported by nearshore littoral currents. Offshore currents also move sediments, albeit more slowly, and large storms stir up bottom sediments all along the shelf.

Major oceanic currents affecting the natural processes and resources in the summer include the southward-flowing California surface current and the northward-flowing California undercurrent (see figures on page 112). These summer currents, reinforced by strong north and northwest winds and the coreolis effect, result in an offshore flow of nearshore waters, with a corresponding upwelling of cold, nutrient-rich waters from the deep. In the winter, south and southwest winds dominate,

GEOLOGIC AND SEDIMENTARY FEATURES OF THE CONTINENTAL MARGIN

WASHINGTON

OREGON

CONTINENTAL SLOPE

2000m

200m

Silt & Mud
Sand
Gravel
Shells
Bedrock

WINTER OCEAN CURRENTS

SUMMER OCEAN CURRENTS
AND UPWELLING

resulting in the northward-flowing Davidson current and downwelling of surface waters. Periodically, this predominant summer-winter cycle is upset by global weather phenomena, such as the strong El Niños that occur on average every eight to nine years. Warmer water conditions, higher sea levels, and reduced biological productivity result, often persisting for many months.

The Marine Ecosystem

Pacific Northwest coastal waters are among the most productive in the world, fueled largely by the upwelling described above. Upwelled, nutrient-rich waters stimulate large "blooms" of phytoplankton throughout spring and summer. These tiny plants, in turn, provide food for marine "grazers" like copepods and euphasids that then serve as food for larger crustaceans and fish, and so on.

The waters of the Pacific Northwest are ecologically significant for another reason. They are an "ecotone"—a boundary region between the subarctic ecosystem to the north and the Californian ecosystem to the south. Populations at the edges of their ranges tend to be more variable and sensitive to changes in environmental conditions. Coho

salmon, more attuned to the subarctic, are an example of such vulnerable species.

This rich oceanic ecosystem is home to large populations of valuable fishery resources, thousands of breeding and feeding seabirds, and diverse marine mammal populations. Ocean commercial fisheries include salmon, ling cod, halibut, sole, rockfish, pink shrimp, crab, tuna, whiting, and sablefish. These fish, together with hundreds of other species, comprise a complex oceanic food web.

More than a dozen species of marine birds breed along the Pacific Northwest coast, including cormorants, auklets, petrels, gulls, murres, oystercatchers, and tufted puffins. Others are regular visitors or migrants, including loons, grebes, albatrosses, shearwaters, pelicans, and numerous ducks and shorebirds. Pollution, human disturbance, and loss of habitat are major concerns.

A variety of whales, dolphins, porpoises, seals, and sea lions are also found in coastal waters of the Pacific Northwest. Common to the nearshore are California gray whales, who migrate south from summer feeding areas in the Arctic to winter calving areas in Baja California, reversing the process in the spring. Many other whale species frequent offshore waters during their migrations. Harbor seals and California sea lions are also common along the Pacific Northwest coast, hauling out on beaches and rocky shores and islands; the endangered Stellar sea lion breeds along the southern Oregon coast. Sea otters, once common throughout the Pacific Northwest coast, are now found only along the rugged Olympic coast of Washington.

Offshore Ownership and Jurisdiction

On March 10, 1983, President Reagan signed a proclamation that established the Exclusive Economic Zone (EEZ), a resource zone that is contiguous to the territorial sea of the United States and its territories (see map below). The EEZ extends 200 nm from the coastal low-water baseline from which the territorial sea is measured. Within the 3-nm territorial sea, coastal states, including Oregon and Washington, own and manage natural resources, although federal jurisdiction remains over many

activities, such as navigation, commerce, and pollution control. EEZ resources in the 3- to 200-nm zone are under exclusive federal ownership and jurisdiction, although federal resource managers must consult with adjacent states and take their concerns into consideration when setting fishing regulations, leasing areas for oil and gas exploration, permitting pollution discharges, and allowing other uses and activities. Beyond the EEZ are the high seas and international seabed, an area governed by international customs and conventions.

Commercial and Recreational Fisheries

Commercial and recreational fisheries in the Pacific Northwest are an important regional industry, whether measured in numbers or pounds of fish caught, dollar value for commercial catches at the dock, or in personal income generated in fishing communities. The bulk of the fish caught and value generated in the industry are from the commercial fisheries in the ocean off Washington and Oregon and in Puget Sound. But the Washington-Oregon distant-water fleet, fishing in a number of important Alaskan fisheries, also contributes substantially to the regional economy.

Diverse fisheries. The fishery resources harvested commercially in local waters by non-Indians are diverse in terms of the numbers of species harvested, areas fished, and the type of gear used. Species fished include five species of salmon (chinook, coho, sockeye, chum, and pink), albacore tuna, groundfish (rockfish, snapper, halibut, ling cod, sablefish, flounders and soles), crab, shrimp, and a variety of other species (including sharks, clams, sea urchins, and shad). Indian treaty rights fisheries for salmon and steelhead are also important commercial and ceremonial fisheries. Aquaculture contributes to the "landings" as well, with salmon and oysters making up most of the harvest.

Some of the ocean fisheries are in very deep water (e.g., albacore, some groundfish), others are nearshore (e.g., crab), while still others are inshore, bay, or river fisheries (see maps on pages 117 and 118). The sizes of boats and type of gear varies with the fishery as well. Groundfish, mid-water schooling fish, and shrimp are caught by trawlers using large nets. Pots are used to fish for crab all along the coast, and are also an alternative method to catch sablefish. Trollers fish with hooks and lines for salmon and albacore, and longliners go after halibut and sablefish.

Commercial fish landings and value. Landings of food fish at Oregon and Washington ports by non-Indian fishers have averaged 309 million pounds annually from 1975 to 1990, although there have been significant year-to-year fluctuations. In 1990, landings were 324 million pounds, with a dockside value of nearly $228 million (see graphs on page 116). This was 2.5 percent of the nation's total by poundage and 4.8 percent by value. Washington accounted for 57 percent of 1990 landings by weight and 69 percent by value, the difference attributed to deliveries of Alaska-caught fish and to the much larger proportion of high-value salmon in the Washington harvest. Based on licenses issued, full-time commercial fishers numbered about 6,500 in Washington and about 6,200 in Oregon in 1990. In addition, fish handling and processing seasonally employ an additional 4,000 to 6,000 in the two states. Major fishing ports include

Bellingham, Westport, and Seattle in Washington, and Newport, Astoria-Warrenton, and Charleston in Oregon.

Recreational fisheries. Recreational fisheries from private boats and passenger-carrying charter boats also make a significant contribution to the region's economy. The recreational fleet included more than five hundred licensed charter boats in 1990 and many more small private craft, fishing mostly in nearshore ocean waters and in Puget Sound. Important ocean recreational fishing ports in coastal Washington include Westport, Ilwaco, Neah Bay, and La Push. In Oregon, Newport, Charleston, Astoria-Warrenton-Hammond, Winchester Bay, Brookings, and other smaller ports support important recreational fisheries. Salmon, principally coho and to a lesser extent chinook, are the prime

WASHINGTON COMMERCIAL FISHERIES LANDINGS
1975-1990

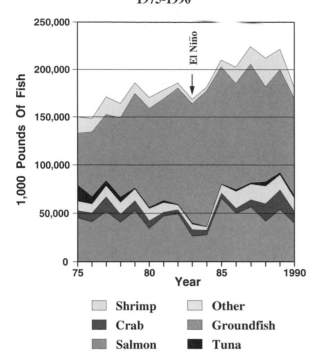

OREGON COMMERCIAL FISHERIES LANDINGS
1975-1990

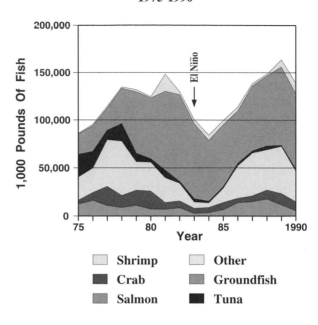

LANDED VALUE OF
WASHINGTON COMMERCIAL FISHERIES
1975-1990

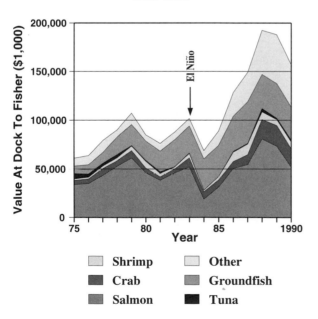

LANDED VALUE OF
OREGON COMMERCIAL FISHI
1975-1990

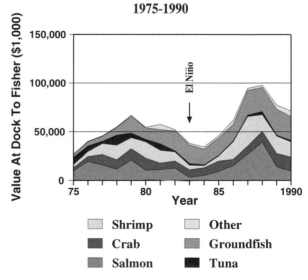

recreational fishing targets, mostly in nearshore waters. However, season and area closures in recent years have led to increased emphasis on recreational groundfishing in nearshore and deeper waters, with rockfish, ling cod, and halibut the new species of interest.

Fisheries problems and management. Although commercial fisheries are an important sector of the economy, they have experienced a number of serious problems, some environmental and some human-induced. The 1982-83 El Niño, for example, changed ocean environmental conditions and resulted in significant declines in salmon and shrimp harvest for several years. Other problems beset the industry as well, including declining stocks and catches and too many fishing boats. Allocation conflicts are also on the increase among commercial groups using different gear, between commercial and recreational fishers, and between Indian and non-Indian fishers. These conflicts have increasingly politicized the fisheries management process.

Responsibility for management varies with the fishery. Inshore fisheries that are primarily within the 3-nm territorial sea (e.g., crab) are managed by the respective states. Most marine fisheries, however, are under the jurisdiction of the Pacific Fisheries Management Council (PFMC), which includes representatives from Washington, Oregon, California, and Idaho, as well as public and industry members. The PFMC was established under the Magnuson Fisheries Conservation and Management Act of 1976 (as were regional councils in other areas). The overall goals of the act are to promote the sustainable harvest of species in the 200-nm Fisheries Conservation Zone (FCZ, now called the EEZ) and "Americanize" fisheries in the zone, which at the time were largely foreign fisheries. The PFMC writes fishery management plans for individual fisheries, such as salmon and groundfish, considering scientific information available on stocks, reproductive capacity, fishing fleet capacity and gear types, and socioeconomic concerns. The halibut fishery is managed by the International Pacific Halibut Commission. A variety of management measures are used to regulate the different fisheries, including selective time and area closures, limited entry schemes, and quotas and other rationing systems.

COMMERCIAL AND RECREATIONAL SALMON FISHING AREAS

Commercial trolling

Recreational

Tribal set net

Customary tribal fishing

Note: Tribal and non-tribal gillnet fisheries exist in certain bays and rivers

Oil and Gas Resources

The offshore geology of the Pacific Northwest is extremely complex. While available geologic information indicates that there are several sedimentary basins where oil and gas may be trapped (see map on facing page), these basins are poorly defined. Following a federal offshore oil and gas lease sale off Washington and Oregon in 1964, twelve wells were drilled at promising offshore sites, and numerous others just inland. However, most wells were dry holes, and while there were "shows" of both oil and gas at a few sites, no recoverable deposits of oil and gas were discovered.

Interest in offshore leasing for oil and gas exploration surfaced again in the 1980s. In 1989, after some debate, both the Washington and Oregon state legislatures placed moratoria on oil and gas leasing in state waters (up to 3 nm from shore) until 1995. In federal waters (between 3 and 200 nm from shore), a 1990 moratorium called a halt to oil and gas leasing until the year 2000. Reasons for the moratoria included insufficient scientific information; concern about potential risks and impacts to economically valuable fisheries and other marine resources; general public opposition because of these risks; and the assessment by industry and federal resource managers that there is very little oil and gas in the area.

Marine Minerals

There are a number of potentially valuable marine mineral resources in the Pacific Northwest, including polymetallic sulfides, placers, and sand and gravel. As with other seabed resources, exploitation of marine minerals is under state jurisdiction inside 3 nm and under federal control in the remainder of the 200-nm EEZ.

Polymetallic sulfides are massive deposits of ore that contain iron, zinc, copper, and other metals. They are deposited in areas of hydrothermal vents along mid-ocean spreading centers. The seafloor off the Pacific Northwest is unique in that two such "mid-ocean" spreading centers are within the 200-mile EEZ boundary—the entire Gorda Ridge and a portion of the Juan de Fuca Ridge. The federal government attempted to lease the Gorda Ridge for mineral exploration in the early 1980s, but the proposal was canceled because of public outcry and a lack of industry interest.

Placers are concentrated deposits of heavy mineral-bearing sands. Placers found off the Oregon and Washington coasts contain magnetite (iron), chromite (a source for chromium), ilmenite (a source of titanium), zircon, garnet, gold, platinum, and other potentially valuable minerals. Historically, gold was mined from beach placers in southern Oregon. In the late 1980s, there was considerable interest by industry and government in exploring for chromite-rich placer deposits offshore. The federal government and Oregon and California formed a technical task force to gather more complete data on the deposits known to occur there. While the research was inconclusive as to economic recoverability, the 1991 Oregon legislature passed a law banning offshore mineral exploration because of potential threat to habitat for fisheries and other living resources. Placer sands off northern Oregon and Washington are mostly iron oxides, the least valuable placer mineral and unlikely to be exploited.

Offshore gravel deposits are estimated to be 1.9-9.8 billion cubic yards offshore the Washington coast and 130-650 million cubic yards offshore Oregon. Gravel is thus the most abundant marine mineral resource. While it is unlikely to be mined soon, offshore gravel may be looked to in the future to supplement dwindling onshore supplies of high quality construction aggregate.

OFFSHORE OIL, GAS, AND MINERAL RESOURCES

Oil and gas sedimentary basins (sediments >15,000 ft. thick)

Sands with >10% heavy minerals

Exploratory oil/gas wells drilled in 1960s (no commercial deposits)

MARINE MAMMALS, SEABIRDS AND PROTECTED AREAS

Flattery Rocks NWR

Quillayute Needles NWR

Copalis NWR

WASHINGTON

Oregon Islands NWR

Cape Meares NWR

Three Arch Rocks NWR

Oregon Islands NWR

OREGON

Oregon Islands NWR

Legend:

- Olympic Coast National Marine Sanctuary
- Northwest Straits National Marine Sanctuary (proposed)
- National Wildlife Refuges (sea birds, marine mammals)
- Sea otter range
- Haulout areas for seals and sea lions
- Gray whale migration route

Marine Resource Protection

Harbor seals and California sea lions are protected under the federal Marine Mammal Protection Act of 1972, and their populations have increased dramatically in the last twenty years. As a consequence, marine mammal conflicts with human activities have also increased, especially with commercial and recreational fisheries. Whales are protected under international agreements and managed by the International Whaling Commission.

Many critical nesting, resting, and migration sites for seabirds and coastal waterfowl are protected along the Oregon and Washington coasts as part of a system of national wildlife refuges. Many of these are offshore rocks and islands that are part of the Oregon Islands National Wildlife Refuge and the Flattery Rocks, Quillayute, and Copalis National Wildlife Refuges off the Washington coast.

In 1992, the Olympic Coast National Marine Sanctuary was established, including all EEZ waters north of Grays Harbor, Washington. While many traditional uses are permitted, oil and gas development is prohibited. Proposals for other sanctuaries in Washington (e.g., the Northwest Straits in Puget Sound) and Oregon have been made, but none have been designated.

Differing degrees of marine resource protection are also provided at national seashores, recreation areas, marine intertidal gardens, estuarine research reserves, and other coastal wildlife refuges. Particular attention is being given to protecting rocky intertidal areas from overuse in Oregon.

Toward a More Integrated Ocean Management

One of the frequent, long-time criticisms of marine resource management is that the United States does not have a coherent "national ocean policy." Critics charge that management of ocean resources at both the state and federal levels is too resource- or use-specific and poorly integrated. The result is increasing conflict among resource users and other interest groups, with no efficient, equitable means for resolution. At the national level, proposals for a comprehensive EEZ management scheme to integrate ocean resource decision making are being discussed. At the state level, actual experiments in integrated ocean management are underway, including innovative ocean planning efforts in Oregon and Washington. In 1990, Oregon produced the nation's first state "ocean management plan."

Further reading

Strickland, R., and D.J. Chasen. 1989. *Coastal Washington: A synthesis of information.* WSG 89-1. Seattle: Washington Sea Grant.

Parmenter, L., and R. Bailey. 1985. *The Oregon Ocean Book.* Salem: Department of Land Conservation and Development.

Oregon Ocean Resources Management Task Force. 1990. *The Oregon Ocean Plan.* Salem, Oregon.

Minerals and Mining

CYRUS W. FIELD

Although the resources and production of the agricultural, fishery, forest, and recreation-tourism industries of the Pacific Northwest are well known and utilized by many, those pertaining to the mining and minerals industry are not as evident or appreciated. The geology and landforms of this region, as noted in a previous chapter, are extraordinarily varied in form, substance, and age. Each of the three major rock groups consisting of igneous, sedimentary, and metamorphic types are abundantly present.

The primary processes involved with the formation of these rocks, in concert with secondary processes involving hydrothermal activity, weathering, and erosion, have resulted in a diverse multitude of mineral deposits including base (copper, lead, zinc), ferroalloy (cobalt, chromium, manganese, molybdeum, nickel, titanium, vanadium), precious (silver, gold), and other metals and a wide spectrum of gem stones and industrial minerals. These deposits range from surficial accumulations of sand and gravel and exposures of commercial grade building stone to less common and intrinsically more valuable occurrences of metals and minerals at variable depths.

Because commercial concentrations of most metals and minerals are unique to a particular type of rock and/or geologic environment, it is not unusual to find multiple occurrences of mineralogically similar deposits within a geographically and geologically restricted area. Examples include lateritic deposits of nickel in weathered ultramafic intrusions of the Klamath-Siskiyou Mountains of southwest Oregon; hydrothermal deposits of copper and molybdenum associated with porphyritic intrusions in the Cascade Mountains of Washington and Northern Rocky Mountains of Idaho; and deposits of lead and zinc in limestones of the Northern Rocky Mountains in northeast Washington.

Deposits of base and precious metals in the Pacific Northwest have formed largely by hydrothermal processes related to magmatic activity and the formation of both plutonic and volcanic igneous rocks. Because such rocks are widespread and document repeated episodes of magmatism throughout the geologic evolution of this region, hydrothermal deposits of one or more metals are widely distributed throughout the Pacific Northwest, although few have proved to be commercially important to date.

In contrast to deposits of the metals and most other minerals, those of sand, gravel, and stone are vastly more numerous and extensive. However, because unit values and profit margins for these materials are generally low, commercial utilization is normally restricted to those in close proximity to construction sites and centers of population and industrial activity.

Mineral Production

The total average annual value of nonfuel mineral production in the U.S. has risen 36.8 percent in the last decade, from $23,351 million in 1980-82 to $31,942 million in 1990-92. This increase is substantially less than that of inflation, which, based on the Consumer Price Index, rose about 76 percent during the same period. Mineral production in the Pacific Northwest has followed the U.S. trend, with average annual values for the region increasing 35.4 percent from about $751 million in 1980-82 to $1,017 million in 1990-92. However, the overall trend and averages ignore some important details about the mineral economy of this region. During this period, the average annual value of mineral production for Idaho decreased, whereas those for both Oregon and Washington increased, but at markedly

Table 25. Average annual value of nonfuel mineral production in the United States and the Pacific Northwest (in millions of dollars)

	1980-82	1985-87	1990-92
U. S.—total	23,351	24,372	31,942
Metals	7,769	6,298	11,566
Industrial minerals	15,582	18,074	20,376
PNW—total	751	789	1,017
Idaho	418	297	338
Oregon	136	139	201
Washington	197	353	478

Table 26. Average annual value of nonfuel mineral production in Idaho, Oregon, and Washington (in thousands of dollars)

	IDAHO			OREGON			WASHINGTON		
	1980-82	1985-87	1990-92	1980-82	1985-87	1990-92	1980-82	1985-87	1990-92
Cement						20,625	89,108	41,074	w
Clays	230	w	w	278	520	1,197	1,641	1,773	2,411
Copper	6,635	1,747	w			179			
Gem stones	70	329	353	517	350	2,038	183	200	126
Gold		27,936	30,886	434					78,644
Lead	22,354	6,335		w					
Phosphate rock	69,946	77,278	83,165						
Pumice			336	439					
Sand & gravel	11,220	18,077	32,041	40,110	40,532	59,876	46,431	76,121	136,956
Silver	191,532	58,982	49,583	32			236		
Stone	6,482	11,674	16,352	45,934	60,515	83,341	18,140	38,311	54,569
Zinc	7,625	98				607			
Combined*	101,546	94,735	125,049	47,811	37,324	32,796	41,567	195,431	205,349
Total	417,640	297,191	337,765	135,555	139,241	200,659	197,306	352,910	478,055

w = withheld
*Combined category includes the value of production for minerals not listed, listed without reported value, and for which information has been withheld.

different rates. The reasons for these divergent trends arc instructive, because they relate not to absolute values of the mineral wealth, but instead to breadth and composition of the mineral resource base, which differ among the three states.

Idaho ranked 32nd among the states in 1991 for nonfuel mineral production and contributed 0.92 percent of the nation's mineral wealth. Idaho has been consistently among the top three producers of antimony, garnet, lead, molybdenum, phosphate rock, silver, and vanadium. Nonetheless, the average annual value of mineral production has decreased 19.1 percent over the past decade from $417.6 million in 1980-82 to $337.8 million in 1990-92. Annual production values have ranged from a high of $522.1 million in 1980 to a low of $269.4 million in 1987. This cyclic and decade-long decline in production values has two major causes. One is the lengthy and deep minerals industry recession of the mid-1980s. The other is the fact that Idaho derives a high percentage of its mineral revenues (between 40 and 60 percent) from metals, the prices of which have been depressed, especially in the case of molybdeum and silver.

VALUE OF MINERAL PRODUCTION
(In Millions Of Dollars)

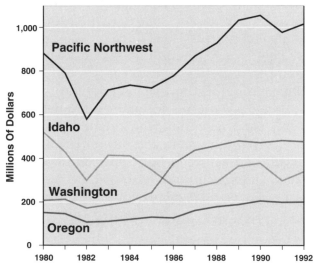

123

PRECIOUS METALS

Ag   **Silver**
Au   **Gold**
☐   **Active Mine**

Revenue losses were compounded by production curtailments and/or closures at several important mines. As of 1992, only the Galena, Lucky Friday, and Sunshine mines continued to operate in the world-famous and silver-rich Coeur d'Alene mining district of Shoshone County. Elsewhere, gold and silver were recovered from ores of the Black Pine (Cassia County), Champagne (Butte County), DeLamar (Owyhee County), and Stibnite and Yellow Pine (Valley County) mines, as was molybdenum from the Thompson Creek mine (Custer County). Various industrial minerals are produced at numerous localities, including phosphate rock used in fertilizers (from which fluorine, gallium, silica, silver, vanadium, and yttrium are also extracted) and garnet of both gem and industrial grades. Other gemstones recovered include aquamarine, jasper, quartz, opal, topaz, and turquoise.

Oregon. The average value of mineral production in Oregon rose from $135.6 million in 1980-82 to $200.7 million in 1990-92, an increase of 47.8 percent, which is somewhat better than the national increase. Annual values for this period ranged from a high of $204.6 million in 1990 to a low of $107.8 million in 1982. Production values for Oregon in recent years are a conservative minimum, because revenues for nickel (as much as $50-60 million in 1992) have not been included. In 1991, the state

ranked 33rd nationally in value of mineral output, and produced 0.88 percent of U.S. mineral wealth. The value of mineral production increased for nearly all commodities, and copper and zinc returned to the list. Oregon is the only primary producer of nickel in the U.S. (about 20 percent of total consumption). It ranks first in the production of pumice, third in diatomite, and contributes significant quantities of zeolite. Gem minerals include the thunderegg (state "rock"), the calcic plagioclase feldspar known as "sunstone," and varying amounts of agate, opal, jasper, and petrified wood. Gold was recovered from small placer operations in northeast and southwest Oregon. Also in southwest Oregon, in Douglas County, the Nickel Mountain mine was reactivated in 1991, and production of copper and zinc with byproduct gold and silver resumed at the Silver Peak mine.

Washington's mineral economy underwent a robust expansion during the past decade. As of 1991, Washington ranked 22nd nationally and generated 1.44 percent of total U.S. nonfuel mineral revenues. Average annual values of mineral production rose from $197.3 million in 1980-82 to $478.1 million in 1990-92, an impressive increase of 142.6 percent. Annual production values for this period ranged from a high of $482.7 million in 1991 to a low of $172.1

BASE METALS

million in 1982. Washington benefited from an expanding economy, a product mix of commodities least impacted by depressed prices, and successful exploration and development of new mineral resources. With the notable exception of gemstones, the annual production value for nearly all mineral commodities rose during this period. Although mineral revenues for the state were dominated by those of sand and gravel, magnesium metal, and stone, those of the precious metals increased dramatically with new output of gold and silver from the Cannon mine in Chelan County and from the Kettle, Key, and Overlook mines added to that of the long-producing Republic (Knob Hill) mine, all in the Republic mining district of Ferry County.

Exploration and Development

Exploration activity in the Pacific Northwest has increased substantially since the minerals recession of the mid-1980s. It has been most pronounced in Idaho and Washington, restrained and unobtrusive in Oregon. The incentives, beyond profit, for such costly efforts include attractive and stable mineral prices and a vast expanse of geologically favorable terrain that has received relatively little attention with modern exploration technology. Disincentives for such expenditures are the increasingly stringent environmental regulations adopted by

some states (for example, Oregon), actual and proposed closures of large and potentially favorable areas to prospecting, and possible forthcoming changes in U.S. mining law.

Recent exploration activities have been widespread throughout Idaho, particularly in the north, north-central, and south parts. Efforts in Oregon have been largely confined to the east and southwest parts of the state. Exploration in Washington has been especially intense to the northeast in and near active or dormant mines of the Metalline and Republic mining districts in Pend Oreille and Ferry counties, respectively, and selectively to the west at several locations along the trend of the Cascade Mountains and adjoining terrain to the east. Although exploration activity for most of the past decade has been dominated by the search for precious metals, the recent price stability for some base metals has led to a renewed interest in copper and zinc.

As a result of some intensive and moderately successful exploration programs in the Pacific Northwest, one or more properties in each of the three states are now in the development stage preparatory to production. Mine development in Idaho is being considered or is underway at the Beartrack (Lemhi County), Grouse Creek (Custer County), Stone Cabin (Owyhee County) and Yellowjacket (Lemhi County) properties for gold

FERROALLOY METALS

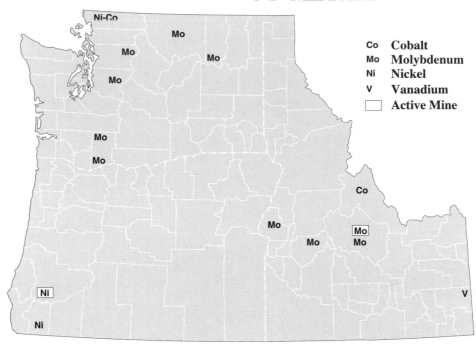

Co   **Cobalt**
Mo **Molybdenum**
Ni   **Nickel**
V   **Vanadium**
☐   **Active Mine**

and silver, and also at the large Dry Valley (Caribou County) phosphate deposit. In Oregon, approval for immediate development is being sought at the Bornite (copper, silver, gold) deposit located on the west side of the Cascade Mountains east of Salem in Marion County, and at the large Grassy Mountain (gold, silver) property south-southwest of Ontario in Malheur County. Nickel ore is now being imported from New Caledonia for processing in the Glenbrook smelter located at the recently reactivated Nickel Mountain mine (Douglas County) south of Roseburg. Apparently the smelter, with access to relatively inexpensive hydroelectric power, is as valuable as the mine itself. New developments in Washington are largely focused on the Republic (silver, gold) mining district in Ferry County, the nearby Crown Jewel (gold, silver, copper) property in Okanogan County, and the proposed reactivation of the now idle Pend Oreille (zinc, lead, silver) mine north of Spokane in Pend Oreille County.

Environmental Problems and Future Trends

The nation has become increasingly focused on environmental concerns and the mining industry is regarded as a prime antagonist in these deliberations. This image is not without justification, but it has been exaggerated beyond reason. Both the Tacoma smelter in Washington and the Bunker Hill smelter at Kellogg, Idaho, are currently Superfund sites resulting from years of pollution by toxic metals. The Delamar mine in southwest Idaho has been cited for violation of the Migratory Bird Treaty Act after the deaths of nearly one hundred waterfowl in a cyanide-bearing tailings pond, in spite of mitigation tactics such as 24-hour surveillance, fencing, propane cannons, radar, and loud rock music. Elsewhere, mills processing phosphate rock in Idaho have had to contend with difficult particulate and radioactive emission standards; tailings from the long-dormant Holden mine near Lake Chelan in Washington have undergone enforced cleanup; and recently the Oregon Environmental Quality Commission imposed new rules, in addition to those of Oregon's Department of Geology and Mineral Industries and the Department of Fish and Wildlife, to restrictively control the heap leaching of gold with cyanide. These regulations, and others relating to quality of ground and surface waters, have caused protracted and costly delays in

INDUSTRIAL MINERALS

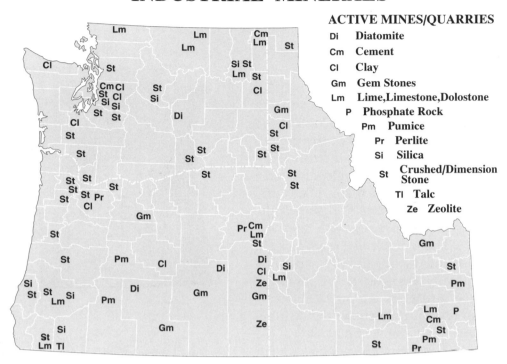

ACTIVE MINES/QUARRIES

Di	Diatomite
Cm	Cement
Cl	Clay
Gm	Gem Stones
Lm	Lime,Limestone,Dolostone
P	Phosphate Rock
Pm	Pumice
Pr	Perlite
Si	Silica
St	Crushed/Dimension Stone
Tl	Talc
Ze	Zeolite

the development of major new mines in Oregon. For such well-publicized reasons, many companies will not conduct exploration in the state. On the other hand, mining companies, working with government agencies, have successfully developed bacterial methods of degrading highly toxic cyanide to harmless carbon dioxide, nitrogen, and water. Coeur d'Alene Mines has won the first DuPont/Conoco Environmental Leadership Award and the highest award given by the Wildlife Habitat Enhancement Council for extraordinary environmental restoration efforts at the now depleted Thunder Mountain gold mine in Idaho. These and other environmentally positive efforts suggest that the mining industry can adapt to the changing times.

Finally, it is likely that the Mining Law of 1872 will soon be modified by Congress. Among the most contentious of changes proposed in the Bumpers/Rahall Bill are the addition of an annual holding fee of $100 per claim, regardless of other exploration expenditures, and the imposition of a royalty tax of at least 8 percent on the gross value of production. Although there are both positive and negative aspects to the impending bill, it is certain that the Mining Law of 1872 warrants change, and that the minerals industry will survive and probably flourish, regardless of current pessimism and uncertainty.

Sources of Information

Production and other statistical data were derived mainly from the Minerals Yearbook, Mineral Commodity Summaries, and State Mineral Summaries published annually by the U.S. Bureau of Mines. Details concerning mineral deposits were obtained from excellent annual summaries of the Idaho Geological Survey, Oregon Department of Geology and Mineral Industries, and the Washington Department of Natural Resources. Industry publications such as the Engineering and Mining Journal, Mining Engineering, and Skillings Mining Review, in addition to several corporate annual reports, provided further useful information.

Manufacturing and Industries

WILLIAM B. BEYERS

The majority of working people in the Pacific Northwest are employed in manufacturing, trade, and service industries. Table 27 shows that 2.9 million people were employed in these industries in 1989, an increase of 1.2 million between 1974 and 1989, a gain of 69 percent. However, this growth rate has been uneven both among industries and geographically. The bulk of this employment gain was in the various service industries, while manufacturing employment grew at less than half the overall regional employment growth rate. The modest growth in manufacturing employment in Idaho and Oregon and the significant expansion in Washington, led by the aerospace sector, compared favorably with the virtual lack of growth nationally.

The first map on this page shows the distribution of private nonagricultural employment at the county level with concentration of employment in the major metropolitan areas of the Pacific Northwest, while the next map shows the percentage change in private nonagricultural employment between 1974 and 1989. Most employment growth was concentrated in the region's major metropolitan areas, but it was more rapid in suburban counties near Portland and Seattle than in central city counties. Smaller nonmetropolitan counties, such as many Idaho Rocky Mountain counties, have experienced employment declines. Much of nonmetropolitan eastern Washington and Oregon, and counties outside the Snake River Plain in Idaho, have grown slowly. Rapid growth in amenity-laden counties such as Blaine in Idaho, Deschutes in Oregon, and San Juan in Washington is also evident in this map.

Manufacturing

The structure of manufacturing employment varies among the Northwest states, as shown in the graph on page 129. Washington's manufacturing sector is larger than those of Oregon and Idaho taken together, and it has expanded more rapidly. Washington's manufacturing sector is led by transportation equipment manufacturing, which is in turn dominated by aerospace employment at the Boeing Company. Food products and forest products sectors are important in all three states, but the latter have experienced declines in

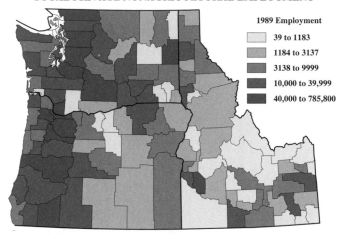

TOTAL PRIVATE NONAGRICULTURAL EMPLOYMENT

1989 Employment
- 39 to 1183
- 1184 to 3137
- 3138 to 9999
- 10,000 to 39,999
- 40,000 to 785,800

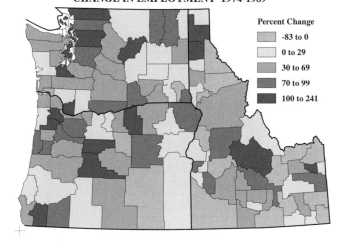

CHANGE IN EMPLOYMENT 1974-1989

Percent Change
- -83 to 0
- 0 to 29
- 30 to 69
- 70 to 99
- 100 to 241

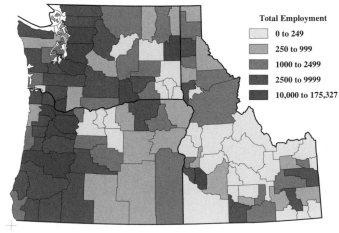

MANUFACTURING EMPLOYMENT 1989

Total Employment
- 0 to 249
- 250 to 999
- 1000 to 2499
- 2500 to 9999
- 10,000 to 175,327

MANUFACTURING EMPLOYMENT BY
MAJOR INDUSTRIAL SECTORS - 1989

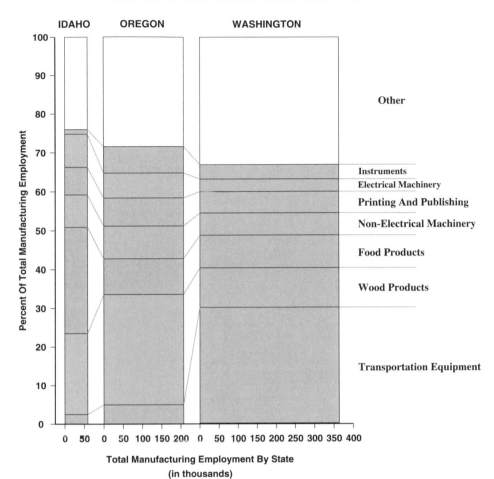

Total Manufacturing Employment By State
(in thousands)

employment in recent years. The graph shows that forest products manufacturing is relatively more important in Idaho and Oregon than in Washington. High-technology sectors have been a basis for growth in all three states. Electrical and non-electrical machinery, transportation equipment, and instruments manufacturing sectors are the most important high-technology sectors in the Northwest, and Table 27 shows that they have exhibited much more rapid employment growth than manufacturing as a whole.

Manufacturing employment is most heavily concentrated in the major metropolitan areas of the region, as shown on the map at the borrom of page 128. The graph on page 131 shows the composition of this employment for the Standard Metropolitan Areas (SMSAs), which account for 75 percent of total manufacturing employment in the Pacific Northwest. It is evident that there are major structural differences in Northwest metropolitan area

economies. Manufacturing employment in the Central Puget Sound region is dominated by the transportation equipment sector; no other metropolitan area in the region exhibits such a concentration of employment in this sector. Interestingly, central office or administrative employment is quite important in Central Puget Sound manufacturing, led by headquarters of corporations such as Weyerhauser and Boeing. The Portland and Spokane metropolitan areas' manufacturing composition is much more diversified.

Smaller metropolitan areas tend to have less diversified manufacturing sectors than larger centers. The manufacturing sector in Medford and Eugene is dominated by lumber and wood products, Boise's by electrical and nonelectrical machinery, the Tri-Cities' by food and chemicals production/nuclear repository management at Hanford, Salem and Yakima's by food and wood products, and Bellingham's by food, wood,

129

Table 27. **Private nonagricultural summary employment data**

	1989 EMPLOYMENT (THOUSANDS)				CHANGE	PERCENT CHANGE			
	ID	OR	WA	Region	1974-89	ID	OR	WA	Region
Total	285.6	976.9	1652.0	2914.5	1192.7	51.1	54.1	83.9	69.3
Ag. services, forestry, fishing	2.4	9.8	16.5	28.7	17.5	80.4	123.2	201.0	156.1
Mining	3.4	1.5	3.1	8.0	2.2	12.6	46.2	72.1	37.0
Construction	15.9	43.6	97.9	157.4	56.5	17.8	20.6	91.0	56.0
Manufacturing total	59.1	207.4	363.4	629.8	144.9	18.1	11.0	46.5	29.9
Food products	16.2	19.1	30.6	65.9	8.2	4.0	5.5	27.2	14.2
Wood products	12.4	59.4	37.0	108.7	-23.8	-13.5	-18.6	-18.4	-18.0
Printing & publishing	4.2	14.9	20.0	39.1	17.2	95.3	86.0	69.7	78.1
Nonelectrical machinery	4.9	17.5	20.7	43.0	15.1	192.8	36.2	53.7	54.0
Electrical machinery	5.0	13.3	11.7	30.0	20.3	703.2	210.1	143.3	208.6
Transportation equipment	1.5	10.4	109.9	121.9	47.5	105.2	21.0	69.1	63.9
Instruments	0.7	14.0	13.5	28.1	14.5	915.4	29.7	389.9	106.8
Other manufacturing	14.2	58.8	120.0	193.1	46.0	- 4.4	14.7	48.3	31.2
Trade & services total	204.8	714.6	1171.1	2090.5	971.6	69.1	76.2	97.9	86.8
Transp., commun., utilities	16.6	61.2	100.9	178.7	64.3	41.9	47.2	65.2	56.3
Wholesale trade	23.3	72.3	113.9	209.6	65.0	29.2	37.8	54.0	45.0
Retail trade	67.8	226.9	361.4	656.1	287.9	53.7	67.0	92.0	78.2
Eating & drinking	22.2	79.1	128.5	230.0	122.2	44.9	54.0	74.9	63.6
Other retail	45.6	147.7	232.9	426.2	165.7	75.8	98.1	133.2	113.4
Finance, insurance, real estate	15.5	63.8	113.2	192.6	65.2	53.6	40.5	57.5	51.1
Producer services	23.1	74.9	128.1	226.0	152.1	235.8	202.0	203.2	205.8
Health services	21.8	89.6	147.1	258.5	135.8	98.0	105.4	116.1	110.7
Other services	36.6	126.0	206.4	369.0	201.6	91.2	103.3	139.1	120.4

nonferrous metals, and petroleum refining. This degree of specialization tends to be even sharper in smaller nonmetropolitan counties.

While manufacturing employment as measured in absolute numbers is highest in the large metropolitan areas, it is nevertheless important to the economies of many smaller places in the Northwest. The map at the foot of page 128 shows some manufacturing employment in most counties in Washington and Oregon, and in northern Idaho and the upper Snake River counties of southern Idaho. The map on page 132, which is based on a cluster analysis of county manufacturing structure, clearly shows the importance of forest products manufacturing to many county economies in the Pacific Northwest. Over much of western Washington and Oregon, much of eastern Oregon, and in the Idaho Rocky Mountain counties, forest products employment is the distinguishing manufacturing component. Frequently it is found along with other categories of manufacturing, including food products, metals, stone/clay/glass, and high technology manufacturing sectors.

Food Products

Food products manufacturing is important in most of the metropolitan area economies and is also found in many nonmetropolitan counties in the Northwest, as shown in the small map on page 132. Major food products sectors include meat and dairy products, canning and freezing of fruits and vegetables, baking, sugar processing, and beverage

MANUFACTURING EMPLOYMENT IN SELECTED M.S.A.'S BY SECTOR

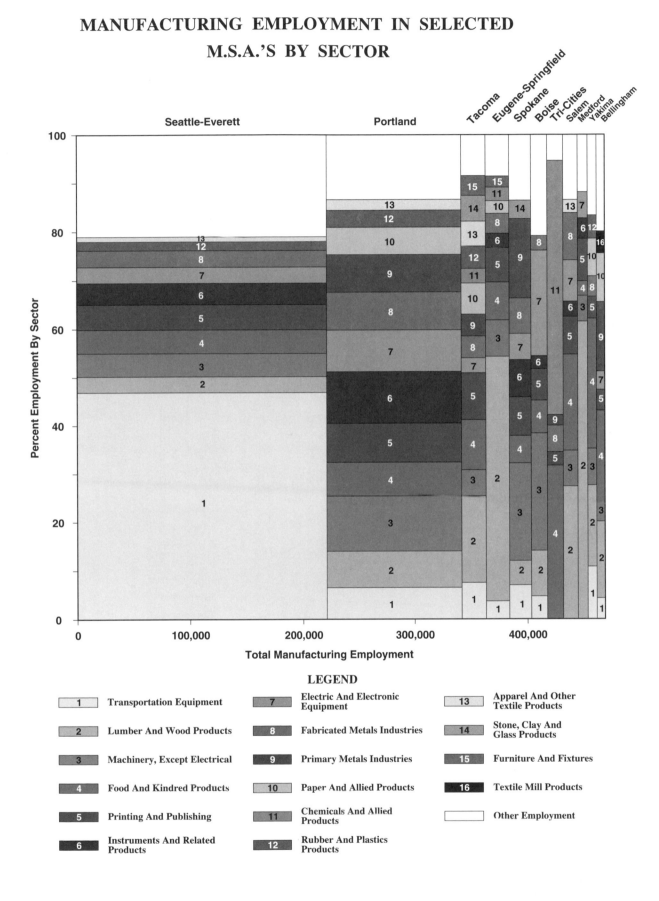

LEGEND

1	Transportation Equipment
2	Lumber And Wood Products
3	Machinery, Except Electrical
4	Food And Kindred Products
5	Printing And Publishing
6	Instruments And Related Products
7	Electric And Electronic Equipment
8	Fabricated Metals Industries
9	Primary Metals Industries
10	Paper And Allied Products
11	Chemicals And Allied Products
12	Rubber And Plastics Products
13	Apparel And Other Textile Products
14	Stone, Clay And Glass Products
15	Furniture And Fixtures
16	Textile Mill Products
	Other Employment

131

production. Production is destined to local consumer markets, and exported to other parts of the United States or abroad. Meat and dairy products production tends to be located near to the region's major metropolitan areas, although specialty dairy products processing establishments are found in rural counties. Canning and freezing plants are located near major agricultural areas in southern Idaho, the Willamette Valley, eastern Washington, and northern Puget Sound. Small bakeries are found in towns around the region, but most employment is associated with large commercial baking establishments in the region's major metropolitan areas. Beet sugar refineries are found in southern Idaho. Beverage production is divided between beer, soft drinks, and wine. Breweries and soft-drink bottling facilities are found in the major metropolitan areas of the region, while wineries are located in the Willamette and Yakima-Columbia valleys close to grape-producing regions, as well as in suburban Seattle, utilizing grapes grown in eastern Washington.

Food products manufacturing industries are part of a larger industrial complex which includes the region's agriculture sector, and a service-sector distribution system which includes transportation services, wholesaling, and retail activities bringing Northwest food products to household consumers in grocery stores and eating and drinking establishments. It also includes manufacturers of packaging materials such as plastics, glass, and paper, establishments in the agricultural services sector, and manufacturers of machinery and equipment used in farming and in the food products processing sectors.

FOOD PRODUCTS MANUFACTURING EMPLOYMENT

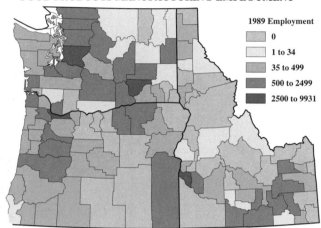

1989 Employment
- 0
- 1 to 34
- 35 to 499
- 500 to 2499
- 2500 to 9931

MANUFACTURING EMPLOYMENT STRUCTURE - 1989

Dominant Employment

- Forest Products
- Food Products
- Metal Products
- Chemical Products
- Stone Products
- High Technology
- D Diverse Manufacturing
- O Other Manufacturing
- Negligible Employment

Forest Products

The forest products industry has historically been the largest manufacturing sector in the Pacific Northwest. It is composed of a number of integrated subsectors, which range from the growing of timber (forestry) to harvesting timber (logging) and processing it into semifinished or finished products. The graph on this page shows the important components of the industry; important manufacturing sectors are logging, sawmills, veneer and plywood, and pulp and paper production. The map at the foot of page 132 shows that the forest products industry is the most important manufacturing sector in many county economies in the Northwest, a reflection of the widespread distribution of commercial forests in the region. The two maps at the top of page 134 show the distribution of employment in wood products and pulp and paper manufacture. Pulp and paper manufacturing is highly localized in comparison to the much broader distribution of employment in the lumber and wood products sector. These maps show that while the forest products industry is locally important east of the Cascades, the primary concentration of employment in these sectors is located west of the Cascade Mountains.

The graph below identifies the market orientation of the Northwest forest products industry. Most production is consumed outside the region, and is split between domestic and foreign markets. In recent years, about one-third of Washington's and about one-sixth of Oregon's timber harvest has been sold in the log export market. The bulk of these shipments have been to Japan and South Korea. Sawmills and veneer/plywood production facilities consume the majority of the balance of the timber harvest, and the output of these mills is primarily

FOREST PRODUCTS INDUSTRIAL COMPLEX

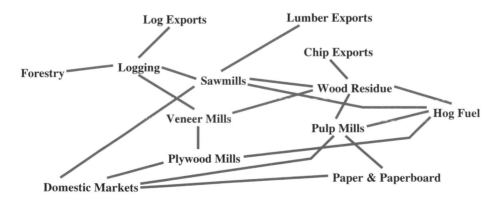

sold in the domestic construction market, although foreign lumber markets have grown in recent years. Residue generated in the lumber and plywood manufacturing process is the primary source of wood fiber for the pulp and paper manufacturing industry, and is also used as hog fuel providing energy for manufacturing in the forest products industry as well as being sold in the regional energy market.

Output in the forest products industry has been cyclical, responding to the fluctuating demand for lumber and wood products through business cycles. Recent supply constraints on federal and state timberlands have magnified the impact of the current recession on the Northwest forest products industry. These impacts, combined with ongoing changes in technology which have saved labor in the production process, have resulted in an ongoing decline in the number of people employed in the forest products industry regionally, as shown in Table 27. This decline has been sharper in western Washington and Oregon than in the interior, as new technologies have made it possible to process smaller diameter (second growth) logs, allowing some expansion of timber harvests and processing in eastern Washington, Oregon, and Idaho.

Printing & Publishing

Printing and publishing manufacturing employment is widely distributed throughout the Pacific Northwest. Newspaper printing and commercial printing are the two most important constituents of this industry, and are found even in relatively small rural counties. Most firms in this sector are small, and the map shows that while there is some employment found in most Northwest counties, the total level in most counties is quite small. The largest concentrations of printing employment are found in the cities where the major daily newspapers are printed.

Chemicals and Petroleum Refining

Chemicals and petroleum refining employment is highly concentrated in the Pacific Northwest. Most counties have no employment in these sectors, as shown on the map on page 135. Petroleum refining primarily occurs at four refineries in Skagit and Whatcom counties in Washington state, utilizing crude oil imported by tanker from Alaska and the

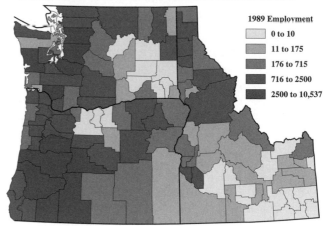

WOOD PRODUCTS MANUFACTURING EMPLOYMENT

1989 Employment
- 0 to 10
- 11 to 175
- 176 to 715
- 716 to 2500
- 2500 to 10,537

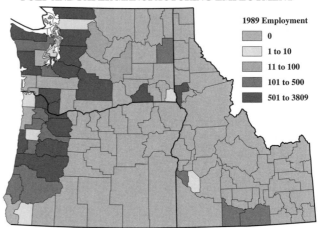

PULP AND PAPER MANUFACTURING EMPLOYMENT

1989 Employment
- 0
- 1 to 10
- 11 to 100
- 101 to 500
- 501 to 3809

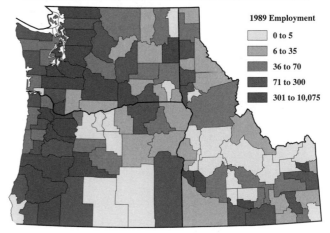

PRINTING AND PUBLISHING INDUSTRY EMPLOYMENT

1989 Employment
- 0 to 5
- 6 to 35
- 36 to 70
- 71 to 300
- 301 to 10,075

CHEMICALS AND PETROLEUM REFINING EMPLOYMENT

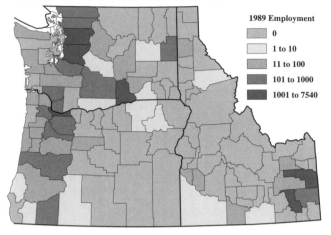

1989 Employment

0

1 to 10

11 to 100

101 to 1000

1001 to 7540

PRIMARY METALS MANUFACTURING EMPLOYMENT

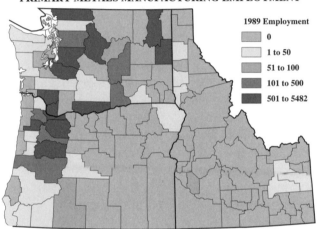

1989 Employment

0

1 to 50

51 to 100

101 to 500

501 to 5482

HIGH-TECHNOLOGY MANUFACTURING EMPLOYMENT

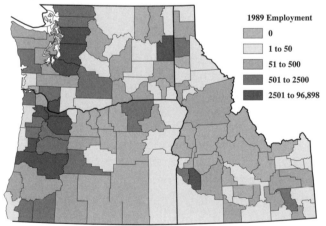

1989 Employment

0

1 to 50

51 to 500

501 to 2500

2501 to 96,898

Far East, and by pipeline from Alberta. Several smaller refineries are also found in the region, along with several asphalt products plants. Major chemicals manufacturing activities are diverse in character. Phosphatic fertilizer and inorganic chemicals are important in southeastern Idaho. And in Benton County, Washington, plutonium production has shifted to waste management. Chlorine and adhesives are made for use by the forest products industry in some westside urban areas.

Primary Metals

The primary metals industry in the Pacific Northwest is dominated by mills in the aluminum reduction industry. Plants are located in Spokane, Ferndale, Wenatchee, Tacoma, Goldendale, The Dalles, Longview, Vancouver, and Troutdale. Alumina, which is used to make aluminum metal, is imported primarily from Australia in bulk carriers, and transported by rail or barge to interior mills. These mills account for about 40 percent of the domestic smelting capacity for primary aluminum; they were located in the Northwest due to the availability of cheap federal hydropower from Columbia and Snake river dams. Today the energy cost has risen, making these plants less competitive. To help keep them economically viable, their energy cost is now linked to the world price for primary aluminum metal. In addition to these primary reduction mills, major aluminum fabricating plants are located in Spokane, Vancouver, Longview, and Troutdale. Millersburg, in Linn County, Oregon, is a major producer of titanium, columbium, and zirconium metals and metal alloys, as well as of silicon metal products. Near Wenatchee, Washington, and Riddle, Oregon, major ferrosilicon plants are located, while a large magnesium production facility is located in Addy, Washington. Historically important copper smelting facilities in Tacoma have been closed due to environmental and technological considerations, while the silver processing facilities in northern Idaho have been closed due to poor market conditions.

Ferrous metals production in the Northwest is based on scrap iron and steel. Primarily located in Portland and Seattle/Tacoma, it uses electrical furnaces to melt scrap, which is primarily used to produce rebar and other shapes for the construction industry (see maps on page 139).

High-Technology Sectors

The Northwest has developed a substantial high-technology manufacturing sector, which is primarily located in or near to the major metropolitan centers of the region. The map at the foot of page 135 shows the location of this employment, which is defined here as the sum of nonelectrical and electrical machinery, transportation equipment, and instruments manufacture (some other sectors often considered high-technology are not included in this grouping). The graph on page 131 showed the composition of employment in the SMSAs of the Northwest. In central Puget Sound, the aerospace sector led by Boeing dominates the high-technology sector, but ship- and boat-building, truck assembly, nonelectrical and electrical machinery, and instruments manufacture are also of importance. The region from Eugene to Vancouver also contains a major concentration of high technology industry, but with a very different character than found in the Puget Sound area. Often dubbed the Silicon Forest, this complex is strongly tied to electronic equipment, computing equipment, instruments, and the manufacture of electronic components. Boise and Spokane have smaller but rapidly growing high-technology sectors. Not shown on the map is the major concentration of navy shipbuilding workers in Bremerton. Computer software has emerged as a major industry in both the Portland and Seattle metropolitan areas; it is classified both in services and in manufacturing. High-technology sectors typically have a large share of nonproduction workers, and a substantial commitment to research and development. Boeing provides a good example of the occupational profile of high-technology manufacturers. Currently, about 35 percent of Boeing's Puget Sound labor force is engaged in blue-collar occupations, while 65 percent are engaged in professional and technical occupations which require high educational and skill levels. Strong ties with regional colleges and universities for research and labor force training are common for high-technology manufacturers. While the Northwest has a combination of indigenous high-technology firms and branch plants of domestic and foreign corporations, entrepreneurs in these firms have often been the source of innovative ideas for new, spin-off, high-technology businesses.

Other Manufacturing

Several other manufacturing industries are found in the Northwest. The largest of these is fabricated metals, which accounts for 4 percent of regional manufacturing employment. Smaller numbers of people work in apparel; furniture; rubber and plastics; stone, clay, and glass; and in other manufacturing.

Services

Service industry employment in the Northwest is the largest component of the regional economy today. As shown in Table 27, service industries have also been the source of most new jobs in the region in recent years, and this trend is expected to continue over the next decade. In contrast to many lines of manufacturing, where producers are drawn to the location of resources such as timber or relatively inexpensive electricity, most service industries are located in proximity to their markets. Thus, the overall pattern of service industry employment mirrors the overall distribution of population in the Northwest. However, there are systematic variations in the structure of service industries as we move from small towns to major metropolitan areas, or from neighborhood shopping centers in cities to major retail malls in suburban centers. While household consumer markets are of primary importance for many lines of service employment, this is not the case for all services. Many lines of service employment are dependent upon businesses or governments as their clients. It is therefore necessary to differentiate among services with differing market orientations.

Consumer-oriented Services

Household consumers are the most important markets for retailing, health services, basic financial, insurance, and real estate services, entertainment, social and educational services, and some repair services. Services such as legal and banking services have mixed business and household markets. Demand for these services is based on people's residential and work locations, and their spatial distribution is related to the size of market needed for a service firm to successfully compete. Services demanded commonly (such as groceries) rely on localized trade areas for their clients, while services which are demanded only occasionally (such as writing pen repair) rely on much larger trade areas for their clients. This results in the development of a hierarchy of trade centers, with clusters of service firms with similar trade areas. In some cases, agglomerations of offices providing specialized services arise, as in the case of specialized health-care services, while in other cases diverse sellers cluster in town centers or urban shopping districts. For people living in the parts of the Northwest with a low population density, these service functions are clustered at the lowest levels of this hierarchy in nearby small towns, while the demand for more specialized service functions is satisfied in nearby medium-sized centers, and the most specialized functions are supplied by businesses located in the region's major metropolitan areas. Within major metropolitan areas, a similar spatial differentiation is found, but because of higher densities of settlement the spacing of suppliers is closer than is the case in the more sparsely populated parts of the region.

A recent analysis of this system of settlements was undertaken by Swanson. The map at the top of this page shows Swanson's classification scheme of Northwest counties by position in the settlement heirarchy. This classification overlooks within-county patterns, including major shopping centers and suburban cities in major metropolitan counties. However, it does suggest the existence of a settlement heirarchy dominated by Portland and Seattle, with mid-level places such as Bend and Pocatello, and a position in this system of distribution and trade for every community found in the Pacific Northwest.

The distribution of retail employment in 1989 shows a pattern very similar to the overall distribution of employment shown in the map on page 128. In recent years, one of the most rapidly growing retailing industries has been eating and drinking establishments, as shown in Table 27. The map shows the relative distribution of employment in this sector in 1989, through the use of location quotients, which show the share of employment in this industry in a given county relative to the share in the U.S. as a whole in 1989. The patterns on this map show a number of counties with more than twice the national average employment in eating and drinking establishments. These are primarily tourist-oriented counties such as Lincoln County, Oregon, and Blaine County, Idaho. They

REGIONAL TRADE CENTER HIERARCHY

- Small Rural Trade Centers
- Subregional Trade Centers
- Regional Trade Centers
- Supra-regional Trade Centers
- Metropolitan Core & Metropolitan Fringe

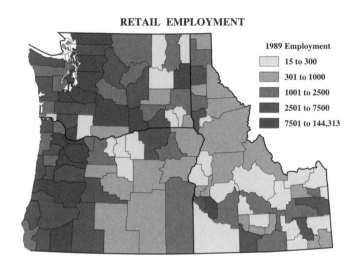

RETAIL EMPLOYMENT

1989 Employment
- 15 to 300
- 301 to 1000
- 1001 to 2500
- 2501 to 7500
- 7501 to 144,313

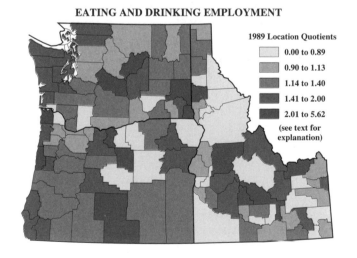

EATING AND DRINKING EMPLOYMENT

1989 Location Quotients
- 0.00 to 0.89
- 0.90 to 1.13
- 1.14 to 1.40
- 1.41 to 2.00
- 2.01 to 5.62

(see text for explanation)

also include counties with large government employment (which was excluded from the data base used to calculate these measures) and little manufacturing employment, such as Whitman County, Washington, where Washington State University is located. The map at the top of this page shows location quotients for another service important to the tourist and recreation industry, hotels and other lodging places, and the pattern is similar.

Other important consumer-oriented services include health, social, educational, cultural, amusement, and repair services. The distribution of employment in these other consumer services is similar to the pattern exhibited by retail trade.

Business-oriented Services

Services which primarily sell their services to other businesses are referred to as the producer services; this group of services includes functions such as legal, architectural and engineering, accounting, and business services such as advertising, computing, and consulting. Table 27 showed that these services had exhibited a very rapid growth rate between 1974 and 1989. The geographical distribution of this group of services is much more concentrated in major urban areas than is the case with consumer-oriented services. The map on this page shows location quotients for producer services, and shows a strong tendency for the most populous counties to have a higher concentration than smaller rural counties. While producer service firms sell most of their services within the region, some are highly specialized businesses which trade their services nationally or internationally, such as computer software or consulting firms.

Wholesale trade also serves a variety of business markets, not only supplying retailers who sell goods to household consumers, but also handling products destined for export markets, or consumed by manufacturers, governments, and service firms within the region. While the overall pattern of wholesale employment (see map on page 139) again mirrors the aggregate distribution of population, the importance of wholesalers in the distribution of agricultural commodities is clearly illustrated in the map below. Fruit and vegetable, grain, and other agricultural commodity storage operations—either in fresh or processed form—are part of the channel of distribution for the Northwest's agriculture sector.

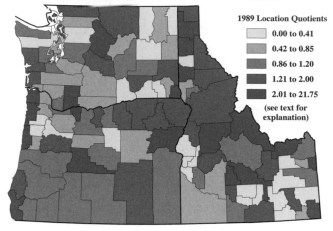

HOTEL AND OTHER LODGING EMPLOYMENT

1989 Location Quotients
- 0.00 to 0.41
- 0.42 to 0.85
- 0.86 to 1.20
- 1.21 to 2.00
- 2.01 to 21.75

(see text for explanation)

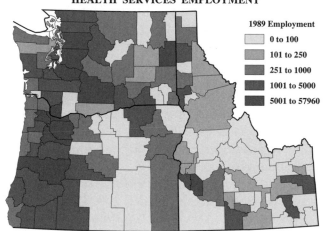

HEALTH SERVICES EMPLOYMENT

1989 Employment
- 0 to 100
- 101 to 250
- 251 to 1000
- 1001 to 5000
- 5001 to 57960

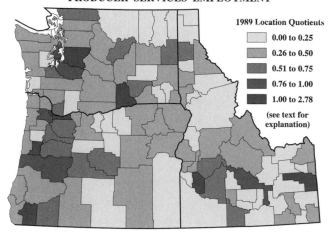

PRODUCER SERVICES EMPLOYMENT

1989 Location Quotients
- 0.00 to 0.25
- 0.26 to 0.50
- 0.51 to 0.75
- 0.76 to 1.00
- 1.00 to 2.78

(see text for explanation)

Two important service sectors have mixed consumer and business markets: transportation services, communications, and utilities; and finance, insurance, and real estate. These services are broadly distributed with population, as illustrated by the map at the top of this page. Electrical utility employment in the Northwest is influenced by our dependence on hydropower from Columbia and Snake river dams. Lower Columbia River and Puget Sound ports play a key role in exporting Northwest grain, as well as handling foreign trade moving through the region. Finance and insurance sectors are organized in large corporations with many branch offices distributed widely throughout the region, with regional headquarter offices located in the largest metropolitan centers.

TRANSPORTATION SERVICES, COMMUNICATIONS, AND UTILITIES EMPLOYMENT

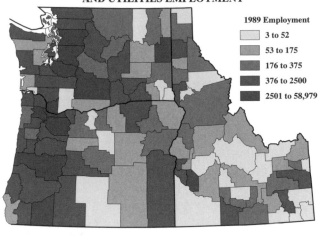

1989 Employment
- 3 to 52
- 53 to 175
- 176 to 375
- 376 to 2500
- 2501 to 58,979

WHOLESALE EMPLOYMENT

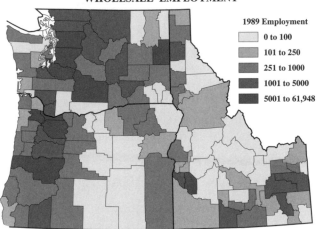

1989 Employment
- 0 to 100
- 101 to 250
- 251 to 1000
- 1001 to 5000
- 5001 to 61,948

STEEL AND FERROALLOY PLANTS

- ● Steel Rolling Mill
- ▲ Other Steel Furnace
- ■ Prereduced Iron Pellet Plant
- ◆ Ferroalloy Plant

Seattle, Wenatchee, Tacoma, Portland, McMinnville, Riddle

WHOLESALE TRADE EMPLOYMENT

1989 Location Quotients
- 0.00 to 0.43
- 0.44 to 0.66
- 0.67 to 1.00
- 1.01 to 1.64
- 1.65 to 5.58

(see text for explanation)

NONFERROUS PLANTS

Aluminum Plants
- ■ Smelter
- ◆ Fabrication

- ■ Zinc Smelter, Lead Smelter And Refinery
- ◆ Zirconium, Titanium, And Columbium
- ▲ Magnesium Reduction
- ★ Silicon Plant

Ferndale, Addy, Wenatchee, Spokane, Kellogg, Tacoma, Longview, Vancouver, Goldendale, Troutdale, The Dalles, Albany, Springfield

Recreation Resources and Tourism

MARY LEE NOLAN

The Pacific Northwest offers a wide variety of outdoor recreation opportunities. These opportunities contribute to quality of life for the residents and form a basis for the region's economically important tourism industry.

Landscape diversity is a principal contributing factor in the region's recreation resources. Broad beaches and rugged headlands, forested hills and snowcapped peaks, placid estuaries and turbulent mountain streams, all provide scenic attractions along the region's westward margins. Eastward, beyond the Cascade Range, high desert plateaus are interspersed with lush green stream valleys and rugged, canyon-cut mountains. In various parts of the region there are mountains to climb, untrammeled wilderness areas to hike, and beaches to comb. Streams, lakes, and estuaries offer bounty to fishing enthusiasts and large expanses of forest and shrub steppe support wildlife populations that attract hunters. These resources provide activity opportunities with little development other than provision for access. In many parts of the region,

recreation possibilities are expanded by developed facilities such as lifts and cleared runs for skiers, launch ramps and marinas to facilitate boating, and numerous campgrounds in scenic surroundings.

The region's ample endowment of natural attractions is supplemented with numerous cultural sites including some of importance to Native American cultures, others associated with European discovery, exploration, and settlement, and yet others that recall the pioneer period. Of particular interest to many tourists are landmarks along the routes of the early nineteenth-century Lewis and Clark expedition, which familiarized Euro-Americans with the region, and the mid-nineteenth-century Oregon Trail, taken by thousands of pioneer settlers from the eastern and central United States.

Management of the region's natural and cultural recreation resources is shared by federal, state, and local government agencies along with private nonprofit and commercial operations. Public

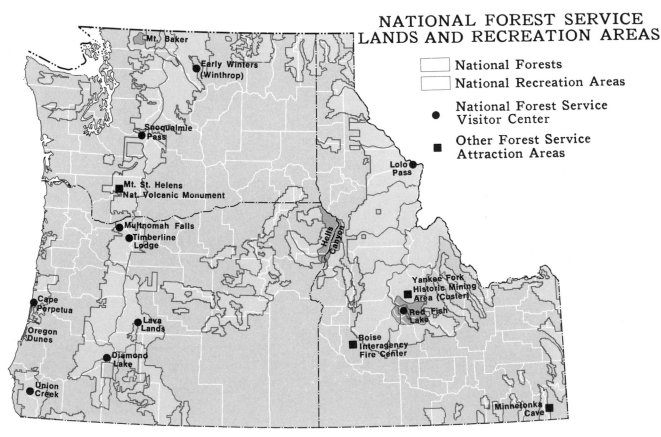

NATIONAL FOREST SERVICE LANDS AND RECREATION AREAS

National Forests
National Recreation Areas
● National Forest Service Visitor Center
■ Other Forest Service Attraction Areas

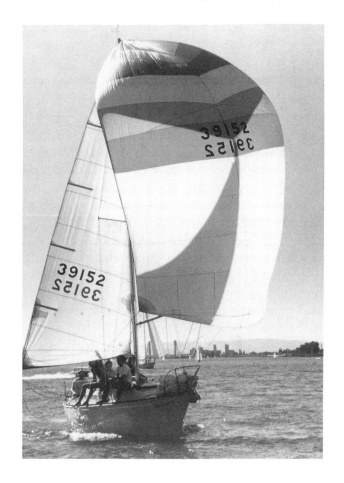

lands, mostly under federal management, make up the bulk of the total area available for recreation. The existence of large, contiguous areas in public ownership has made it possible to develop extensive trails systems and designate numerous Scenic River and Wilderness Areas. Although the abundance of recreation opportunities on public lands may have reduced the region's potential for commercial recreation development, their presence has stimulated the growth of tourism; this, in turn, has enabled private enterprise to invest profitably in the services required by tourists and to develop resorts and highly specialized recreation facilities that are not provided for on public lands.

Expenditures by tourists from other parts of the country and abroad add billions of dollars each year to the region's economy. In all three states, tourism ranks as one of the three most important generators of outside income. In addition to economic considerations, the region's recreation resources are important to Northwesterners as part of a high-quality environment.

National Park Resources in the Pacific Northwest

Several of the most outstanding scenic and historic resources in the Pacific Northwest are administered by the National Park System. In addition to large areas of major significance entitled National Parks, the system includes other parks with a variety of designations such as National Monuments, National Historic Sites, and National Recreation Areas. National Recreation Areas are usually found in association with landscapes that have been greatly modified by human activities, such as the reservoirs behind dams. All these well-publicized attractions are important in drawing tourists to the region and also provide a travel and recreation focus for the region's residents.

Parks Emphasizing Natural Features

Crater Lake National Park, Oregon. About 6,000 years ago, fiery eruptions led to the collapse of Mount Mazama's volcanic peak. The near-circular deep blue lake which lies in the caldera left by the eruption is dramatically encircled by steep slopes of multicolored volcanic material. The park covers more than 160,000 acres in the southern Oregon Cascades.

Mount Rainier National Park, Washington. This park centers on a giant volcano that rises 14,410 feet above sea level. Its peak is covered with glaciers and the lower slopes are decorated with flowered subalpine meadows and dense forests. The entire mountain is included in this park of more than 235,000 acres.

North Cascades National Park, Washington. The heavily glaciated peaks of the North Cascades loom above an alpine region of meadows, forests, fast-running streams and spectacular waterfalls. The park's 504,785 acres are rich in wildlife.

Olympic National Park, Washington. Only trails penetrate this mountain wilderness in the heart of the Olympic Range. Temperate rainforest vegetation thrives on the Pacific slopes of these mountains, where rainfall exceeds 100 inches per year. The park's 901,216 acres also includes 50 miles of coastal headlands and beaches.

Craters of the Moon National Monument, Idaho. The volcanic landscape in this 53,545-acre park includes cinder cones, jagged lava flows, and lava caves.

John Day Fossil Beds National Monument, Oregon. A vividly eroded landscape exposes plant and animal fossils spanning most of the Cenozoic from the Eocene epoch to the late Pleistocene. This priceless record of ancient North American life is preserved in three separate park units covering 14,402 acres.

Oregon Caves National Monument, Oregon. This fascinating labyrinth of underground passages developed in the Siskiyou Mountains of southwestern Oregon as groundwater dissolved the marble and limestone bedrock over eons of time. The park comprises 465 acres.

Mount St. Helens National Volcanic Monument, Oregon. The approximately 110,000 acres devastated by the May 18, 1980, eruption of this volcano are preserved for scientific research and compatible uses.

Historical Parks

Fort Clatsop National Memorial, Oregon. A replica of the log fort where the Lewis and Clark expedition spent the winter of 1805-06 is the principal attraction in this park.

Fort Vancouver National Historic Site, Washington. Fort Vancouver on the Columbia River was the western headquarters of the Hudson's Bay Company. Between 1825 and 1846 it was the center of fur-trading and political activity in the Pacific Northwest. Vancouver Barracks, a U.S. military post established in 1848, took over the fort in 1860. It remained an active military reservation until 1949.

Klondike Gold Rush National Historic Park, Washington. This park in downtown Seattle commemorates the city's historic role as the major embarkation point for the Alaskan gold fields.

McLoughlin House National Historic Site, Oregon. Dr. John McLoughlin, who lived in this house from 1847 until 1857, was in charge of the strategic Fort Vancouver through most of the second quarter of the nineteenth century. In this role, he was important in the development of the Pacific Northwest and gave substantial aid to early settlers from the United States. The site is owned and administered by the McLoughlin Memorial Association in affiliation with the National Park Service.

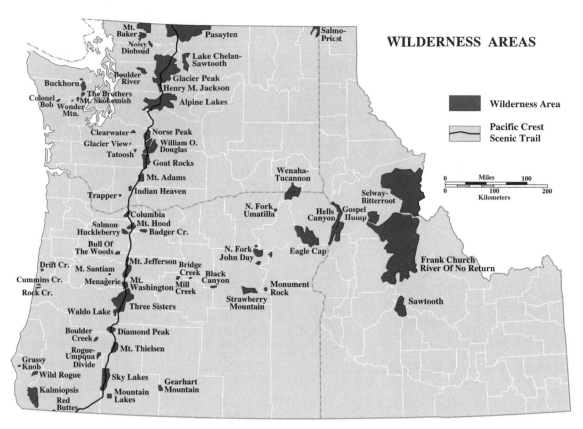

WILDERNESS AREAS

■ Wilderness Area

Pacific Crest Scenic Trail

Miles 0 ___ 100
Kilometers 0 ___ 100 ___ 200

Nez Perce National Historical Park, Idaho. The scattered sites in central western Idaho which make up this park are dedicated to the commemoration, interpretation, and preservation of important features of history and culture in the Nez Perce Indian country.

San Juan Island National Historical Park, Washington. British and American military campsites are included in a park that commemorates the peaceful relations between the United States, Great Britain, and Canada since an 1872 boundary dispute in the islands.

Whitman Mission National Historic Site, Washington. Marcus and Narcissa Whitman established a mission here in 1836. Until they were killed by Indians in 1847, the Whitmans provided aid to Oregon-bound pioneers. The site includes a monument to the couple.

National Recreation Areas

Coulee Dam National Recreation Area, Washington. This 100,059-acre park centers on the 130-mile-long Franklin D. Roosevelt Lake that was created by the construction of the Grand Coulee Dam, a part of the Columbia River Basin project.

Lake Chelan National Recreation Area, Washington. Glacially caved Lake Chelan in the beautiful Stekhkin Valley is the principal feature of this recreation area, which joins North Cascades National Park.

Ross Lake National Recreation Area, Washington. This reservoir in the Skaget River drainage is surrounded by mountains and lies between the north and south units of North Cascades National Park.

Wilderness Recreation

The Pacific Northwest has relatively extensive amounts of wild land and numerous areas that have been proclaimed as formal wilderness. According to the 1964 National Wilderness Act, wilderness is defined as an area where "the earth and its community of life are untrammeled by man, where man himself is a visitor who does not remain." To qualify for inclusion in the wilderness system, an area must be large (usually at least 5,000 acres), generally unaffected by human activity including permanent improvements and places of human habitation, and characterized by outstanding opportunities for primitive recreation and solitude. Many wilderness areas also contain

WILD AND SCENIC RIVERS
(River Sections Highlighted in Color)

(1) *Big Marsh Cr.*	(14) *Malheur*
(2) *Clackamas*	(15) *N. Fk. Malheur*
(3) *Crescent Cr.*	(16) *McKenzie*
(4) *Crooked*	(17) *Metolius*
(5) *N. Fk. Crooked*	(18) *Minam*
(6) *Eagle Cr.*	(19) *North Powder*
(7) *Grande Ronde*	(20) *Powder*
(8) *Imnaha*	(21) *Quartzville Cr.*
(9) *N. Fk. John Day*	(22) *Rapid*
(10) *S. Fk. John Day*	(23) *Roaring*
(11) *Joseph Cr.*	(24) *Salmon*
(12) *Little Deschutes*	(25) *Sandy*
(13) *Lostine*	(26) *Squaw Cr.*
	(27) *Wenaha*
	(28) *White*
	(29) *N. Fk. of M. Fk.*
	Willamette

important geological and ecological features with educational, scenic, historic, or scientific value. Wilderness areas must be on federal lands, but can be administered by any one or a combination of several agencies including the National Park Service, the United States Forest Service, and the Bureau of Land Management.

Recreational uses of wilderness areas include backpacking, horse and llama packing, nature study, mountain climbing, and river running. Float trips and rapid running are possible on many of the region's rivers, and certain particularly remote and/or scenic stretches of free-flowing rivers have been established as Wild and Scenic Rivers in accordance with 1968 legislation. These sections of rivers and their shorelines are maintained in a natural condition.

Trails through wilderness areas are ordinarily followed on foot or on horseback. The Pacific Crest Trail, which extends from the Canadian border to Mexico, is the region's longest hiking trail. Numerous shorter hiking and horse trails exist in the Pacific Northwest, primarily on federal lands.

The region's only National Seashore, which protects parts of the extensive Oregon Dunes, is administered by the U. S. Forest Service. There are also several Oregon State Parks in the dunes. Parts of the Oregon Dunes National Seashore are set aside for hiking and nature study. In other areas, dune buggies and dirt bikes are permitted.

Indian Reservation Attractions

Throughout the United States Native Americans have turned to tourism development as a way of improving reservation economies and as a means of sharing a part of their heritage with other Americans. Places with the most highly developed tourism attractions include Oregon's Warm Springs Reservation with its Kah-Nee-Hah Lodge and Resort, Idaho's Nez Perce National Historical Park, and Washington's Yakima Reservation, which features a museum, restaurant and annual pow wow. The Seattle area boasts a number of Native American attractions including the Daybreak Star Arts Center, owned and operated by the United Indians of All Tribes Foundation, the Kwakiutl Indian Family House at the Pacific Science Center, and the Suquamish Museum with its reconstruction of Chief Seattle's longhouse. Chief Seattle Days, generally held at Suquamish on the third weekend in August, feature a salmon bake, dugout canoe races, and traditional dances.

SELECTED WINTER SPORTS AREAS

Other Recreation Activities

The most popular recreation activities for residents of the Pacific Northwest include pleasure walking, picnicking, swimming, camping, bicycling, sightseeing, fishing, various kinds of boating, and outdoor games. State parks provide a setting for many of these activities. These parks range from small wayside areas with a few picnic tables to larger parks with campgrounds, nature trails, interpretive centers and other facilities.

Camping is a popular recreation activity in the region. Campgrounds are most numerous in particularly scenic areas, especially along the coast and in the Cascade Mountains. Campgrounds in Idaho are clustered in the scenic Rocky Mountain region north of Boise and in the northern panhandle. Campgrounds are also found along major highway routes where they serve the needs of travelers who prefer camping to staying in hotels and motels. The majority of Pacific Northwest campgrounds are managed by the U.S. Forest Service, though the Bureau of Land Management, the Army Corp of Engineers, and the National Park Service also maintain campgrounds. Many state parks have campgrounds, as do some city and county parks. Commercial campgrounds play a role by providing campers with special kinds of facilities and offering camping opportunities in areas where few public campgrounds have been developed.

Popular winter sports in the Pacific Northwest include downhill and cross-country skiing along with snowmobiling, snowshoeing, and snow-camping. Facilities for these activities are primarily found in mountainous regions.

Some of the region's more unusual recreational opportunities have an international reputation. The Columbia Gorge, particularly in the area around Hood River, has become a mecca for windsurfers from all over the world because of the nearly constant winds. Washington's Puget Sound, and especially the area around the San Juan Islands, offers some of the best pleasure boating waters in the United States. Sailboats and motor craft can be chartered at numerous marinas in the area. Malheur Wildlife Refuge in southeastern Oregon attracts birdwatchers from all over the United States and abroad, particularly in the spring. The Pacific Northwest is also rich in lapidary materials. Sites yielding agates, jaspers, and semi-precious stones such as garnets attract rockhounds from all over North America and as far away as New Zealand.

LAPIDARY MATERIAL SITES

Oregon

1. Vernonia—agate, jasper (Nehalem River gravels)

2. Hardman—agate, opal in thundereggs

3. Wecoma Beach to Florence—agate, jasper, sagenite

4. Antelope—agate, jasper

5. Willowdale—thundereggs (Priday Ranch, Kennedy Ranch, and Friends Ranch)

6. Ashwood—agate, petrified wood, thundereggs

7. Spray—jasper, agate (Corncob Ranch)

8. John Day River—agate, petrified wood (China Diggin's, Sunshine Flat, Lick Creek, Windy Point, and Howard Meadows)

9. Calapooya River—sagenite, amethyst-agate, petrified wood

10. Lebanon—carnelian, agate, petrified wood

11. Sweet Home—petrified wood, agate

12. Ochoco Mountain—thundereggs, agate, jasper

13. Crook River—plum agate (Carey Ranch and Eagle Rock)

14. Beak Creek—agate, jasper

15. Peterson's Rock Garden—rock exhibit

16. South Fork Crook River—agate "limb casts"

17. Harper—thundereggs, petrified wood (20-30 miles south)

18. Jamison—bog agates, petrified wood (8 miles N.E.)

19. Hampton Butte—agate, jasper, petrified wood

20. Glass Butte—red and black obsidian (near Humpton)

21. Buchanan Lane—agate, jasper, petrified wood

22. Burns—large obsidian flow (7 miles west)

23. Riverside—agate, jasper, petrified wood

24. Stinkingwater Mountain—agate, petrified wood (north and south of Highway 20)

25. Succor Creek—thundereggs, jasper

26. Jordan Valley—petrified wood

27. Dry Creek—petrified wood, agate

28. Bandon to Gold Beach—petrified wood

29. Harney Lake—petrified wood, oolite (2 miles south)

30. Kerby—oregonite, grossulanite garnet

31. Rome—"snakeskin agate" (15 miles S.W.)

32. McDermitt—petrified wood (15 miles west)

33. Camp White-Eagle Point—agate (dendrites), sagenite

34. Paisley—agate (Chewancan River)

35. Lakeview—thundereggs (Dry Creek), petrified wood (Quartz Mountain)

36. Plush—feldspar (Rabbit Creek), jasper, agate, opal (Hart Mountain)

Washington

1. Crescent Bay—jasper

2. Anacortes, San Juan Islands—jasper

3. Concrete—jade (23.8 miles east)

4. Issaquah—amber (7 miles S.E.)

5. Republic—garnet, agate (15 miles east

6. Salmon River—agate

7. Cashmere—rose quartz

8. Lake Cle Elum—geodes, quartz crystals

9. Thorp—crystal geodes (Frost Mountain)

10. Nisqually—petrified wood

11. Ellensburg—agate (Jack Creek), petrified wood (Saddle to Kittias, one of the world's most extensive deposits)

12. Toledo—jasper, bloodstone (25 miles N.E.)

13. Adna—petrified wood, carnelian, jasper

14. Beverly—petrified wood (5 miles south)

15. Chehalis—carnelian, petrified wood

16. Tono—agate

17. Yakima—petrified wood (5 miles south)

18. Aberdeen—jasper

19. Porter—fossil crab (south of town)

20. Sunnyside-Bickleton-Roosevelt—petrified wood, agate, jasper

21. Stevenson—jasper, bloodstone (Wind River)

Idaho

1. Fernwood—garnet (in Emerald Creek)

2. Bovill—garnet

3. Moscow—garnet

4. Lewiston—opal (in rims 6 miles west)

5. Pierce—garnet (Rhodes, Oro Fino creeks)

6. Riggins—jasper, agate (John Day Creek, 12 miles north), garnet (Salmon River placers)

7. Warren—topaz, quartz crystals (Paddy Creek)

8. New Meadows—rhodonite (near Tamarack, 6 miles south), sapphire (near Rock Flat)

9. Yellow Pine—agate (Hog Creek, 10-15 miles N.W.)

10. Chehalis—jasper, agate (in low hills)

11. Weiser—agate (Hog Creek, 10-15 miles N.W.)

12. Emmet—opal, agate, jasper, petrified wood (Pearl and Willow creeks)

13. Idaho City—opal (Moore Creek)

14. Marshing—opal (Givern Springs, 15 miles south), jasper, queenstone (10 miles south on U.S. 95)

15. Bellevue—agate (dendritic and moss), sagenite (Muldoon Summit and Little Wood River Res.)

16. Firth—black tempsiki (20 miles R.)

17. Silver City—agate, corundum

18. Bruneau—amethyst, agate, jasper

19. Rogerson—thundereggs, agate (dendritic), sagenite

20. Montpelier, Bear—jasper

21. Paris—jasper

Hunting and Fishing

GORDON E. MATZKE

The Pacific Northwest has wild land and water resources in sufficient supply to support substantial populations of many fish and game species. Since much of the wild land is in public ownership, even non-landowners have access to considerable hunting and fishing opportunities.

A primary management tool used by states to regulate harvest and raise revenues for fish and game work is the sale of licenses which authorize an individual to attempt to harvest specified species. The trend in sales of licenses in the three-state area shows participation rates in fishing generally increasing as the population grows while the number of hunters is declining from the highs of the early 1980s. Many reasons are suggested for this latter trend, including the decline in mule deer populations throughout the region in the late 1980s, a smaller population of residents reared in rural areas where hunting norms are strongest, and a higher proportion of female-headed households, which produce fewer hunting recruits than households headed by males. The drop in the numbers of licensed hunters is causing revenue difficulties for the state agencies which use the income to support much of the game management budget.

The likelihood that an individual will participate in hunting or fishing varies according to a combination of factors including previous experience, the abundance of game, and the accessibility of recreation sites. Participation rates decline with increased urbanization of the population. In the context of the Pacific Northwest, this means that Idaho residents are most likely to hunt or fish while people from Washington are least likely to participate in these sports. The statewide averages mask substantial variation in participation between groups within the general population. For example, studies have shown about 95 percent of hunters and 68 percent of fishers are males. In the United States as a whole, whites are twice as likely to hunt or fish than nonwhites and the dominance of the urban residence pattern for Blacks in the Pacific Northwest suggests they would have even lower participation rates in this part of the country.

FISHING LICENSE HOLDERS 1960-1990

(In Thousands)

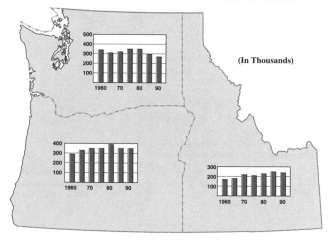

HUNTING LICENSE HOLDERS 1960-1990

(In Thousands)

Table 28. License holders as a percent of population over 16 years old, 1990

	FISHING	HUNTING
Idaho	57%	33%
Oregon	34%	16%
Washington	26%	7%

Hunting

The abundance of fish and game available for harvest varies greatly from place to place and over time in any one place. The variation in waterfowl harvest is an excellent illustration. The size of the annual migration fluctuates with changing conditions on the northern breeding grounds, the hunting pressure en route, and the quality of the wintering habitats. The distribution of the harvest within the Pacific Northwest is strongly associated with traditional migratory flight lines, resting and feeding areas, and the attractiveness of refuge areas. Although every county shares in the waterfowl harvest, higher than average numbers are harvested in the counties along the Columbia, Snake, and Willamette rivers and in the Puget Sound area. The largest harvests occur in two counties with especially large wetland habitats: Washington's Grant County (the Potholes Reservoir) and Oregon's Klamath County (the Klamath Marsh).

Wildlife management in the Pacific Northwest has achieved some notable successes in assisting the recovery of game populations which were devastated by the early part of the 20th century. All three states have large populations of deer and elk which owe their existence to extensive restoration efforts such as restocking, protection, and controlled harvests. These efforts continue in an attempt to restore several other big game species. The mountain goat—which had disappeared from most of Idaho and Washington and was extinct in Oregon—now has at least a small wild population in each state, and all three states have active programs aimed at restoring the mountain sheep to portions of its former range. Now populations are secure enough to allow some tightly controlled harvesting of rams in all three states.

The success of restoration operations is nowhere more obvious than in the level and pattern of deer and elk harvest. Nearly every suitable piece of habitat produces harvestable surpluses of deer, while management efforts are still needed to expand the range of elk in only a few locations, most notably in western Oregon. In many places, the former problems of low to nonexistent populations have been replaced by problems of big game abundance. Hence, timber interests complain of seedling damage caused by game animals and ranchers complain of the competition for forage when game descends onto the limited winter range of the interior valleys.

DISTRIBUTION OF WATERFOWL HARVEST

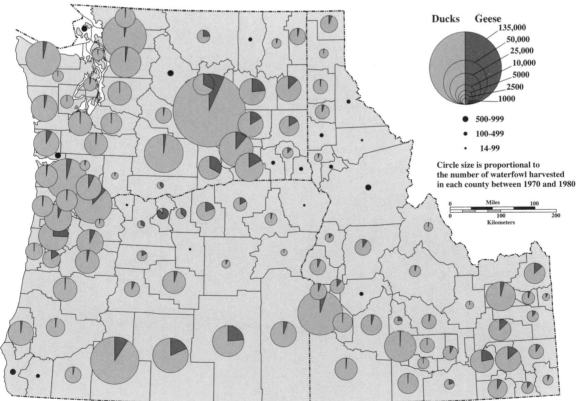

Ducks Geese
135,000
50,000
25,000
10,000
5000
2500
1000

● 500–999

● 100–499

· 14–99

Circle size is proportional to the number of waterfowl harvested in each county between 1970 and 1980

DEER AND ELK HARVEST BY MANAGEMENT UNIT

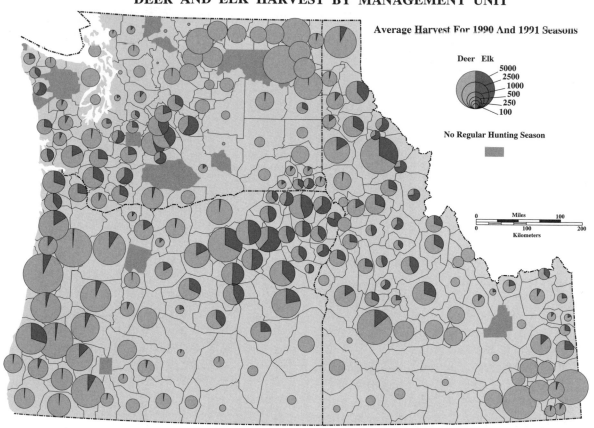

Average Harvest For 1990 And 1991 Seasons

Deer Elk

5000
2500
1000
500
250
100

No Regular Hunting Season

Miles
0   100
0   100   200
Kilometers

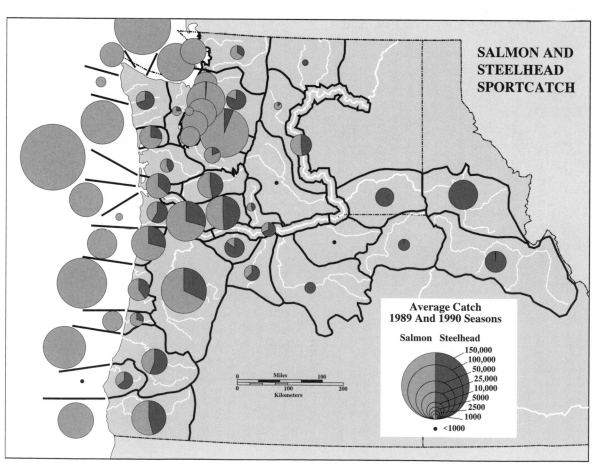

SALMON AND STEELHEAD SPORTCATCH

Average Catch
1989 And 1990 Seasons

Salmon Steelhead

150,000
100,000
50,000
25,000
10,000
5000
2500
1000

• <1000

Miles
0   100
0   100   200
Kilometers

Harvest management attempts to balance the desire of hunters for more deer and elk against the preference of ranching and timber interests for lower populations.

The spatial pattern of big game harvest exhibits several characteristics, including the scarcity of deer and total absence of elk in the driest regions, heavy elk harvests in northeastern Oregon and in a few locations in the Oregon Coast Range, and a widespread large-scale deer harvest with exceptionally heavy takes in most areas of Oregon, northeastern Washington, and the accessible fringes of the Idaho mountains. These patterns are the result of a combination of management policy, habitat quality, accessibility, and population size.

Fishing

Sport fishing is a major recreational activity in all three states. Fishing opportunities are as varied as anywhere in the world, with both cold and warm freshwater fisheries as well as the Pacific Ocean. In addition, nine species of anadromous fish move back and forth between fresh and salt water throughout the still accessible portions of the Columbia River drainage and most of the coastal streams.

The anadromous fishery, including both salmon and steelhead, shows an interesting geographic pattern. Sport fishers compete for salmon against a heavy commercial fishing effort, especially in the ocean, and with Indian Treaty fishing rights on certain rivers, particularly in Washington. The near absence of saltwater steelhead catch is due to the species' ocean movements and elusive behavior. In fact, the only steelhead caught in the ocean are accidental landings by fishers seeking other species. Since salmon flesh is in its best condition during the saltwater part of the life cycle, salmon fishers concentrate on the saltwater harvest, and most are taken by hook and line methods before they enter fresh water.

The total anadromous fish catch declines dramatically with distance from the sea. The decline is so great that there is no salmon season in Idaho and only a few thousand steelhead are taken. This decrease reflects the combined influence of heavy oceanward fishing pressure, the dominance of downstream hatchery production in the fish reproduction picture, the destruction of river habitat,

151

GENERAL PRESENT AND PAST DISTRIBUTION
OF ANADROMOUS FISH

Present Distribution

Access Blocked By Water Project

Historically Inaccessible

Major Obstruction To Fish Passage

and the difficulties of passage (in both directions) through dams and associated impoundments (see map on page 152). The decrease in the wild Columbia River anadromous fish stocks is sufficiently alarming that four of those originating in Idaho streams were listed for protection under the Endangered Species Act in 1992. Dealing with the maintenance and improvement of endangered anadromous fish stocks will involve much more than limitations on sport fishing. Commercial and Indian fishers, hatchery managers, livestock owners, irrigators, power producers, timber harvesters, dam operators, and a variety of industrial water users will likely have to adjust to the needs of the fish. Without successful recovery efforts, upstream fishing for wild Columbia River anadromous fish will be relegated to a footnote in the history of sportfishing.